WHO
RULES
AMERICA?

WHO RULES AMERICA?

POWER AND POLITICS

FOURTH EDITION

G. WILLIAM DOMHOFF
University of California, Santa Cruz

Boston   Burr Ridge, IL   Dubuque, IA   Madison, WI   New York
San Francisco   St. Louis   Bangkok   Bogotá   Caracas   Kuala Lumpur
Lisbon   London   Madrid   Mexico City   Milan   Montreal   New Delhi
Santiago   Seoul   Singapore   Sydney   Taipei   Toronto

McGraw-Hill Higher Education

A Division of The **McGraw-Hill** Companies

1 2 3 4 5 6 7 8 9 0 MAL/MAL 0 9 8 7 6 5 4 3 2 1

Credits: Figure 2.1 From *Lean and Mean* by Bennett Harrison. Copyright © 1994 by Bennett Harrison. Reprinted by permission of Basic Books, a member of Basic Books, LLC. **Table 2.2** Glynn, Jeannett E., ed., *Who Knows Who 1997: Networking Through Corporate Boards*. Reprinted by permission.

Domhoff, G. William.
    Who rules America : power and politics / G. William Domhoff.—4th ed.
        p. cm.
    Includes bibliographical references and index.
    ISBN 0-7674-1637-6
    1. Elite (Social sciences)—United States. 2. Power (Social sciences)—United States. 3. Social classes—United States. 4. United States—Politics and government—1993– 5. United States—Economic conditions—1981– 6. United States—Social conditions—1980– I. Title.
HN90.E4 D652 2001
305.5'2'0973—dc21

                                                                        2001030228

Sponsoring editor, Serina Beauparlant; production editor, Carla Kirschenbaum; manuscript editor, Patricia Ohlenroth; design manager, Jean Mailander; text designer, Leigh McLellan; cover designer, Laurie Anderson; art manager, Robin Mouat; illustrator, Judith Ogus; manufacturing manager, Randy Hurst. The text was set in 10/12 New Aster by TBH Typecast, Inc. and printed on acid-free 50# Re-Conn Matte by Malloy Lithographing, Inc.

www.mhhe.com

Contents

7 How the Power Elite Dominates Government   147

8 The Big Picture   181

Appendix A: How to Do Research on Power   199

Appendix B: Indicators of Upper-Class Standing   207

Preface

This new edition of *Who Rules America?* is even more accessible to students than the previous one. It has been streamlined, reorganized, and updated. The book is more inviting at the outset due to a brief introduction clearly explaining what it is about. The discussion of competing theories has been refined and moved to the final chapter. Now students new to the topic can assimilate the argument and findings before seeing how other theories relate to the one in this book.

Methodological issues concerning network analysis and content analysis have been moved to an appendix, which is organized as a step-by-step guide to conducting power structure research. A detailed guide for studying a local power structure has been added. The appendix also includes an emphasis on how students can use the resources now available on the Internet to do their own research projects, and students are introduced to an exciting new sociological Web site: *Who Rules: An Internet Guide to Power Structure Research.*

The empirical chapters have been updated. There are discussions of the Bush Cabinet, the electoral challenge by Ralph Nader and the Green Party, and the "new economy." There are new sections on the Supreme Court and the Occupational Safety and Health Administration, and a new comparative-historical discussion of why corporations are more powerful in the United States than in Europe. Recent research on public opinion has been incorporated. There is a more focused and sustained discussion of the origins of the Social Security Act and the environmental movement. The analysis of the Democratic Party is richer and more nuanced. The latest statistics on agribusiness, elected officials, campaign finance, and the wealth distribution are included.

This new edition greatly benefited from the editorial comments of Rhonda F. Levine of Colgate University, who also conveyed the reactions of students in classes in which she used the book. The Appendix was much improved by thoughtful comments from Val Burris at the University of Oregon, who created the Web site for power structure research. John Higley of the University of Texas, Austin, and Michael Burton of Loyola College in Maryland made many improvements to the discussion of elite theory in Chapter 8. The book also benefited from the helpful suggestions of the several anonymous reviewers, who turned out to be Dan Clawson of the University of Massachusetts, Amherst; James M. Cook of the University of Arizona; J. William Gibson of California State University, Long Beach; Anne Kane of the University of Texas, Austin; Jerry Lembcke of Holy Cross College; and Brett C. Stockdill of California Polytechnic University, Pomona. Jeff Manza of Northwestern University corrected the discussion of the Social Security Act on key points, and John Campbell of Dartmouth provided useful answers to several questions posed to him in a letter.

Introduction

WHY BOTHER TO READ THIS BOOK?

Do corporations have far too much power in the United States? Does the federal government ignore the interests of everyday people? The great majority of Americans—70 to 75 percent in some surveys—answer "yes" to both questions.[1] This book explains why their answers are accurate even though there is freedom of speech, the possibility of full political participation, and increasing equality of opportunity due to the civil rights and women's movements. In other words, it attempts to resolve a seeming paradox that has bedeviled social scientists and political activists for a long time: How is it possible to have such extreme corporate domination in a democratic country?

This paradox is made all the more striking because corporations do not have as much power in most other democratic countries. The wealth and income differences between people at the top and the bottom are not as great, and the safety net for those who are poor, ill, or elderly is stronger. Why does the richest nation in the world also have the most poverty compared to any other democratic country?

Using a wide range of systematic empirical findings, this book shows how the owners and top-level managers in large companies work together to maintain themselves as the core of the dominant power group. Their corporations, banks, and agribusinesses form a *corporate community* that shapes the federal government on the policy issues of interest to it, issues that have a major impact on the income, job security, and well-being of most other Americans. At the same time, there is competition within the corporate community for profit opportunities, which can lead to highly visible policy conflicts among rival corporate leaders that are sometimes fought out in Congress. Yet the corporate community is cohesive on the policy issues that affect its general welfare, which is often at stake when political challenges are made by organized workers, liberals, or strong environmentalists. The book therefore deals with another seeming paradox: How can a highly competitive group of corporate leaders cooperate enough to work their common will in the political and policy arenas?

None of this means the corporate executives have complete and total power, that their success in each new policy conflict is a foregone conclusion, or that they never lose. For example, lawyers and other highly trained professionals with an interest in consumer or environmental issues are able to use lawsuits, lobbying, or publicity to win governmental restrictions on some corporate practices and even to challenge whole industries. Wage and salary workers, when they are organized into unions and have the right to strike, can gain pay increases and such social benefits as health insurance. Even the most powerless of people occasionally develop the capacity to bring about some redress of their grievances through sit-ins, demonstrations, and other forms of strategic nonviolent disruption.

Moreover, one of the great triumphs of the Civil Rights Movement, the Voting Rights Act of 1965, began a process that could make it possible for liberal, black-brown-white voting coalitions to challenge the corporate community in the electoral arena. Although this book demonstrates that the corporate community became even more powerful after the 1960s, it also shows that the potential for limiting corporate power has developed at the same time, due to the gradual (and far from complete) transformation of the Democratic Party from the political arm of the Southern rich and big-city political machines to the party of liberals, minorities, women, and labor unions. And thus another paradox: During the period from 1965 to 1999, when top executive salaries went from 42 times an average worker's pay to 475 times as much, new political openings for social change that did not exist before also developed.[2] These openings are discussed in the final chapter.

Partly because the owners and high-level managers within the corporate community share great wealth and common economic interests, but also due to political opposition to their interests, they band together to develop their own social institutions—gated neighborhoods, private schools, exclusive social clubs, debutante balls, and secluded summer resorts. These social institutions create social cohesion and a sense of group belonging, a "we" feeling, and thereby mold wealthy people into a *social upper class*. In addition, the owners and managers supplement their small numbers by financing and directing a wide variety of nonprofit organizations—e.g., tax-free foundations, think tanks, and policy-discussion groups—to aid them in shaping public policy. The highest-ranking employees in these nonprofit organizations become part of a general leadership group for the corporate community and the upper class, a group that is discussed at the end of Chapter 4.

Corporate owners and their top executives enter into the electoral arena as the leaders of a *corporate-conservative coalition*, which they control through large campaign contributions, the advocacy of policy options developed by their hired experts, and easy access to the mass media. They are aided by a wide variety of patriotic, antitax, and single-issue organizations that celebrate the status quo and warn against "big government." These opinion-shaping organizations are funded in good part by the corporate community but have some degree of independence due to direct-mail appeals and modest donations by a large number of middle-class conservatives. The corporate conservatives play a large role in both of the major political parties at the presidential level and succeeded in electing a conservative majority to Congress throughout the twentieth century. Historically, the conservative majority in Congress consisted of Northern Republicans and Southern Democrats, but that arrangement changed gradually after the Voting Rights Act of 1965 made it possible for a coalition of African-Americans and white liberals to push the most conservative Southern Democrats into the Republican Party.

During the last quarter of the twentieth century, the corporate-conservative coalition formed an uneasy alliance with the New Christian Right, which consists of a wide range of middle-class religious groups concerned with a variety of social issues, including abortion, prayer in schools, teenage sexual behavior, homosexuality, and pornography. The alliance is best described as an uneasy one because the corporate community and the New Christian Right do not have quite the same priorities, except for a general antipathy to liberalism and government-supported social services. Many leaders in the corporate community worry that the New Christian Right is not winning over as many voters as its publicists and fundraisers claim.

Despite their preponderant power in the federal government and the many useful policies it carries out for them, leaders within the corporate community are constantly critical of government because of its potential independence and its ability to aid their opponents. In particular, they are wary of the federal government due to its capacity to aid average Americans by (1) creating government jobs for the unemployed, (2) making health, unemployment, and social security benefits more generous, (3) helping employees gain greater workplace rights and protections, and (4) supporting efforts by employees to form unions. All of these initiatives are opposed by the corporate community on the grounds that they might increase taxes or wages.

However, this book suggests that the major issue is not really taxes or government spending, although that is what the corporate community complains about the most. The deeper issue is power. Most of all, corporations oppose any government support for unions because unions are a potential organizational base for advocating a whole range of polices that threaten corporate power. In a phrase, *control of labor markets* is the crucial issue in the eyes of the corporate community, which rightly worries that government policies could alter the power over labor markets it now enjoys.

The opponents of the corporate-conservatives—union leaders, locally based environmental organizations, most minority-group communities, liberal churches, and liberal university communities—sometimes work together on policy issues as a *liberal-labor coalition*. However, this coalition is extremely difficult to hold together because its members have divergent and sometimes clashing interests. It also has far less money to spend on political campaigns than the corporate-conservatives, although this fact may become much less important in the future for reasons explained in Chapter 6. Despite the fact that unions have represented a declining percentage of working people since the 1950s, with a precipitous drop after 1975, they still have over 16 million members and are the largest and best-financed part of the coalition. They also cut across racial and ethnic divisions more than any other institutionalized sector of American society.

The liberal-labor alliance enters into the electoral arena through the liberal wing of the Democratic Party, sometimes fielding candidates in party primaries to stake out its policy goals. Contrary to the strident warnings of conservatives and the fond hopes of liberals, this coalition never has had a major voice in the Democratic Party at the national level and never even had the possibility of such a voice as long as the Southern rich were a key element in the party. Although there is now the potential for new political openings, union leaders and liberals probably had more impact from the late 1930s to the early 1970s than they have had ever since.

In the 1990s, unions spent approximately $50 million a year on political campaigns, and in 2000 they spent an estimated $75 million.[3] They also urge their officials and members to work at the grass roots in political campaigns—making telephone calls, stuffing envelopes, and going door-to-door to bring out the vote. However, their political clout has been hurt since the 1970s by the fact that some of them are slow to accept women and minorities, and often oppose environmental initiatives out of fear that jobs might be lost. Unions also have limited impact because they are not able to shape the voting behavior of their members. In some elections, including the 2000 presidential election, half or more of their white male members were likely to vote Republican.[4] Nor are unions beyond reproach from the vantage point of their liberal coalition partners, because they are often controlled by a few top leaders who pay themselves very high salaries, ignore the initiatives of ordinary members, and sometimes enter into shady dealings with organized crime.[5]

The liberal-labor coalition is on occasion aided by the organizing skills and militancy of political leftists, who are steeled by the hope and determination they gain from their strong socialist or communist convictions. Historically, these left activists played a significant role in the struggle for women's suffrage, the building of industrial unions, and the success of the Civil Rights Movement. However, leftists are also strong critics of the liberal-labor coalition and they usually advocate the creation of a third party to replace the Democrats. Moreover, some leftists advocate or use violence against people or property, which alienates a large majority of Americans, who opt for the Republican Party in the face of such actions.[6]

The major policy conflicts between the corporate-conservative and liberal-labor coalitions are best described as *class conflicts* because they concern the distribution of profits and wages, the rate and progressivity of taxation, the usefulness of labor unions, and the degree to which business should be regulated by government. The liberal-labor side wants corporations to pay higher wages to employees and higher taxes to government. It wants government to regulate a wide range of business practices and help employees to organize unions. The corporate-conservative side rejects all these policy objectives, claiming they endanger the freedom of individuals and the efficient workings of the economic marketplace. The conflicts these disagreements generate can manifest themselves in many different ways: workplace protests, industrywide boycotts, massive demonstrations in cities, pressure on Congress, and voting preferences.

Social conflict over abortion, homosexuality, and other social issues favored by liberals and vigorously opposed by the New Christian Right are not part of this overall class conflict. They do not affect the power of the corporate community. They are therefore of little or no concern to most of the policy-planning organizations funded by corporate leaders. However, these social issues are an important part of the competition between the corporate-conservative and liberal-labor coalitions in the electoral arena, where they are raised by conservatives in an attempt to win over voters who are liberal on economic issues.

Neither the corporate-conservative nor the liberal-labor coalition elicits the strong loyalty of a majority of the American population. Both consist primarily of organization leaders, policy experts, financial donors, politicians, political consultants, and party activists. They are therefore in constant competition for the allegiance of the general citizenry, most of whom are focused on the positive aspects of their everyday lives: love and concern for their families, the challenges of their jobs, or the enjoyment of a hobby or athletic activity. The typical American pays little attention to most policy issues, focuses on political candidates only around the time of elections, and has a mixture of liberal and conservative opinions that seems contradictory to members of the rival coalitions. In exit polls after the 2000 election, 20 percent of voters identified themselves as liberals, 50 percent as moderates, and 29 percent as conservatives.[7]

The seeming apathy or ignorance ascribed to ordinary citizens by many public commentators actually makes practical sense in terms of the compelling nature of everyday life, the difficulties of bringing people into agreement on new policy initiatives, and the amount of time and effort it takes to change government policies. The net result is that a majority of voters may be open to an attractive candidate or well-crafted policy appeal from the liberal-labor alliance. More often than not, however, the corporate-conservative coalition triumphs in both the electoral and policy arenas. The hows and whys of these triumphs are the key issues of the following chapters. So, why bother to read this book? Because it explains the corporate domination that most Americans sense to be their lot, and its suggests what to look for on the part of liberals and conservatives in the near future.

1

Class and Power in America

What do everyday Americans and social scientists mean when they talk about *social class* or *power,* and how do their views compare? This chapter answers these two questions. It also explains the methods used to study these two concepts and presents a preliminary look at the American upper class.

WHAT IS A SOCIAL CLASS?

Most Americans don't like the idea that there might be social classes. Classes imply that people have relatively fixed stations in life. They fly in the face of beliefs about equality of opportunity and seem to ignore the evidence of upward social mobility. Even more, Americans tend to deny that classes might be rooted in wealth and occupational roles. They talk about social class, but with euphemisms like "the suits," "the blue bloods," "Joe Sixpack," and "the other side of the tracks."

   American dislike for the idea of class is deeply rooted in the country's colonial and revolutionary history. Colonial America seemed very different from other countries to its new inhabitants because it was a rapidly expanding frontier country with no feudal aristocracy or rigid class structure. The sense of difference was heightened by the need for solidarity among all classes in the war for freedom from the British. Revolutionary leaders from the higher classes had to concede greater freedom and equality for common people to gain their support. One historian states the power equation succinctly: "Leaders who did not fight for equality accepted it in order to win."[1]

Although large differences in wealth, income, and lifestyle already existed in revolutionary America, particularly in port cities and the South, these well-understood inequalities were usually explained away or downplayed by members of the middle classes as well as by the merchants, plantation owners, and lawyers who were at the top of the socioeconomic ladder. As shown by a historical study of diaries, letters, newspapers, and other documents of the period, Americans instead emphasized and took pride in the fact that any class distinctions were small compared with Europe. They recognized that there were rich and poor, but they preferred to think of their country "as one of equality, and proudly pointed to such features as the large middle class, the absence of beggars, the comfortable circumstances of most people, and the limitless opportunities for those who worked hard and saved their money."[2]

The fact that nearly 20 percent of the population was held in slavery and that 100,000 Native Americans lived in the western areas of the colonies was not part of this self-definition as a middle-class, egalitarian society. It is clear, however, that the free white majority nonetheless defined itself in terms of the potentially dangerous slaves on the one hand and the warlike "savages" on the other. This made their shared "whiteness" a significant part of their social identity. In fact, race is the first of many factors that make the class-based nature of American society less salient than it might otherwise be.

Even members of the upper class preferred this more democratic class system to what had existed for many centuries in Europe. To emphasize this point, a study of the democratic revolutions in North America and Europe begins with a letter written from Europe in 1788 by a young adult member of a prominent American upper-class family. After the young man registered his disgust with the hereditary titles and pomp of the European class system, and with the obsequiousness of the lower classes, he stated his conviction that "a certain degree of equality is essential to human bliss." As if to make sure the limits of his argument were clear, he underlined the words *a certain degree of equality*. He then went on to argue that the greatness of the United States was that it had provided this degree of equality "without destroying the necessary subordination."[3]

Two hundred years later, in response to sociologists who wanted to know what social class meant to Americans, a representative sample of the citizenry in Boston and Kansas City expressed ideas similar to those of the first Americans. Although most people are keenly aware of differences in social standing and judge status levels primarily in terms of income, occupations, and education (but especially income), they emphasize the openness of the system. They also argue that a person's social standing is in good part determined by such individual qualities as initiative and the motivation to work hard. Moreover, many of them feel the importance of class is declining. This belief is partly due to their conviction that people of all ethnic and religious backgrounds are being treated with greater respect and decency whatever their occupational and educational levels, but even more to what they see as material evidence for social advancement in the occupations and salaries of their families and friends.[4] In short, a tradition of public social respect for everyone and the existence of social mobility are also factors in making class less important in the everyday thinking of most Americans. People are very aware of basic economic and educational differences, and they can size up social standing fairly well from such outward signs as speech patterns, mannerisms, and style of dress, but the existence of social classes is nonetheless passed over as quickly as possible.

People of the highest social status share a general distaste for talking about social class in an open and direct way. Nevertheless, they are very conscious of the fact that they and their friends are set apart from other Americans. In the study of Boston and Kansas City residents, an upper-class Bostonian said, "Of course social class exists—it influences your thinking." Then she added, "Maybe you shouldn't use the word 'class' for it, though—it's really a niche that each of us fits into."[5] In a classic study of social classes in New Haven, a person in the top category in terms of neighborhood residence and educational background seemed startled when asked about her class level. After regaining her composure, she replied, "One does not speak of classes; they are felt."[6] As part of a study of thirty-eight upper-class women in a large Midwestern city, a sociologist bluntly asked her informants at the end of the interview if they were members of the upper class. The answers she received had the same flavor of hesitation and denial:

> I hate (the term) upper class. It's so non-upper class to use it. I just call it "all of us," those of us who are well-born.
>
> I hate to use the word "class." We're responsible, fortunate people, old families, the people who have something.
>
> We're not supposed to have layers. I'm embarrassed to admit to you that we do, and that I feel superior at my social level. I like being part of the upper crust.[7]

SOCIAL CLASS ACCORDING TO SOCIAL SCIENTISTS

Social scientists continue to debate among themselves at great length about how social classes should be defined and even about the value of theorizing in terms of social classes. While there is considerable overlap on some of the main issues, there is no firm consensus.[8]

For purposes of this book, the following general guidelines provide a sufficient starting point.

Class is a two-dimension concept. First and foremost, the term refers to an intertwined economic and power relationship between two or more groups of people who have specific roles in the economic system. Owners of businesses and the employees of those businesses are the most obvious examples of this dimension in the nation-states of the Western world, but not all societies have economies that feature owners and their employees. Second, class is a category that refers to the social institutions, social relationships, and lifestyle within the various economic groups: common neighborhoods, common clubs and recreational activities, and a strong tendency to interact primarily with people from one's own economic class. It is in this latter sense that Americans usually use the term.

However, the degree to which a given *economic class* is also a *social class* can vary widely from place to place and time to time. Class as a relationship is always operating, but the people in any given economic category may or may not live in the same neighborhoods or interact socially. They may or may not think of themselves as being members of one or another class. Historically, it is the members of the most powerful class in a society who organize themselves socially and develop a common class awareness that is an important part of their social identity.[9]

The empirical study of the degree to which a given economic category is also a social class begins with a search for connections among the people and institutions that are thought to constitute it. This procedure is called *membership network analysis,* which boils down to a matrix in which social institutions are arrayed along one axis and individuals along the other. Then the cells created by each intersection of a person and a social institution are filled in with information revealing whether or not the person is a member. This information is used to create two different kinds of networks, one organizational and the other interpersonal. An *organizational network* consists of the relationships among organizations, as determined by their common members. These shared members are sometimes called *overlapping* or *interlocking members.* An *interpersonal network,* on the other hand, reveals the relationships among individuals, as determined by their common organizational affiliations.*

To provide a concrete example of the type of analysis that appears throughout this book, suppose a researcher has the membership

---

* These and other methodological issues are explained in more detail, with the help of diagrams and tables, in Appendix A.

lists for several exclusive social clubs. By determining which members are common to each pair of clubs, it is possible to see which clubs are part of an organizational network defined by the overlapping members. In addition, it can be said that the most central clubs in the network are those with members in common with many other clubs, whereas a peripheral club in the network might have common members only with a club that itself is one or two steps removed from the central clubs. Furthermore, some clubs may have no members in common with any of the others, which reveals they are not part of that social network.

The same procedure can be repeated with alumni lists from preparatory schools and Ivy League colleges, and with guest lists from debutante balls and other social functions. Then the membership overlaps among all these different types of social institutions can be compiled. In effect, this network analysis provides a systematic overview of the social institutions that define the social upper class in the United States.

A membership network analysis is in principle very simple, but it is theoretically important because it contains within it the two types of human relationships of concern in sociological theorizing: interpersonal relations and memberships in organizations. Thus, these networks contain "a duality of persons and groups."[10] For analytical purposes, the interpersonal and organizational networks are often treated separately, and some social scientists talk of different levels of analysis, but in the reality of everyday life the two levels are always intertwined. Hence the phrase, "a duality of persons and groups."

IS THERE AN AMERICAN UPPER CLASS?

If the owners and managers of large income-producing properties in the United States are also a social upper class, then it should be possible to create a very large network of interrelated social institutions whose overlapping members are primarily wealthy families and high-level corporate leaders. These institutions should provide patterned ways of organizing the lives of their members from infancy to old age and create a relatively elite style of life. In addition, they should provide mechanisms for socializing both the younger generation and new adult members who have risen from lower social levels. If the class is a sociological reality, the names and faces may change somewhat over the years, but the social institutions that underlie the upper class must persist with only gradual change over several generations.

Four different types of empirical studies establish the existence of such an interrelated set of social institutions and social activities in the United States: historical case studies, quantitative studies of biographical directories, open-ended surveys of knowledgeable observers, and interview studies with members of the upper-middle and upper classes. These studies not only demonstrate the existence of an American upper class, they also provide what are called *indicators* of upper-class standing, which are useful in determining the degree of overlap between the upper class and the corporate community or between the upper class and various types of nonprofit organizations. They can be used to determine the amount of involvement members of the upper class have in various parts of the government as well.

In the first major historical case study, the wealthy families of Philadelphia were traced over a period of 200 years, showing how they created their own neighborhoods, schools, clubs, and debutante balls. Then their activities outside of that city were determined, which demonstrated that there are nationwide social institutions where wealthy people from all over the country interact with each other. This study led to the discovery of an upper-class telephone directory called the *Social Register*, published for thirteen large cities from Boston to San Francisco between 1887 and 1975.[11] The guide to the thirteen city volumes, the *Social Register Locator*, contained about 60,000 families, making it a very valuable indicator of upper-class standing.

Using information on private school attendance and club membership that appeared in 3,000 randomly selected *Who's Who in America* biographies, along with listings in the *Social Register*, another study provides a statistical analysis of the patterns of memberships and affiliations among dozens of prep schools and clubs. The findings from this study are very similar to those from the historical case study. Still another study relied on journalists who cover high society as informants, asking them to identify the schools, clubs, and social directories that defined the highest level of society in their city. The replies from these well-placed observers reveal strong agreement with the findings from the historical and statistical studies.[12]

A fourth and final method of establishing the existence of upper-class institutions is based on intensive interviews with a cross-section of citizens. The most detailed study of this type was conducted in Kansas City. The study concerned people's perceptions of the social ladder as a whole, from top to bottom, but it is the top level that is of relevance here. Although most people in Kansas City can point to the existence of exclusive neighborhoods in suggesting that there is a class of "blue bloods" or "big rich," it is members of the upper-middle class and the upper class itself whose reports demonstrate that clubs and similar social institutions as well as neighborhoods give the class an institutional existence.[13]

The specific schools and clubs discovered by these and related investigations are listed in Appendix B. The *Social Registers* and other blue books are listed as well, but are now utilized primarily for historical investigations because they became less popular and shrank in size in the last third of the twentieth century.

Although these social indicators are a convenient tool for research purposes, they are far from perfect in evaluating the class standing of any specific individual because they are subject to two different kinds of errors that tend to cancel each other out in group data. *False positives* are those people who qualify as members of the upper class according to the indicators, even though further investigation would show that they are not really members. Scholarship students at private secondary schools are one example of a false positive. Honorary and performing members of social clubs, who usually are members of the middle class, are another important type of false positive. *False negatives*, on the other hand, are people who do not seem to meet any of the criteria of upper-class standing because they shun social registries and do not choose to list their private school or their club affiliations in biographical sources.

Private schools are especially underreported. Many prominent political figures do not list their private secondary schools in *Who's Who in America*, for example; even former president George H. W. Bush removed mention of his private school from his entry in the 1980–1981 edition when he became vice president in the Reagan Administration. More generally, studies comparing private school alumni lists with *Who's Who* listings suggest that 40 to 50 percent of corporate officers and directors do not list their graduation from high-prestige private schools. Membership in social clubs may also go unreported. In a study of the 326 members of a prestigious private club with a nationwide membership who are listed in *Who's Who in America*, 29 percent did not include this affiliation.[14]

The factors leading to false positives and false negatives raise interesting sociological questions deserving of further study. Why are scholarship students sought by some private schools, and are such students likely to become part of the upper class? Why aren't private schools and clubs listed in biographical sources by some members of the upper class? Why are some middle-class people taken into upper-class clubs? Merely to ask these questions is to suggest the complex social and psychological reality that lies beneath this seemingly dry catalog of upper-class indicators. More generally, the information included or excluded in a social register or biographical directory is an autobiographical presentation that has been shown to be highly revealing concerning religious, ethnic, and class identifications.[15]

WHAT IS POWER?

As might be expected, American ideas about power have their origins in the struggle for independence. What is not so well known is that these ideas owe as much to the conflict within each colony about the role of ordinary citizens as they do to the war itself. It is often lost from sight that the average citizens were making revolutionary political demands on their leaders as well as helping in the fight against the British. Before the American revolution, governments everywhere had been based on the power and legitimacy of religious leaders, kings, self-appointed conventions, or parliaments. The upper-class American revolutionary leaders who drafted the constitutions for the thirteen states between 1776 and 1780 expected their handiwork to be debated and voted upon by state legislatures, but they did not want to involve the general public in a direct way.

It was members of the "middling" classes of yeoman farmers and artisans who gradually developed the idea out of their own experience that power is the possession of all the people and is delegated to government with their consent. They therefore insisted that special conventions be elected to frame constitutions, and that the constitutions then be ratified by the vote of all free, white males without regard to their property holdings. They were steeled in their resolve by their participation in the revolutionary struggle and by a fear of the potentially onerous property laws and taxation policies that might be written into the constitutions by those who were known at the time as their betters. So the idea of the people as the constituent power of the new United States arose from the people themselves.[16]

In the end, the middle-level insurgents only won the right to both a constitutional convention of elected delegates and a vote on subsequent ratification in Massachusetts in 1780. From that time forth, however, it has been widely agreed that power in the United States belongs to "the people." Since then, every liberal, radical, populist, or ultraconservative political group has claimed that it represents "the people" in its attempt to wrest arbitrary power from the "vested interests," the "economic elite," the "cultural elite," "the media," the "bureaucrats," or the "politicians in Washington." Even the Founding Fathers of 1789, who were far removed from the general population in their wealth, income, education, and political experience, did not try to promulgate their new constitution, designed to more fully protect private property and commerce, without asking for the consent of the governed. In the process, they were forced to add the Bill of Rights to insure its acceptance. In a very profound cultural sense, then, no group or class has power in America, but only influence. Any small group or class that has power over the people is therefore perceived as illegitimate. This may explain why those with power in America always deny they have any.[17]

THE SOCIAL SCIENCE DEFINITION OF POWER

Like social class, the meaning of *power* is still disputed among social scientists, within the context of rough agreement on some issues. For purposes of this book, power can be defined as "the ability to achieve desired social outcomes."[18] This broad definition encompasses two intertwined dimensions. First, power is the overall capacity of a group, class, or nation to be effective and productive. Here, the stress is on power as the degree to which a collectivity has the technological resources, organizational forms, and social morale to achieve its general goals. In that sense, most nations have become more powerful in recent decades than they were in the past.

Second, power is also the ability of a group, class, or nation to be successful in conflicts with other groups, classes, or nations on issues of concern to it. Here, the stress is on *power over,* which is also called *distributive power.* In this book, the distributive dimension of power is the sole concern. More specifically, the book seeks to show that a social upper class of owners and high-level executives, with the help of conservative, single-issue groups and the New Christian Right, has the power to institute the policies it favors even in the face of organized opposition from the liberal-labor coalition.

Unfortunately, it is not an easy matter to study the distributive power of a social class. A formal definition does not explain how a concept is to be measured. In the case of distributive power, it is seldom possible to observe interactions that reveal its operation even in small groups, let alone to see one class affecting another. People and organizations are what can be seen in a power struggle, not classes. It is therefore necessary to develop what are called *indicators of power.*

Although distributive power is first and foremost a relationship between two or more contending classes, for research purposes it is useful to think of distributive power as an underlying trait or property of a social class. As with any underlying trait, it is measured by a series of indicators, or signs, that bear a probabilistic relationship to it. This means that all of the indicators do not necessarily appear each and every time the trait is manifesting itself. It might make this point more clear to add that the personality traits utilized by psychologists to understand individual behavior and the concepts developed to explain findings in the natural sciences have a similar logical structure. Whether a theorist is concerned with friendliness, as in psychology, or magnetism, as in physics, or power, as in the case of this book, the nature of the investigatory procedure is the same. In each case, there is an underlying concept whose presence can be inferred only through a series of diagnostic signs or indicators that vary in their strength under differing conditions. Research proceeds, in this view, through a series of *if-then* statements. *If* a group is powerful, *then* at least some of the indicators of this power should be present.[19]

THREE POWER INDICATORS

Since each indicator of power may not necessarily appear in each and every instance where power is operating, it is necessary to have several indicators. Working within this framework, three different types of power indicators are used in this book. They are called (1) Who benefits? (2) Who governs? and (3) Who wins? Each of these empirical indicators has its own strengths and weaknesses. However, the potential weaknesses of each indicator do not present a serious problem because all three of them have to point to the owners and managers of large income-producing property as the most powerful class for the case to be considered convincing.

Who Benefits?

Every society has material objects and experiences that are highly valued. If it is assumed that everyone would like to have as great a share of these good things of life as possible, then their distribution can be utilized as a power indicator. Those who have the most of what people want are, by inference, the powerful. Although some value distributions may be unintended outcomes that do not really reflect power, the general distribution of valued experiences and objects within a society still can be viewed as the most publicly visible and stable outcome of the operation of power.

In American society, for example, wealth and well-being are highly valued. People seek to own property, to have high incomes, to have interesting and safe jobs, to enjoy the finest in travel and leisure, and to live long and healthy lives. All of these values are unequally distributed, and all may be utilized as power indicators. In this book, however, the primary focus with this type of indicator is on the wealth and income distributions. This does not mean that wealth and income are the same thing as power, but that income and the possession of great wealth are visible signs that a class has power in relation to other classes.

The argument for using value distributions as power indicators is strengthened by studies showing that such distributions vary from country to country, depending upon the relative strength of rival political parties and trade unions. One study reports that the degree of equality in the income distribution in Western democracies varied inversely with the percentage of social democrats who had been elected to the country's legislature since 1945.*[20] The greater the social democratic presence, the greater the amount of income that goes to the lower classes. In a study based on eighteen Western democracies, it was found that strong trade unions and successful social democratic parties are correlated with greater equality in the income distribution and a higher level of welfare spending.[21] Thus, there is evidence that value distributions do vary depending on the relative power of contending groups or classes.

Who Governs?

Power also can be inferred from studying who occupies important institutional positions and takes part in important decision-making groups. If a group or class is highly overrepresented or underrepresented in relation to its proportion of the population, it can be inferred that the group or class is relatively powerful or powerless, as the case may be. For example, if a class that contains 1 percent of the population has 30 percent of the important positions in the government, which is thirty times as many as would be expected by chance, then it can be inferred that the class is powerful. Conversely, when it is found that women are in only a small percentage of the leadership positions in government, even though they make up a majority of the population, it can be inferred that they are relatively powerless in that important sector of society. Similarly, when it is determined that a minority group has only a small percentage of its members in leadership positions, even though it comprises 10 to 20 percent of the population in a given city or state, then the basic processes of power—inclusion and exclusion—are inferred to be at work.

This indicator is not perfect because some official positions may not really possess the power they are thought to have, and some groups or classes may exercise power from behind the scenes. Once again, however, the case for the usefulness of this indicator is strengthened by the fact that it has been shown to vary over time and place. For example, the decline of landed aristocrats and the rise of

* Social democrats come from a tradition that began with a socialist orientation and then moved in a more reformist direction. For the most part, social democratic parties have only slightly more ambitious goals than the liberal-labor coalition in the United States; the left wing of the liberal-labor coalition would feel at home in a strong social democratic party in western Europe.

business leaders in Great Britain has been charted through their degree of representation in Parliament.[22] Then, too, as women, African-Americans, Latinos, and Asian-Americans began to demand a greater voice in the United States in the 1960s and 1970s, their representation in positions of authority began to increase.[23]

Who Wins?

There are many issues over which the corporate-conservative and liberal-labor coalitions disagree, including free trade, taxation, unionization, business regulation, and Social Security. Power can be inferred on the basis of these issue conflicts by determining who successfully initiates, modifies, or vetoes policy alternatives. This indicator, by focusing on relationships between the two rival coalitions, comes closest to approximating the process of power contained in the formal definition. It is the indicator preferred by most social scientists. For many reasons, however, it is also the most difficult to use in an accurate way. Aspects of a decision process may remain hidden, some informants may exaggerate or downplay their roles, and people's memories about who did what often become cloudy shortly after the event. Worse, the key concerns of the corporate community may never arise as issues on the public agenda because it has the power to keep them nonissues through a variety of means that are explained throughout later chapters.

Despite the difficulties in using the *Who wins?* indicator of power, it is possible to provide a theoretical framework for analyzing governmental decision-making that mitigates many of them. This framework encompasses the various means by which the corporate community attempts to influence both the government and the general population in a conscious and planned manner, thereby making it possible to assess its degree of success very directly. More specifically, there are four relatively distinct, but overlapping processes (discovered by means of membership network analysis) through which the corporate community controls the public agenda and then wins on most issues that appear on it. These four power networks, which are discussed in detail in later chapters, are as follows:

1. The *special-interest process* deals with the narrow and short-run policy concerns of wealthy families, specific corporations, and specific business sectors. It operates primarily through lobbyists, company lawyers, and trade associations, with a focus on congressional committees, departments of the executive branch, and regulatory agencies.

2. The *policy-planning process* formulates the general interests of the corporate community. It operates through a policy-planning network of foundations, think tanks, and policy-discussion groups, with a focus on the White House, relevant congressional committees, and the high-status newspapers and opinion magazines published in New York and Washington.

3. The *candidate-selection process* is concerned with the election of candidates who are sympathetic to the agenda put forth in the special-interest and policy-planning processes. It operates through large campaign donations and hired political consultants, with a focus on the presidential campaigns of both major political parties and the congressional campaigns of the Republican Party.

4. The *opinion-shaping process* attempts to influence public opinion and keep some issues off the public agenda. Often drawing on policy positions, rationales, and statements developed within the policy-planning process, it operates through the public relations departments of large corporations, general public relations firms, and many small opinion-shaping organizations, with a focus on middle-class voluntary organizations, educational institutions, and the mass media.

WHAT'S IN STORE?

With the definitions and indicators for class and power in mind, it is now possible to outline the steps that are taken in each of the following chapters. Using membership network analysis, this book attempts to show there is a corporate community (Chapter 2) that is the basis for a social upper class (Chapter 3). This intertwined corporate community and social upper class have developed a policy-planning network (Chapter 4) and an opinion-shaping network (Chapter 5) that give them the means to win a majority of seats in the electoral process (Chapter 6) and to shape the policies of interest to them within the federal government (Chapter 7). Chapter 8 discusses the theoretical framework that fits best with these findings and then compares it with the main alternatives offered in the social sciences. Chapter 8 also explains why the corporate community is so powerful by comparing American and European history, and concludes with a discussion of the cracks and openings that developed in the power structure as a result of the Civil Right Movement.

2

The Corporate Community

It may seem a little strange at first to think about the few hundred big corporations that sit astride the American economy as any sort of community, but in fact corporations have many types of connections and common bonds. They include shared ownership, long-standing patterns of supply and purchase, the use of the same legal, accounting, advertising, and public relations firms, and common (overlapping) members on the boards of directors that have final responsibility for how corporations are managed. The large corporations share the same goals and values, especially the profit motive. As noted in the introduction, they also develop a closeness because they are all opposed and criticized to some degree by the labor movement, liberals, leftists, strong environmentalists, and other types of anticorporate activists.

For research purposes, the interlocks created when a person sits on two or more corporate boards are the most visible and useful of the ties among corporations. Since membership on a board of directors is public information, it is possible to use membership network analysis to make detailed studies of interlock patterns extending back into the early nineteenth century. The organizational network uncovered in these studies provides a rigorous research definition for the term *corporate community*. It consists of all those profit-seeking organizations connected into a single network by overlapping directors.

However, it is important not to overstate the actual importance of these interlocks. They are valuable for communication among corporations, and they give the people who are members of several boards a very useful overview of the corporate community as a whole.

But the effects of interlocks on the economic performance of corporations are rather small, if any. Corporate interlocks should be thought of as the best starting points that outsiders can use to understand the overall corporate community.

Once the bare outlines of the corporate community are established, it is possible to extend the membership network analysis to determine the other types of organizational affiliations maintained by corporate directors. Such studies show that members of the corporate community create two types of organizations for purposes of relating to each other and government. First, they develop trade associations made up of all the businesses in a specific industry or sector of the economy. Thus, there is the American Petroleum Institute, the American Bankers Association, the National Association of Home Builders, and hundreds of similar organizations that focus on the narrow interests of their members through the special-interest process discussed briefly at the end of the previous chapter.

Second, the corporate community is pulled even closer together by organizations like the National Association of Manufacturers, the U.S. Chamber of Commerce, and the Business Roundtable, which look out for its general interests and play a role in the policy-planning process. In the case of the National Association of Manufacturers and its many state affiliates, for example, one of its foremost concerns since 1903 had been all-out opposition to labor unions in any part of the economy. As for the Business Roundtable, it is the organization that has coordinated the corporate community against a wide range of challenges from the liberal-labor coalition since the 1970s.

THE UNEXPECTED ORIGINS
OF THE CORPORATE COMMUNITY

Standard historical accounts sometimes suggest that the first American businesses were owned by individual families and only slowly evolved into large corporations with common ownership and many hired managers. In fact, the corporate community had its origins in jointly owned companies in the textile industry in New England in the late eighteenth and early nineteenth centuries. At that time, the common directors reflected the fact that a small group of wealthy Boston merchants were joining together in varying combinations to invest in new companies. By 1845, a group of eighty men, known to historians as the *Boston Associates,* controlled 31 textile companies that accounted for 20 percent of the nationwide textile industry. Seventeen of these men served as directors of Boston banks that owned 40 percent of the city's banking capital, twenty were directors of 6 insurance companies, and eleven sat on the boards of 5 railroad companies.[1]

Meanwhile, wealthy investors in other major cities were creating commonly owned and directed companies as well. In New York, for example, the 10 largest banks and 10 largest insurance companies in 1816 were linked into one network; 10 of the companies had from eleven to twenty-six interlocks, 6 had six to ten interlocks, and 4 had one to five interlocks. In 1836, all but 2 of the 20 largest banks, 10 largest insurance companies, and 10 largest railroads were linked into one common network, with 12 of the 38 companies having an amazing eleven to twenty-six interlocks, 10 having six to ten interlocks, and 16 having one to five interlocks. Even at that time, which is often romanticized as one of small businesses, the 10 largest banks had 70 percent of the bank assets in New York City and 40 percent of the bank assets in the entire state.[2]

These big-city networks of financial companies and railroads persisted in roughly their mid-century form until they were transformed between 1895 and 1904 by a massive merger movement, which created a national corporate network that included huge industrial corporations for the first time.[3] Until that point, industrial companies had been organized as partnerships among a few men or families. They tended to stand apart from the financial institutions and the stock market. Detailed historical and sociological studies of the creation of this enlarged corporate community reveal no economic efficiencies that might explain the relatively sudden incorporation of industrial companies. Instead, it seems more likely that industrial companies had to adopt the corporate form of organization for a variety of historical, legal, and sociological reasons. The most important of these reasons seems to have been a need to (1) regulate the competition among themselves that was driving down profits, and (2) gain better legal protection against the middle-class reformers, populist farmers, and socialists who had mounted an unrelenting critique of *the trusts*, meaning agreements among industrialists to fix prices, divide up markets, and/or share profits. When trusts were outlawed by the Sherman Anti-Trust Act of 1890, which was coincidentally followed by a major depression and many strikes by angry workers, the stage was set for industrialists to resort to the legal device called a *corporation*.[4]

Several studies show that the corporate community remained remarkably stable after the merger movement ended. Since then, it always has included the largest corporations of the era, and financial companies are always at the center. Three changes in the patterns of corporate interlocks between 1904 and the present seem to reflect gradual economic and financial changes. First, railroads became more peripheral as they gradually declined in economic importance. Second, manufacturing firms became more central as they increased in economic importance. Third, as corporations became more independent of banks, the banks became less likely to place their top officers on non-bank boards and more likely to receive officers of nonbank corporations on their own boards; this reversal of flow may reflect the gradual transformation of banks from major power centers to places of coordination and communication.[5]

In short, large American businesses always have been owned and controlled by groups of well-to-do people, who share common economic interests and social ties even more than kinship ties. Moreover, the deposits and premiums held by banks and insurance companies for ordinary people were used for investment purposes and the expansion of corporations from the beginning. Then too, control of corporations by directors and high-level executives was an early feature of the American business system, not a change that occurred when stockholders allegedly lost control of companies to bankers or managers in the first half of the twentieth century. Contrary to the usual claim that corporate growth and restructuring is a sensible and efficient response to changing technology and markets, a claim that leaves no room for any concern with power, careful research suggests big corporations are a response to class conflict and legal changes, even though it is also true that improvements in transportation and communication made such changes possible.

Before taking a detailed look at the corporate community of today, it is necessary to say a few words about the board of directors.

THE BOARD OF DIRECTORS

The board of directors is the official governing body of the corporation. Usually composed of ten to fifteen members, but including as many as twenty-five in the case of commercial banks, it meets for a day or two at a time about ten times a year and receives reports and other information between meetings. Various board committees meet periodically with top managers as well. A smaller executive committee of the board often meets more frequently, and the most important individual members are sometimes in daily contact with the management that handles the day-to-day affairs of the corporation. The major duty of the board of directors is to hire and fire high-level executives, but it also is responsible for accepting or rejecting significant policy changes. Boards seem to play their most critical role when there is conflict within management, the corporation is in economic distress, or there is the possibility of a merger or acquisition.[6]

The board is the official governing body, but the company executives on the board, who are called *inside directors*, sometimes play a role in shaping the board's decisions. These inside directors, perhaps in conjunction with two or three of the nonmanagement directors, called *outside directors*, are able to set the agenda for meetings, shape board thinking on policy decisions, and select new outside directors. In those situations, the board may become little more than a rubber stamp for management, with the top managers having great influence in naming their successors in running the company.

Although the exact role of the board varies from corporation to corporation, boards of directors in general embody the complex power relations within the corporate community. In addition to their role in selecting high-level management and dealing with crises, their importance manifests itself in a number of ways. They speak for the corporation to the rest of the corporate community and to the public at large. New owners demand seats on boards to consolidate their positions and to have a "listening post." Conflicts over hostile merger attempts may be concluded by electing the top officers of the rival corporations to each other's boards. Commercial bankers may seek seats on boards to keep track of their loans and to ensure that future business will be directed their way. The chief executives of leading companies take time from their busy schedules to be on two or three other boards because it is a visible sign that their advice is respected outside their home company. Their board memberships also provide them with general intelligence on the state of the business world.[7] Then, too, the presence of investment bankers, corporate lawyers, and academic experts on a board is a sign that their expertise is respected by the corporations. The appointment of a university president, former government official, well-known woman, or highly visible minority group leader is a sign that their high status and respectability are regarded as valuable to the image of the corporation.[8]

Boards of directors are important for another reason. In the broadest sense, they are the institutionalized interface between organizations and social classes in the United States. For the purposes of this book, they are viewed more specifically as the intersection between corporations and the upper class. As such, they are one of the means by which the book attempts to synthesize a class-based theory and insights from organizational theory. From the standpoint of organizational theory, boards are important because they allocate scarce resources, deal with situations where there is uncertainty, and link with other organizations that are important to the organization's future success. The organizational perspective is represented on the board of directors by the inside directors, who are fulltime employees of the corporation. They are concerned that the organization survive and that any new initiatives have a minimal effect on routine functioning. They see outside directors as the ambassadors of the organization, who help to reduce uncertainty in the organization's environment.

Table 2.1 Number of Network Connections for 1,029 Corporations in 1996

Number of Connections	Frequency	Cumulative Percent
28–45	28	2.7
20–27	65	9.0
15–19	102	19.0
10–14	146	33.1
5–9	226	55.1
2–4	241	78.5
1	93	87.6
0	128	100.0

Source: Who Knows Who (Detroit: Gale Research Inc., 1997), chap. 4.

The class perspective is represented by those outside directors who are members of the upper class. Such directors want to insure that any given corporation fits well with their other profit-making opportunities and does not jeopardize new policy initiatives or general public acceptance in the political realm. Outside directors have a number of resources that make it possible for them to represent a class perspective: their own wealth, their connections to other corporations and nonprofit organizations, their general understanding of business and investment, and their many connections to other wealthy people, fundraisers, and politicians. Such resources make it possible for them to have a very real impact when new leadership must be selected or new policy directions must be undertaken.[9]

THE CORPORATE COMMUNITY TODAY

Two different studies, one for the 1970s and one for the late 1990s, provide a detailed overview of the modern-day corporate community. It is first of all very large, encompassing 90 percent of the 800 corporations studied for the 1970s and 87.6 percent of the 1,029 reviewed for 1996. Furthermore, most corporations are within three or four steps, or links, to any other.[10] Although large, the network is not generally very dense because most corporations have only one to nine connections to the rest of the network. On the other hand, the largest corporations usually have ten or more connections, and some have as many as forty-five. The exact figures for the number of connections among the top 1,029 corporations in 1996 are presented in Table 2.1.

The corporations and banks in the corporate community control a great proportion of the country's economic activity. Just five giant corporations—General Electric, General Motors, Ford Motor, IBM, and Exxon—have 28 percent of all industrial assets, and the top 100 have almost 75 percent. Eleven banks have 33 percent of all commercial banking assets; the top 50 have 62 percent. The levels of concentration are roughly the same for other major business sectors, such as insurance and public utilities, although retailing is somewhat less concentrated.[11] These figures reflect a gradual increase in economic concentration over the span of the twentieth century.

In general, the corporations with the most connections are also the corporations that are in the center of the network. This point is first of all demonstrated by studying the number of connections that the most highly connected firms have with each other. Table 2.2 presents the interconnections for the 28 companies with twenty-eight or more interlocks. Twenty-four of the 28 companies have three or more connections with each other; American Express and Sara Lee head the list with nine ties each in the top group; Chase Manhattan Bank, General Motors, and Procter and Gamble follow with eight; and Prudential Insurance, Minnesota Mining and Manufacturing, and Mobil Oil have seven. Of the 4 companies with two or fewer connections within the top 28, 2 are banks in San Francisco that have most of their many connections to corporations located on the West Coast. The other 2 are railroad companies.

The most highly connected corporations are usually financial ones—banks, insurance companies, and credit-card companies. As already noted, the centrality of financial companies is one of the network's most striking and consistent features, dating back to the earliest years for which information can be assembled. There is some evidence that these financial institutions do not have quite as many connections to the other corporations as they did twenty or thirty years ago, but they are still at the center of the network.[12]

The centrality of the 28 firms with the most connections also is shown by their connections to other highly connected corporations. Of the 313 firms with between ten and twenty-seven connections, 226 (72.2 percent) have at least one connection to the top 28. In addition, every one of the 81 corporations without a connection to the top 28 has at least one connection (and most have three or more) to the other 226. More generally, a representative sample of 400 companies in the overall network showed that 39 percent of them had at least one direct link to the central group of 28. This means that the network tends to radiate out in concentric circles from its central core, but even that image does not capture the full picture because even some corporations with only two or three connections are linked directly to the top 28. Still more

Table 2.2 The 28 Most Connected Corporations for 1996 and Their Connections to Each Other (Financial Companies Marked by Asterisks)

Company	Total Number of Connections	Connections among the Top 28
Chase Manhattan Bank*	45	8
Wells Fargo Bank*	41	2
American Express*	40	9
Prudential Insurance*	39	7
Sara Lee Foods	39	9
Minnesota Mining and Manufacturing	37	7
General Motors	33	8
Kroger Stores	33	5
Ashland Oil	32	3
Bank of America*	32	1
CSX (railroad)	32	2
Bell Atlantic	31	6
Coca-Cola	31	3
Procter and Gamble	31	8
Spring Industries	31	6
AMR	30	4
Mobil Oil	30	7
TRW	30	3
Xerox	30	4
Ameritech	29	5
Bell South	29	3
Union Pacific	29	6
Westinghouse Electric	29	4
Burlington Northern	28	2
Cummins Engine	28	4
Kellogg	28	6
Kmart	28	4
AOL Time Warner	28	6

Source: Who Knows Who (Detroit: Gale Research, Inc., 1997), p. 749.

Table 2.3 Examples of How Corporations with One Connection Link to the Top 28

Company	Linking Corporation	Linking Corporation's Connection to the Top 28
A. G. Edwards	Helig-Meyers	CSX
Ascend	Silicon Graphics	Mobil, Prudential, Sara Lee
Bally Co.	First Union Bank	Bell Atlantic
Dimm Co.	First Union Bank	Bell Atlantic
Big Flowers Press	Host Marriott	AMR
First Federal Savings	Teledyne	Wells Fargo & Co. Bank
Glendale Federal Savings	Teledyne	Wells Fargo & Co. Bank
Unitrin	Teledyne	Wells Fargo & Co. Bank

Source: Who Knows Who (Detroit: Gale Research, Inc., 1997).

are only one step removed from it. Examples of this two-step relationship for 8 corporations with only one network tie are given in Table 2.3.

Aside from some tendency to regional concentrations, there are no subgroups or cliques within the corporate community, at least as measured by director interlocks. Instead, as the findings in the previous paragraphs reveal, there tends to be a very general core, with smaller corporations around the periphery. One further piece of evidence for this conclusion is the fact that corporate connections broken by the death or retirement of a director are not very often restored by a new director from closely related companies, which is what would be expected if the companies were part of a subgroup. New directors usually come from a small general pool of people who are highly visible in the corporate community; they often have several directorships already.[13] Thus, the main constants in the network are its large size, the centrality of financial firms and top industrials, and slight shifts in the degree of a corporation's interlocks when directors are replaced.

THE DIRECTOR NETWORK AS AN INNER CIRCLE

Who are the directors who create a corporate community through their presence on boards of directors? They are 90 to 95 percent men, 95 percent white, 3 to 4 percent African-American, and 1 to 2 percent Latino and Asian-American. Most are business executives, commercial bankers, investment bankers, and corporate lawyers, but there are also a significant minority of university administrators, foundation presidents, former elected officials, and representatives of ethnic and racial minorities.

Compared to three or four decades ago, there is today greater diversity in the corporate community in terms of the number of women and minorities, a response to the social movements that emerged in the 1960s. There is irony in this diversity, however, because the social class and educational backgrounds of the women and minorities tend to be similar to those of their white male counterparts. They also share the Christian religion and Republican politics with most of the white males. In the case of African-American and Latino corporate directors, they tend to have lighter skin color than leaders within their own communities. Based on this and other information, there is reason to believe that white male directors select new women and minority directors who are similar to them in class, education, and skin color. There is also evidence that women and minority directors usually share the same perspectives on business and government with other directors.[14] The next chapter presents information on the social and educational backgrounds of all corporate directors and executives.

Approximately 15 to 20 percent of all present-day directors sit on two or more corporate boards, thereby creating the corporate community as it is defined for purposes of this book. This percentage has proven to be very stable over time. The figure was 24 percent for New York banks and insurance companies in 1816 and 18 percent in 1836. For the 55 companies studied for 1891 and 1912, the figures were 13 percent and 17 percent, respectively. A larger sample of companies for the period 1898 to 1905 found that 12 percent of the directors were on two or more boards.[15]

These people are called the *inner circle* of the corporate community. They do not differ demographically from other directors, but they do sit on more nonprofit boards, as shown in chapters 4 and 5, and are appointed more frequently to government positions, as explained in chapter 7. Thus, the inner circle contributes disproportionately to the general leadership group that represents the corporate community as a whole.[16]

The extensive corporate network created by interlocking directors provides a general framework within which common business and political perspectives can gradually develop. It is one building block toward a more general class awareness that is reinforced in settings that are discussed in the next several chapters. The understanding gained by studying interlocking directors and the corporate network is therefore a useful starting point in understanding corporate power. But it is no substitute for showing how policy views are formed and how government is influenced on specific issues for which there is conflict.

STRATEGIC ALLIANCES/PRODUCER NETWORKS

Firms in the corporate community not only have numerous complex ties to each other, but also to multinational firms in other countries and smaller firms in both the United States and abroad. The relations to the multinationals are called *strategic alliances;* the relations with smaller companies create *producer networks.* Both types of ties developed more rapidly in the late twentieth century than they had previous to that time, in part due to increasing world economic competition, including competition within the United States from Japanese and Western European producers of automobiles and steel. This new competition forced American corporations to seek greater flexibility through internal reorganizations, changes in labor relations, and new relations with other companies.[17]

Strategic alliances with foreign multinationals usually focus on a very specific issue, such as research and development, or the creation of one particular product. Thus, IBM, Toshiba (Japan), and Siemens (Germany) entered into an alliance for research and development on a new kind of microchip. General Motors and Toyota developed a joint venture to produce small cars in a plant in Fremont, California, using advanced technology and more cooperative labor-management relations. The several types of alliances that five separate American companies created with Siemens are shown in Figure 2.1. Such alliances

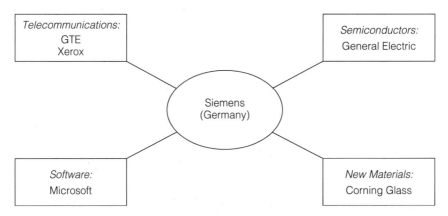

Figure 2.1 Types of Alliances Developed with Siemens by Five American Corporations. *Source:* Bennett Harrison, *Lean and Mean* (New York: Basic Books, 1994), p. 137.

make it possible for large corporations to (1) bypass political barriers blocking their entry into new foreign markets, (2) create new products more quickly by pooling technical know-how, and (3) avoid the expense of start-up costs and head-on competition.

Producer networks, on the other hand, provide supplies and services to big corporations. These networks give large companies the flexibility to rearrange their internal bureaucracies and cut back on employees. In particular, they allow corporations to subcontract, or outsource, for many of the parts and services they need. The corporations are thereby able to outflank unions, which often have difficulty organizing when there are many small companies. Eliminating unions has the effect of lowering wage and benefit costs, and allowing less costly health, safety, and work rules.

Thanks to outsourcing, the large corporations continue to maintain or enlarge their share of sales and profits while decreasing the size of their workforces. Even with these cutbacks, however, the largest 1 percent of manufacturing companies still account for 70 percent of all manufacturing jobs. Nor does outsourcing reduce the power of the big corporations. Based on a detailed investigation of all new corporate strategies, one economist concluded: "Production may be decentralized into a wider and more geographically far-flung number of work sites, but power, finance, and control remain concentrated in the hands of the managers of the largest companies in the global economy."[18]

Outsourcing first seemed to be a feasible option for reducing union power as far back as 1961, but it took a decade for corporations to make use of its potential in the face of liberal-labor opposition. The conflict began when the federal government's National Labor Relation Board, controlled at the time by Republican appointees, ruled that outsourcing did not violate union contracts. The ruling was vigorously opposed by liberals and union leaders, and was overturned one year later by the liberal appointees put on the board by the incoming Democratic president. Convinced that this new ruling was the opening round in a liberal-labor attack on "management prerogatives," the entire corporate community began to mobilize against any further growth in union power; this mobilization included companies that had maintained formally positive relations with unions for over a decade.

Top executives from these companies claimed they were willing to bargain with unions over wages, hours, and working conditions, but not over an issue that involved their rights as managers, including their right to weaken unions. Their successful battle, won through court cases and influence on appointments to the National Labor Relations Board, culminated in 1971 with a series of rulings against any collective bargaining over management decisions. These decisions opened the way for greater outsourcing, plant relocations, and plant closings. The organization that has coordinated the corporate community on policy issues since the 1970s, the Business Roundtable, had its origins in the committees and study groups set up to overturn the original pro-union ruling on outsourcing.[19]

THE NEW ECONOMY: NOT NEW IN TERMS OF POWER

Computers, faxes, and the Internet are sometimes said to be the basis for a new economy that soon will displace the old corporate community. They create networks of electronic devices that make possible high-speed, low-cost information storage and transmittal, thereby improving productivity, warehousing, shipping, and customer service. The result is a new group of semiconductor, telecommunication, and dot.com companies created by young entrepreneurs from allegedly modest social backgrounds. In 1998, the CEO of one of the hottest of these companies, Cisco, which makes products that link communication networks, claimed that the Internet would "change everything," and have "every bit as much impact on society as the Industrial Revolution," all in a span of seven years.[20]

Whether or not there is a new economy developing that will change everything, there is nothing about the organization of these companies, or their methods of operation, that is incompatible with the current corporate community on any dimension discussed in this book. The new companies are financed in many cases by already-established wealth. Their high-level executives come from the same socioeconomic and educational backgrounds as other executives. For example, Steve Case, the CEO of AOL Time Warner, is a typical example, not the exception. Called "middle class" in newspaper stories, his father is a corporate lawyer and his mother a descendant of a sugar plantation owner. He grew up in an exclusive Honolulu neighborhood, attended a high-status private school in his teens, and graduated from Williams College, his father's alma mater. He received his start at the company that later became AOL through his older brother, already established as an investment banker and a member of the company's board of directors.[21]

Nor do the owners of the biggest companies act any differently than empire builders in the past. For example, Microsoft claims to be a highly innovative company built on sheer brain power, but it began as a quick and timely assemblage of newly developed ideas and techniques taken from others before software was patentable. Windows® and Word® came from the Xerox Research Center, Excel® from a little company named Software Arts, and Internet Explorer® from Netscape. As the retired founder of the Xerox Research Center concludes,

Table 2.4 The Corporate Interlocks of 6 New-Economy Companies in 1998

Apple (4)	Microsoft (5)
Citigroup	BankAmerica
DuPont	Hewlett-Packard
Mallinckodt	Mattel
U.S. Waste Services	Safeco
	Washington Mutual

Cisco (5)	Oracle (6)
Air Touch Communications	Air Touch Communications
Cadence Design Systems	American Bankers Insurance
El Paso Natural Gas	Cadence Design Systems
Lockheed Martin	Exxon
Raychem	Lucent Technologies
	Sports Authority

Intel (8)	Sun Microsystems (7)
Air Touch Communications	BankAmerica
Boise Cascade	Federal Express
Cirrus Logic	Gap
Edison International	General Mills
McKesson	Knight-Ridder
Solectron	Nike
Transamerica	Rockwell International
Varian Associates	

Source: Who Knows Who (Detroit: Gale Research, Inc., 1998).

the head of Microsoft, Bill Gates, was "immensely successful in positioning himself between the innovators and the users, taking from one and selling to the others."[22]

Moreover, the largest of the new-economy corporations have numerous interlocks with the corporate community. The most integrated are Automatic Data Processing, with sixteen corporate connections, Dell Computer with fifteen, Varian Associates with thirteen, and Silicon Graphics with twelve in 1998. Table 2.4 shows the specific interlocks for six other prominent high-tech companies. The integration of the new economy with the corporate community can further be seen in the unhappy history of ICG, which provided dial-up links between Internet companies and their customers. Its bonds were underwritten by a leading Wall Street investment bank, Morgan Stanley Dean Witter, and one of the top mutual funds, Fidelity, was the largest purchaser of these bonds. AT&T and Lucent Technologies, a spin-off from AT&T, provided financing for the equipment they sold the company. When ICG collapsed in the fall of 2000, all of these companies lost tens of millions of dollars.[23] As for the many retailing start-ups on the Internet, they are being purchased or pushed aside by established corporations like Walmart.com and Target.com, which can use their huge cash flows to market aggressively and capitalize on their brand-name recognition.[24]

Although many new-economy executives claim they have no need for government, they are in fact as dependent upon it as the rest of the corporate community. The Internet itself was created by the Pentagon's Defense Advanced Research Project Agency in the late 1960s.[25] Other projects financed by the agency "helped create many of the nation's most impressive computers, the chips used in cellular phones, and vital networking technologies like the ability to send simultaneous signals of many wavelengths down a single optic cable."[26] Nor would they have been able to benefit from the Internet if the Telecommunications Act of 1996 and rulings by the Federal Communications Commission had not taken telephone lines from the monopoly grip of the telephone companies.[27]

New-economy companies benefit handsomely from tax breaks that lobbyists worked very hard to obtain through the special-interest process. Due to strong lobbying, backed up by a Senate resolution sponsored by Senator Joseph I. Lieberman, who became the Democratic Party's vice presidential nominee in 2000, companies can take a tax deduction for money their employees earn when they exercise their option to sell stock that the company allowed them to purchase.* This practice keeps earnings artificially high. Giving employees stock options also encourages them to work for lower wages, which also raises profits. If options were counted as costs, Cisco's reported profits for 1999 would have been 24 percent lower, Gateway, Inc.'s would have been 26 percent less, and Dell Computer's 13 percent less. Thanks to

---

*A stock option is an arrangement by which an employee is allowed to buy company stock at any point within a future time period at the price of the stock when the option is granted. If the price of the stock rises, the executive purchases it at the original low price, often with the help of a low-interest or interest-free loan from the corporation. He or she then may sell the stock at the market value, realizing a large capital gain that is taxed at a far lower rate than ordinary income.

this tax break, neither Cisco nor Microsoft paid any federal income taxes in 1999.[28]

Another important piece of special-interest legislation allows new-economy companies to bring 195,000 foreign high-tech workers a year into the country for six-year periods. Not only do these employees have to leave the country at the end of six years, but they cannot easily change jobs without losing their visas. This arrangement comes close to indentured servitude, giving companies access to skilled employees without any risk that they might quit the company or join in unionization efforts.[29]

The final old-fashioned secret to the new economy's economic success is massive resistance to any attempts at unionization. Great success in this regard is critical in maintaining low-wage assembly plants. The absence of a unionized labor force also allows for a steady stream of low-income immigrant workers and means there is no challenge to the right to move assembly plants to Third World countries. Subcontracting is another means of avoiding unionized workers. The firms in California's Silicon Valley use as many temporary software designers as possible and contract with employment agencies to hire janitors at $15,000 a year.[30]

THE CORPORATE LAWYERS

Lawyers specializing in corporate law go back to the beginnings of American corporations. Comprising only a few percent of all lawyers, they generally practice as partners in large firms that have hundreds of partners and even more associates—that is, recent law school graduates who work for a salary and aspire to an eventual partnership. Partners routinely earn several hundred thousand dollars each year, and top partners may make several million.

Corporate law firms grew in size and importance in tandem with the large corporations that developed in the second half of the nineteenth century. Their partners played the central role in creating the state-level laws in New Jersey and Delaware that made the corporate form an attractive and safe haven for companies under pressure from reformers and socialists, who were trying to pass laws at the national level that would break up or socialize large businesses.[31]

In more recent times, corporate lawyers prepare briefs for key legal cases but rarely appear in court. They advise corporations on how widely or narrowly to interpret requests for information when facing lawsuits over the dangers of their products. They are central to mergers and acquisitions by corporate executives. They also serve as important go-betweens with government, sometimes as heads of major departments of the executive branch, sometimes as White

House counsel. After government service, they return to their private practices with new knowledge and contacts that make them even more valuable to their corporate clients.

Despite these close ties with corporations, some social scientists have argued that corporate lawyers are professionals with a code of ethics and concern over the public at large that set them apart from the corporate community. However, a detailed analysis of four large corporate law firms in Chicago provides convincing evidence that these lawyers are an integral part of the corporate community. They have a strong loyalty to their clients, not to their profession or code of ethics. The sociologist who did this study concludes:

> My central thesis is that lawyers in large firms adhere to an ideol-
> ogy of autonomy, both in their perception of the role of legal insti-
> tutions in society and the role of lawyers vis-à-vis clients, but that
> this ideology has little bearing in practice. In the realm of practice
> these lawyers enthusiastically attempt to maximize the interests of
> clients and rarely experience serious disagreements with clients
> over the broader implications of a proposed course of conduct. The
> dominance of client interests in the practical activities of lawyers
> contradicts the view that large-firm lawyers serve a mediating func-
> tion in the legal system.[32]

Although closely tied to their clients, and in that sense not inde-pendently powerful, corporate lawyers are nonetheless important in shaping law schools, the American Bar Association, courts, and politi-cal institutions. The same author quoted above concludes that corpo-rate lawyers "maintain and make legitimate the current system for the allocation of rights and benefits," and that they do so for the benefit of their clients: "The influence of these organizations in the legal system derives from and can only serve the interests of corporate clients."[33]

The socialization that creates a business-oriented mentality in corporate lawyers has been studied in great detail at Harvard Law School. Based on interviews and classroom observations, the sociolog-ical investigator reports that students end up actively participating in building collective identities within law school that all but insure they will become members of the corporate community as a result of a gru-eling socialization process. As a key part of this socialization, students learn there is no such thing as right or wrong, only differing shades of gray. Summer internships provide the students with a taste of the cor-porate world. They come to feel they must be special to be attending a high-status law school and be sought after by powerful law firms that offer starting salaries of $100,000 a year or more. Thus, even though some students enter prestigious law schools with an interest in public-interest law, all but a few percent end up in corporate law firms.[34]

Not all young lawyers follow the corporate path, of course, and those from lower-status schools are very unlikely to do so. Some become trial lawyers who represent aggrieved or injured individuals or groups in cases against corporations. They are often viewed as the major enemies of corporate lawyers. They have been so successful that corporate and Republican leaders call for tort reform, which includes limits on liability. Many trial lawyers have become major donors to the Democratic Party in the face of this counterattack by the corporate community.[35] Other young lawyers go to work for the government as prosecutors and public defenders. Still others focus on environmental, civil rights, or labor law, in effect joining the liberal-labor coalition in many instances.

Given this diversity of interests and viewpoints among lawyers, it makes little sense in terms of a power analysis to talk about lawyers in general as part of a profession that is separate from business and other groups in society, as some social scientists do. Although lawyers share some qualities that make them useful mediators and politicians, it is important to ascertain what kind of law a person practices for purposes of power studies, and to realize that corporate lawyers are the hired guns of the corporate community.

DO PENSION FUNDS HAVE CORPORATE POWER?

About half of the stock issued by large corporations is now owned by what are called *institutional investors*. The term encompasses a mixture of entities, such as mutual funds, bank trust departments, corporate pension funds, union pension funds, and public employee pension funds. They are expected to invest other people's money in a financially responsible manner. Although public employee pension funds have grown dramatically, most institutional funds are controlled by organizations in the corporate community, as Table 2.5 shows. Given the large amount of stock held by these institutional investors, do they exercise any power independent of the corporate community?

During the late 1980s and early 1990s, several public employee and union pension funds seemed to be flexing their muscles in corporate meeting rooms, attempting to force policy changes and even changes in management. Their actions raised the possibility of an *investor capitalism* in which government employees and unions could challenge the prerogatives and power of the traditional owners and executives inside the corporate community.[36] But other pension fund managers never joined the effort, and such a challenge has appeared increasingly less likely since its high point in the early 1990s.

The idea of public pension funds as active participants in corporate governance arose in the mid-1980s when partners at the invest-

Table 2.5 Percentage of Market Value Held by Five Major Categories for All Corporate Stock in the United States

Type of Holder	1975	1985	1994
Households (privately held)	57	51	48
Personal Bank Trust Funds	11	7	3
Mutual Funds	4	5	12
Corporate Pension Funds	13	20	18
Public Pension Funds	3	5	8
Total for Five Categories	88	88	89

Source: Mary Blair, *Ownership and Control* (Washington, D.C.: The Brookings Institution, 1995), p. 46, Table 2.1.

Note: The percentages do not add up to 100 percent because the holdings of commercial banks, savings and loan institutions, insurance companies, closed-end funds, brokers and dealers, and foreign groups are not included.

ment firm of Kohlberg, Kravis, Roberts convinced the head of the state employee pension fund in Oregon to contribute major sums to their takeover projects. Other public pension funds were soon drawn into the action. Then a wealthy Republican maverick, serving as the pensions administrator in the Department of Labor in 1984 and 1985, made it government policy that institutional shareholders had a fiduciary duty to behave as owners. He encouraged the liberal treasurer of California and the head of the New Jersey Division of Investment to take advantage of his ruling by holding boards of directors accountable for delivering maximum shareholder value, meaning the highest possible stock prices. In 1985, these three men together urged several public employee and union pension funds to form a group called the Council of Institutional Investors that would help them influence corporate governance through their voting power. The leaders of the New York City Employees Retirement System and the State of Wisconsin Investment Board also supported an activist approach.[37]

The rise and decline of these efforts is mirrored in the career of one of its leaders, Dale Hanson, a long-time state employee in Wisconsin who was appointed head of the California State Employees Retirement System (known as Calpers) in 1987. Hanson made several efforts to influence corporate behavior by introducing various shareholder resolutions calling for more responsiveness to stockholders' concerns. All of them were overwhelmingly defeated, although a few corporations did alter their policies to allow confidentiality in voting on stockholder resolutions. In 1989, at a secret meeting with members of the

Business Roundtable, Hanson and other institutional investors were quietly urged to criticize General Motors for its poor profit performance. Shortly after this attack began, the CEO at General Motors was ousted and new policies were put in place. There followed several other successful public campaigns against CEOs whose companies were performing poorly, and the movement seemed to be launched.[38]

But public pension fund managers are beholden to a board of directors that is in part appointed by governors and state legislators, so it was not long before Hanson and other activists were facing criticism at home. Since Calpers was viewed as the leader of the insurgency, business leaders complained directly to the state's Republican governor. Hanson became especially vulnerable when Calpers itself did not do well in its investment returns for a year or two. By 1993, he was taking a quieter approach. In May 1994, he resigned to become head of American Partners Capital, an investment firm funded by a Republican fundraiser, and a director of ICN Pharmaceuticals, a large California company with 2,500 employees. Faced with similar criticisms from politicians and appointed board members, leaders of other public pension funds adopted a slower and quieter approach, simply meeting with individual CEOs or directors to express their concerns, or merely publishing lists of underperforming companies.[39]

The reining in of the public pension funds was reinforced in 1996 by leadership changes at the Council of Institutional Investors, which by then included insurance companies, mutual funds, and corporate pension funds as well as public and union funds. Although pension-fund activists opposed the selection of a corporate pension-fund representative to preside over the council, the majority of members expressed their lack of enthusiasm for activism by electing the director of the TRW Pension Fund as president.* The vote was widely interpreted as a rebuff to the leaders of union funds and activists at public employee funds.[40]

Looking back at the most vigorous days of the movement, from roughly 1988 to 1992, it is clear that very little was accomplished. It is now possible for small stockholders to communicate with each other more easily, thanks to a ruling by the Securities and Exchange Commission in 1992, and corporate executives more readily meet with institutional investors. The leaders of the movement also believe that boards of directors are now generally more responsive to stockholder concerns. However, no stockholder resolution relating to corporate governance came close to passing.

---

*TRW, a manufacturing company, was the 125th largest corporation in the country in the mid-1990s.

Reflecting on their efforts in September 2000, many of the leading activists expressed disappointment with the cautious approach adopted by most institutional investors. The head of the Council of Institutional Investors said that they had "won the easy battles," such as being able to have nonbinding shareholder proposals sent out along with company proxies, but that they are in danger of ending up merely writing letters asking executives why they ignore the proposals. She notes that "We are seriously thinking about closing shop because we may be wasting money. We are at a turning point. The more (companies) ignore shareholder proposals, the more they realize they can do that, if they can withstand the embarrassment."[41]

In the end, the success of activists in charge of public employee pension funds depends upon the success of the liberal-labor coalition in electing legislators and governors who are supportive of, or at least willing to tolerate, challenges to the management of private corporations. When the Republican governor and conservative legislators in California began to question the activities of Hanson and Calpers, it was not long before the pension fund gradually began to lower its profile.

No one can be sure, but it seems unlikely that institutional investors from public employee and union pension funds ever will be able to create a coalition of institutional investors that could do anything more than chide, chastise, or confer with directors and executives from the large corporations in which they invest. Institutional investors are not a threat to the current power relations in the corporate community. They play their largest role when rival private investors vie for their voting support in takeover battles.[42]

FROM SMALL FARMS TO GIANT AGRIBUSINESSES

In the last half of the nineteenth century, when the farm vote was a critical one in state and national elections, farmers often provided major opposition for the rising national corporations. Many angry farmers were part of an anticorporate populist movement that started in the 1870s and formed its own political party in the 1880s to challenge both Democrats and Republicans. Several of the reforms advocated by the populists—such as a government commission to set railroad rates, the direct election of senators, and the federal income tax—were eventually adopted.

But the day of farmers as challengers to the corporate community is long past. The populists were defeated at the turn of the twentieth century by a coalition of prosperous farmers and local business leaders. As the farm population declined and the average size of farms increased, farm owners became an interest group rather than a large popular movement. Moreover, the large-scale family farmers of the Midwest and Great Plains increasingly joined with the plantation owners of the South and the ranchers of California as employers of wage labor, especially part-time migrant labor, and identified themselves as business owners. The periodic attempts since the 1930s by farm workers to organize labor unions, often aided and encouraged by liberals and leftists, intensified the farm owners' sense of opposition to the liberal-labor coalition.[43]

Although most of the 2.19 million farms in existence today are still family owned, with less than 1 percent owned by large corporations in other business sectors, the overwhelming majority of them are extremely small. Approximately 55 percent of farms have less than $10,000 a year in sales, and 66 percent have less than $40,000 in sales. The people on these small farms earn over 90 percent of their income in off-farm jobs, many in manufacturing and service firms that relocated to rural areas to take advantage of lower wages. Moreover, one-third of farm sales are made to large corporations under fixed-price contracts, moving many farmers closer to the status of corporate wage-workers.[44]

At the other end of the farm ladder, the well-to-do among farmers, the 15.9 percent with sales of $100,000 or more a year, control 55.9 percent of the farm acreage, and the few percent of farms with over $250,000 in sales account for 72 percent of all agricultural sales. Many of the largest farms are part of agribusiness complexes, particularly for farm commodities where a few companies control most of the market. Roughly 85 percent of all eggs and poultry, for example, come from 20 corporations and the farmers under contract to them.[45] Just 43 farm companies control one-third of the American market for pork; they own 1.74 million sows that produce over 30 million pigs each year. There are 400 companies with $10 million or more in farm sales each year: 114 produced beef, 75 produced poultry, 70 raised vegetables, and 54 produced eggs.[46]

The biggest farms also differentially benefit from the federal subsidy payments made to farmers each year through a variety of programs. Although the government has not made it easy to assemble figures on farm subsidies since the passage of the Freedom to Farm Act in 1996, the Environmental Working Group, a nonprofit watchdog group, used the Freedom of Information Act to obtain copies of the checks for $30 billion sent to farmers between 1996 and 1999. It found that the top 10 percent of recipients, just 202,678 individuals, some of whom are husband and wife, or siblings, received 63 percent of all subsidy payments in that time period, and that the top 20 percent received 81 percent.[47] Thus, the subsidy program serves to strengthen large farms and push more small farms out of business.

These farmers with over $100,000 in yearly sales are organized into a wide variety of associations that look out for their interests. Some of these organizations are commodity groups, made up of those who produce a particular crop. There are also two or three general farm groups, the most important of which is the American Farm Bureau Federation. The Farm Bureau, as it is known, and most other farm groups usually align with business trade associations in the political arena. The Farm Bureau in particular is an important part of the corporate-conservative coalition. It has its own insurance company and includes related agribusinesses and local businesses among its members.[48] There is, however, one farm organization, the National Farmers Union, that usually has allied itself with the liberal-labor coalition. Its historical origins are in wheat farming in the Great Plains.[49]

Farmers, then, are no longer an independent base of power in the United States. They are few in number, and most of those few do not have enough income from their farms to have any political impact. At the same time, average farmers are becoming contract producers, working for a set price for the handful of giant corporations that are on their way to controlling food production. The small percent of large-scale farmers who produce most of the cash crops are integrated into the agribusiness complex within the corporate community through commodity groups and the Farm Bureau.

SMALL BUSINESS: NOT A COUNTERWEIGHT

There are approximately 22 million small businesses in the United States, defined as businesses with less than 500 employees. By contrast, there are only 14,000 companies with 500 or more employees. Because small businesses make 52 percent of all sales and employ 54 percent of the private labor force, they are sometimes claimed to be a counterweight to the power of the corporate community. They have an important place in the American belief system because they are thought to embody the independence and initiative of all Americans, and since the 1980s they have been extolled as the primary force in creating new jobs in the economy.[50]

But the owners of small businesses are too large in number, too diverse in size, and too lacking in financial assets to have any collective power that could challenge the corporate community. One-third of American businesses are part-time operations run from the home or as a sideline from a regular job, and another one-third are solo efforts. Others exist in immigrant ethnic enclaves and have no contacts with businesspeople outside their community. As a result of these problems, small businesspeople have not formed their own associations to lobby for them.

There are organizations that claim to represent small business, especially the National Federation of Independent Business, which has 560,000 members. In fact, these organizations are actually businesses created by political entrepreneurs as a way to make profits on membership dues and at the same time have a basis for lobbying for their policy preferences. In the case of the National Federation of Independent Business, the most visible of these organizations, it is actually a lobbying organization for the corporate-conservative coalition, drawing much of its leadership and staff from the Republican Party. Although it is now a nonprofit organization, it was created as a for-profit organization and controlled by its founder from its beginning in 1943 until his retirement. Now it is controlled by a small board of directors made up of wealthy business owners who pay the top officers several hundred thousand dollars a year to manage 700 employees and oversee $58 million in revenues. There are still no general meetings or votes for officers. Memberships are sold by traveling sales representatives who receive a commission for each new member they recruit. The turnover in membership is very great. The organization reflects the opinions of the most conservative of small business owners.

The claims by small business organizations notwithstanding, the small businesses that go beyond the part-time and one-person levels are most often part of trade associations that receive most of their funding and direction from large corporations. They are also part of the two largest general business organizations in the country: the U.S. Chamber of Commerce, which claims 180,000 companies and 2,800 state and local chambers as members, and the National Association of Manufacturers, which claims 12,500 companies and subsidiaries as members. These are figures that go well beyond the several hundred companies in the corporate community and the 14,000 companies with 500 or more employees.

Many small businesses are part of economic networks that have large corporations at the center. The most visible and longstanding examples of small businesses tied to large corporations are the 600,000 franchise businesses that sell products and services to the general public—convenience stores, fast-food outlets, mall shops, automobile repair shops, and many more. Owners pay fees of $10,000 to $40,000 to the parent company to obtain a franchise, plus monthly royalties. Between 1967 and 2000, the percentage of all sales made by franchise outlets went from 10 to nearly 50 percent.*[51]

---

*Many of these big franchise companies, such as Subway, Midas Muffler, and Thrifty Car Rental, take advantage of guaranteed loans at low interest rates from the federal government's Small Business Administration, which is only supposed to help small companies. In 1996, for example, 14 hotel and motel companies received $209 million in low-interest loans to open nearly 260 new outlets.

As for the small manufacturing companies sometimes said to be sources of innovation and new jobs, they are often part of the producer networks that sell parts and services to large corporations. The fact that many of these firms start with 100 or more employees suggests the importance of their subcontracts for their existence and survival. Not all small manufacturing firms are directly tied to large corporations, however. Many are part of what one author calls "the minor industrial revolution" that brought small firms into southern states in search of low-wage, nonunionized labor.[52] Still others owe their origins to discoveries and patents that were developed in large universities, especially in the electronic and biotechnology industries.

When all is said and done, then, there is no "small business community" in the United States to provide any opposition to the corporate community. The relatively few small businesses that are full-time operations and have more than a handful of employees are incorporated into the power networks of the corporate community (1) by belonging to trade associations dominated by larger businesses; (2) as franchise outlets for larger businesses; and (3) as suppliers and service providers for big corporations. These ties place severe market and political constraints on most small businesses in relation to the large corporations. Small business is too poor and fragmented to be a counterweight to the .3 percent of businesses that have 59 percent of total business assets.[53]

LOCAL BUSINESSES FORM GROWTH COALITIONS

The most important small businesses in the United States are organized into local growth coalitions whose members share a common interest in intensifying land use in their geographical locale. The most typical way of intensifying land use is growth, which usually expresses itself in a constantly rising population. In economic terms, the *place entrepreneurs* at the heart of local growth coalitions are trying to maximize rents from land and buildings, which is a little different than the goal of the corporate community, maximizing profits from the sale of goods and services:

> Unlike the capitalist, the place entrepreneur's goal is not profit from production, but rent from trapping human activity in place. Besides sale prices and regular payments made by tenants to landlords, we take rent to include, more broadly, outlays made to realtors, mortgage lenders, title companies, and so forth. The people who are involved in generating rent are the investors in land and buildings and the professionals who serve them. We think of them as a special class among the privileged, analogous to the classic "rentiers" of a former age in a modern urban form. Not merely a residue of a disappearing social group, rentiers persist as a dynamic social force.[54]

Local growth coalitions and the corporate community, as owners of income-producing properties, have much in common and often work together. The basis for their cooperation is revealed by the fact that the primary way to intensify land use is to attract corporate investments to the area. The place entrepreneurs are therefore very much attuned to the needs of corporations, working hard to provide them with the physical infrastructure, municipal services, labor markets, and political climate they find attractive. The growth caused by corporate investments—and investments by universities and government agencies—then leads to housing development, increased financial activity, and increased consumer spending, all of which make land and buildings even more valuable.

Still, the relationship between the growth coalitions and the corporate community is not without its conflicts. This is primarily because corporations have the ability to move if they think that regulations are becoming too stringent or taxes and wages too high. A move by a major corporation can have a devastating impact on a local growth coalition. Moreover, this ability to move contributes to the constant competition among rival cities for new capital investments, creating tensions between growth coalitions as well as between individual growth coalitions and the corporate community. The net result is often a "race to the bottom" as cities offer tax breaks, less environmental regulation, and other benefits to corporations in order to tempt them to relocate. Ironically, most studies of plant location suggest that environmental laws and local taxes are of minor importance in corporate decisions concerning the location or relocation of production facilities. A union-free environment and low-cost raw materials are the major factors.[55]

Local growth coalitions face a third source of potential tension and conflict: disagreements with neighborhoods about expansion and development. Neighborhoods are something to be used and enjoyed in the eyes of those who live in them, but they are often seen as sites for further development by growth coalitions, who justify new developments with a doctrine claiming the highest and best use for land. Thus, neighborhoods often end up fighting against freeways, wider streets, highrises, and commercial buildings. This conflict between *use value* and *exchange value* becomes a basic one in most successful cities, especially when the downtown interests try to expand the central business district, often at the expense of established low-income and minority neighborhoods. Between 1955 and 1975, for example, a government program called *urban renewal* ended up removing housing from thousands of acres of land so that central business districts and downtown universities could be expanded.[56] This process contributed greatly to inner-city tensions in the following decades.

The success rate of neighborhoods in conflicts with the growth coalitions is very low. Since the primary focus of residents is on their everyday lives, they often do not persist in their protests, and seldom join larger coalitions with other neighborhoods in the city. Moreover, as explained in Chapter 6, the reorganization of local elections in the early twentieth century by growth coalition leaders served to minimize the impact of neighborhood politics. As a result of these changes, neighborhoods usually lose after sometimes causing delays or changes in the plans.

A local growth coalition sometimes includes a useful junior partner, namely, construction unions. Despite a general allegiance to the liberal-labor coalition at the national level, these unions see their fate tied to the growth coalition in the belief that growth creates jobs. They are often highly visible on the side of the growth coalition in battles against neighborhood groups, environmentalists, and university faculty, staff, and students. Although local growth does not create new jobs in the economy as a whole, which is a function of corporate and governmental decisions beyond the province of any single community, it does determine where the new jobs will be located. Local construction unions therefore find it in their interest to help the growth coalition in its competition with other localities. Jobs are the ideal unifying theme for bringing the whole community together behind just about any growth project. The goal of the growth coalition is never said to be moneymaking, but jobs for the citizens of the community.

STRUCTURAL POWER AND ITS LIMITS

What does all this mean in terms of corporate power? First, none of the other economic interests studied in this chapter—public pension funds, small farmers, small businesses, and local growth coalitions—provide the organizational base for any significant opposition to the corporate community. To the degree that the corporate community faces any direct challenges, they come from the union movement and the relatively small number of liberals and leftists in universities, religious communities, and literary/artistic communities. Members of this liberal-labor coalition are often highly visible and vocal through their writing and media appearances, giving an initial impression of considerable strength. This image is reinforced by repeated ultraconservative claims in the media about the great power of liberals. Whether this image is accurate or not is discussed at different points in later chapters.

The power exercised by corporate leaders through their companies is considerable. For example, they can invest their money when and where they choose. If they feel threatened by new laws or labor unions, they can move or close their factories and offices. Unless restrained by union contracts, which now cover less than 10 percent of employees in the private sector, they can hire, promote, and replace workers as they see fit, often laying off employees on a moment's notice. These economic powers give them a direct influence over the great majority of Americans, who are dependent upon wages and salaries for their incomes, and therefore often hesitant to challenge corporations politically. Economic power also gives the corporate community indirect influence over elected and appointed officials because the growth and stability of a city, state, or the country as a whole can be jeopardized by a lack of business confidence in government.

In short, the sheer economic power of the corporate community can influence government without any effort on the part of corporate leaders. Because businesspeople have the legal right to spend their money when and as they wish, and government officials dare not try to take over the function of investing funds to create jobs, the government has to cater to business. If government officials do not give corporate leaders what they want, there are likely to be economic difficulties that would lead people to desire new political leadership. Since most government officials do not want to lose their positions, they do what is necessary to satisfy business leaders and maintain a healthy economy.[57]

In this manner, private control over the investment function provides leaders within the corporate community with a structural power that is independent of any attempts by them to influence government officials directly. While such power is very great, it is not sufficient in and of itself to allow the corporate community to dominate government, especially in times of economic or political crisis. First, it does not preclude the possibility that government officials might turn to nonbusiness constituencies to support new economic arrangements. Contrary to claims by conservative economists, there is no necessary relationship between private ownership and markets.[58] Improbable though it may seem to most readers, it would be possible for government to create firms to compete in the market system and thereby revive a depressed economy, or to hire unemployed workers in order to increase their ability to spend. In fact, the liberal-labor coalition mounted a legislative effort of roughly this sort shortly after World War II, only to be defeated by the conservative Congressional coalition of Southern Democrats and Northern Republicans.[59]

Second, structural power does not guarantee that employees will accept an ongoing economic depression without taking over factories or destroying private property. In such situations, however rare, the corporate leaders need government to protect their private property. They have to be able to call on the government to keep unauthorized persons from entering and using their factories and equipment. In short, structural power primarily concerns the relationship between the corporate community and government officials. It is not always able to contain the volatile power conflict between owners and workers that is built into the economy. In point of fact, such conflicts did arise in the Great Depression of the 1930s, leading to both new labor legislation and the frequent use of police forces to subdue striking workers and union organizers.[60]

There is uncertainty in the relationship between the corporate community and government because there is no guarantee that the underlying population and government officials will accept the viewpoint of corporate owners under all economic circumstances. This makes it risky for corporate officials to refuse to invest or to remain passive in an economic depression. Leaders within the corporate community thus feel a need to have direct influence on both the public at large and government officials. They have developed a number of ways to realize those objectives. As a top corporate leader replied to a sociologist who suggested to him during a research interview that his company probably had enough structural economic power to dispense with its efforts to influence elected officials: "I'm not sure, but I'm not willing to find out."[61]

To fully explain how the owners and top-level managers are able to organize themselves in an effort to create new policies, shape public opinion, elect politicians they trust, and influence government officials, it is first necessary to examine the relationship between the corporate community and the social upper class.

3

The Corporate Community and the Upper Class

Why does it matter whether or not the corporate community and the upper class are intertwined? If the corporate community and the upper class are essentially one and the same in terms of people and objectives, then it is more likely that they have the wealth, social cohesion, and awareness of their common interests to organize themselves well enough to dominate government. If they are separate, the wealth and status of the upper class might form a rival power base and make the power structure more open.

The nationwide social upper class has its own exclusive social institutions and is based in the ownership of great wealth. The social cohesion that develops among members of the upper class provides another basis for the creation of policy agreements within the policy-planning network discussed in the next chapter. This social cohesion is based in the two types of relationships found in a membership network: common membership in specific social institutions and friendships based on social interactions within those institutions. Research on small groups in laboratory settings suggests that social cohesion is greatest when (1) the social groups are seen to be exclusive and of high status; and (2) when the interactions take place in relaxed and informal settings.[1] Many of the social institutions of the upper class fit these specifications very well. From the viewpoint of social psychology, the people who make up the upper class can be seen as members of numerous small groups that meet at private schools, social clubs, retreats, and resorts.

Social cohesion is important because other research suggests that the most socially cohesive groups are the ones that do best in arriving at consensus when dealing with a problem. The members are proud of their identification with the group and come to trust each other through their friendly interactions, so they are more likely to listen to each other and seek common ground.[2] If these findings can be generalized beyond the psychology laboratory, as seems very likely, then social bonding can be seen as another reason why the upper class is cohesive enough to dominate the rest of society despite its small size —less than 1 percent of the population.

The more extravagant social activities of the upper class—the expensive parties, the jet-setting to spas and vacation spots all over the world, the involvement with exotic entertainers—may seem like superfluous trivialities. However, these activities play a role both in solidifying the upper class and in maintaining the class structure. Within the upper class itself, these occasions provide an opportunity for members to show each other that they are similar to each other and superior to the average citizen. It remains the case, as a classic 1941 study of the upper class in New York concluded, that "the elaborate private life of the plutocracy serves in considerable measure to separate them out in their own consciousness as a superior, more refined element."[3]

In addition, the values upon which the class system is based are conveyed to the rest of the population through this conspicuous consumption. Such activities make clear that there is a gulf between members of the upper class and ordinary citizens, reminding everyone of the hierarchical nature of the society. Social extravaganzas bring home to everyone that there are great rewards for success, helping to stir up the personal envy that can be a goad to competitive striving. In sociological terms, the upper class comes to serve as a kind of reference group: "Numerically insignificant . . . the upper class is nonetheless highly influential as a 'reference group': a membership to which many aspire and which infinitely more consciously or unconsciously imitate."[4]

PREPPING FOR POWER

From infancy through young adulthood, members of the upper class receive a distinctive education. This education begins early in life in preschools that sometimes are attached to a neighborhood church of high social status. Schooling continues during the elementary years at a local private school called a day school. The adolescent years may see the student remain at day school, but there is a strong chance that at least one or two years will be spent away from home at a boarding school in a quiet rural setting. Higher education is obtained at one of a small number of prestigious private universities. Although some upper-class children may attend public high school if they live in a secluded suburban setting, or go to a state university if there is one of great esteem and tradition in their home state, the system of formal schooling is so insulated that many upper-class students never see the inside of a public school in all their years of education. This separate educational system is important evidence for the distinctiveness of the mentality and lifestyle that exists within the upper class, because schools play a large role in transmitting the class structure to their students.

The linchpins in the upper-class educational system are the dozens of boarding schools developed in the last half of the nineteenth and the early part of the twentieth centuries, coincident with the rise of a nationwide upper class whose members desired to insulate themselves from an inner city that was becoming populated by lower-class immigrants. They become surrogate families that play a major role in creating an upper-class subculture on a national scale in America.[5] The role of boarding schools in providing connections to other upper-class social institutions is also important. As one informant explained to a sociologist doing an interview study of upper-class women: "Where I went to boarding school, there were girls from all over the country, so I know people from all over. It's helpful when you move to a new city and want to get invited into the local social club."[6]

It is within these several hundred schools that a unique style of life is inculcated through such traditions as the initiatory hazing of beginning students, the wearing of school blazers or ties, and participation in esoteric sports such as lacrosse, squash, and crew. Even a different language is adopted to distinguish these schools from public schools. The principal is a headmaster or rector, the teachers are sometimes called masters, and the students are in forms, not grades. Great emphasis is placed upon the building of character. The role of the school in preparing the future leaders of America is emphasized through the speeches of the headmaster and the frequent mention of successful alumni.

Thus, boarding schools are in many ways the kind of highly effective socializing agent called *total institutions*, isolating their members from the outside world and providing them with a set of routines and traditions that encompass most of their waking hours. The end result is a feeling of separateness and superiority that comes from having survived a rigorous education. According to one retired corporate executive:

> At school we were made to feel somewhat better (than other people) because of our class. That existed, and I've always disliked it

intensely. Unfortunately, I'm afraid some of these things rub off
on one.[7]

Virtually all graduates of private secondary schools go on to college, and most do so at prestigious universities. Graduates of the New
England boarding schools, for example, historically found themselves
at three or four large Ivy League universities: Harvard, Yale, Princeton, and Columbia. However, that situation changed somewhat after
World War II as the universities grew and provided more scholarships.
An analysis of admission patterns for graduates of 14 prestigious
boarding schools between 1953 and 1967 demonstrated this shift by
showing that the percentage of their graduates attending Harvard,
Yale, or Princeton gradually declined over those years from 52 to 25
percent. Information on the same 14 schools for the years 1969 to
1979 showed that the figure had bottomed out at 13 percent in 1973,
1975, and 1979, with some schools showing very little change from the
late 1960s and others dropping even more dramatically.[8] Now many
upper-class students attend a select handful of smaller private colleges, most of which are in the East, but a few in the South and West
as well.

Graduates of private schools outside of New England most frequently attend a prominent state university in their area, but a significant minority go to eastern Ivy League and top private universities in
other parts of the country. For example, the Cate School, a boarding
school near Santa Barbara, California, is modeled after its New England counterparts and draws most of its students from California and
other western states. In the four years between 1993 and 1996, 35 percent of the 245 graduates went to one of fifteen prestigious Ivy League
schools, with Middlebury (12), Harvard (10), and Brown (7) topping
the list. The other leading destinations for Cate graduates were the University of California (27), Stanford (9), University of Colorado (9),
Georgetown (8), Duke (7), Vanderbilt (6), and University of Chicago (5).
Or, to take another example, St. John's in Houston is a lavishly endowed
day school built in the Gothic architecture typical of many universities.
From 1992 through 1996, 22 percent of its 585 graduates went to the fifteen Ivy League schools used in the Cate analysis, with Princeton (27),
the University of Pennsylvania (15), Cornell (13), Harvard (12), and
Yale (12) the most frequent destinations. As might be expected, 105
graduates went to the University of Texas (18 percent), but Rice (49),
Vanderbilt (33), and Stanford (15) were high on the list. Few graduates
of either Cate or St. John's went to less prestigious state schools.[9]

Most private school graduates pursue careers in business, finance, or corporate law, which is the first evidence for the intertwining of the upper class and the corporate community. Their

business-oriented preoccupations are demonstrated in the greatest detail in a study of all those who graduated from Hotchkiss between 1940 and 1950. Using the school's alumni files, the researcher followed the careers of 228 graduates from their date of graduation until 1970. Fifty-six percent of the sample are either bankers or business executives, with 80 of the 91 businessmen serving as president, vice-president, or partner in their firms. Another 10 percent of the sample are lawyers, mostly as partners in large firms closely affiliated with the corporate community.[10]

The involvement of private school graduates on boards of directors is demonstrated in a study for this book of all alumni over the age of 45 from one of the most prestigious eastern boarding schools, St. Paul's. Using *Poor's Register of Corporations, Directors and Executives*, and *Who's Who in America*, it shows that 303 of these several thousand men are serving as officers or directors in corporations in general, and that 102 are directors of 97 corporations in the *Fortune* 800. Their involvement is especially great in the financial sector. Most striking of all, 21 graduates of St. Paul's are either officers or directors at J. P. Morgan Bank, which for a time was one of the five largest banks in the country until it merged with Chase Manhattan Bank in late 2000. This finding suggests that the alumni of particular schools may tend to cluster at specific banks or corporations.

SOCIAL CLUBS

Private social clubs are a major point of orientation in the lives of upper-class adults. These clubs also have a role in differentiating members of the upper class from other members of society. The clubs of the upper class are many and varied, ranging from family-oriented country clubs and downtown men's and women's clubs to highly specialized clubs for yachtsmen, sportsmen, gardening enthusiasts, and fox hunters. Downtown men's clubs originally were places for having lunch and dinner, and occasionally for attending an evening performance or a weekend party. As upper-class families deserted the city for large suburban estates, a new kind of club, the country club, gradually took over some of these functions. The downtown club became almost entirely a luncheon club, a site to hold meetings, or a place to relax on a free afternoon. The country club, by contrast, became a haven for all members of the family. It offered social and sporting activities ranging from dances, parties, and banquets to golf, swimming, and tennis. Special group dinners were often arranged for all members on Thursday night, the traditional maid's night off across the United States.

Initiation fees, annual dues, and expenses vary from a few thousand dollars in downtown clubs to tens of thousands of dollars in some country clubs, but money is not the primary barrier in gaining membership to a club. Each club has a very rigorous screening process before accepting new members. Most require nomination by one or more active members, letters of recommendation from three to six members, and interviews with at least some members of the membership committee. Negative votes by two or three members of what is typically a 10- to-20-person committee often are enough to deny admission to the candidate. The carefulness with which new members are selected extends to a guarding of club membership lists, which are usually available only to club members. Research on clubs therefore has to be based on out-of-date membership lists that have been given to historical libraries by members or their surviving spouses.

Men and women of the upper class often belong to clubs in several cities, creating a nationwide pattern of overlapping memberships. These overlaps provide evidence for social cohesion within the upper class. An indication of the nature and extent of this overlapping is revealed in a study of membership lists for 20 clubs in several major cities across the country, including the Links in New York, the Duquesne in Pittsburgh, the Chicago in Chicago, the Pacific Union in San Francisco, and the California in Los Angeles. There is sufficient overlap among 18 of the 20 clubs to form three regional groupings and a fourth group that provides a bridge between the two largest regional groups. The several dozen men who are in three or more of the clubs, most of them very wealthy people who also sit on several corporate boards, are especially important in creating the overall pattern.[11]

The overlap of this club network with corporate boards of directors provides important evidence for the intertwining of the upper class and corporate community. In one study, the club memberships of the chairpersons and outside directors of the 20 largest industrial corporations were counted. The overlaps with upper-class clubs in general are ubiquitous, but the concentration of directors in a few clubs is especially notable. At least one director from 12 of the 20 corporations is a member of the Links Club, which is the New York meeting grounds of the national corporate establishment. Seven of General Electric's directors are members, as are four from Chrysler, four from Westinghouse, and three from IBM. In addition to the Links, several other clubs have directors from four or more corporations. Another study, using membership lists from 11 prestigious clubs in different parts of the country, confirms and extends these findings. A majority of the top 25 corporations in every major sector of the economy have directors in at least one of these clubs, and several have many more. For example, all of the 25 largest industrials have one or more directors in these 11 clubs. The Links in New York, with 79 connections to 21 industrial corporations, has the most.[12]

The Bohemian Grove as a Microcosm

One of the most central clubs in the club network, the Bohemian Club of San Francisco, is also the most unusual and widely known club of the upper class. Its annual two-week retreat in its 2,700-acre Bohemian Grove, 75 miles north of San Francisco, brings together members of the upper class, corporate leaders, celebrities, and government officials for relaxation and entertainment. They are joined by several hundred so-called associate members, who pay lower dues in exchange for producing plays, skits, artwork, and other forms of entertainment. There are also 50 to 100 professors and university administrators, most of them from Stanford University and campuses of the University of California. This encampment provides the best possible insight into the role of clubs in uniting the corporate community and the upper class. It is a microcosm of the world of the upper class.

The pristine forest setting called the Bohemian Grove was purchased by the club in the 1890s after twenty years of holding the retreat in rented quarters. Bohemians and their guests number anywhere from 1,500 to 2,500 for the three weekends in the encampment, which is always held during the last two weeks in July. However, there may be as few as 400 men in residence in the middle of the week because most return to their homes and jobs after the weekends. During their stay the campers are treated to plays, symphonies, concerts, lectures, and commentaries by entertainers, scholars, corporate executives, and government officials. They also trapshoot, canoe, swim, drop by the Grove art gallery, and take guided tours into the outer fringe of the mountain forest. But a stay at the Bohemian Grove is mostly a time for relaxation and drinking in the modest lodges, bunkhouses, and even teepees that fit unobtrusively into the landscape along the two or three dirt roads that join the few developed acres within the Grove. It is like a summer camp for corporate leaders and their entertainers.

The men gather in little camps of from 10 to 30 members during their stay, although the camps for associate members are often larger. Each of the approximately 120 camps has its own pet name, such as Sons of Toil, Cave Man, Mandalay, Toyland, Owl's Nest, Hill Billies, and Parsonage. Some camps are noted for special drinking parties, brunches, or luncheons to which they invite members from other camps. The camps are a fraternity system within the larger fraternity.

There are many traditional events during the encampment, including plays called the High Jinx and the Low Jinx. The most memorable event, however, is an elaborate ceremonial ritual called the Cremation of Care, which is held the first Saturday night. It takes place at the base of a 40-foot owl shrine, constructed out of poured concrete and made even more resplendent by the mottled forest mosses that cover much of it. According to the club's librarian, who is also a historian at a large university, the event "incorporates druidical ceremonies, elements of medieval Christian liturgy, sequences directly inspired by the Book of Common Prayer, traces of Shakespearean drama and the 17th century masque, and late nineteenth century American lodge rites."[13] Bohemians are proud that the ceremony has been carried out for 128 consecutive years as of 2000.

The opening ceremony is called the Cremation of Care because it involves the burning of an effigy named Dull Care, who symbolizes the burdens and responsibilities that these busy Bohemians now wish to shed temporarily. More than 250 Bohemians take part in the ceremony as priests, elders, boatmen, and woodland voices. After many flowery speeches and a long conversation with Dull Care, the high priest lights the fire with the flame from the Lamp of Fellowship, located on the Altar of Bohemia at the base of the shrine. The ceremony, which has the same initiatory functions as those of any fraternal or tribal group, ends with fireworks, shouting, and the playing of "There'll Be a Hot Time in the Old Town Tonight." And thus the attempt to create a sense of cohesion and in-group solidarity among the assembled is complete.

The retreat sometimes provides an occasion for more than fun and merriment. Although business is rarely discussed, except in an informal way in groups of two or three, the retreat provides members with an opportunity to introduce their friends to politicians and hear formal noontime speeches from political candidates. Every Republican president of the twentieth century was a member or guest at the Bohemian Grove.

Two separate studies demonstrate the way in which this one club intertwines the upper class with the entire corporate community. The first uses the years 1970 and 1980, the second compares 1971 and 1991. In 1970, according to the first study, 29 percent of the top 800 corporations had at least one officer or director at the Bohemian Grove festivities; in 1980 the figure was 30 percent As might be expected, the overlap was especially great among the largest corporations, with 23 of the top 25 industrials represented in 1970, 15 of 25 in 1980. Twenty of the 25 largest banks had at least one officer or director in attendance in both 1970 and 1980. Other business sectors had somewhat less representation.[14]

Table 3.1 Corporations with Three or More Directors Who Were
Members of the Bohemian Club in 1991

Corporation	Number of Directors in Bohemian Club
Bank of America	7
Pacific Gas and Electric	5
AT&T	4
Pacific Enterprises	4
First Interstate Bank	4
McKesson Corporation	4
Carter-Hawley-Hale Stores	3
Ford Motor	3
FMC	3
Safeco Insurance	3
Potlatch Industries	3
Pope and Talbot	3
General Motors	3
Pacific Bell Telephone	3

Source: Peter Phillips, *A Relative Advantage: Sociology of the San Francisco Bohemian Club.* Ph.D. Dissertation, University of California, Davis, 1994, p. 77.

An even more intensive study, which includes participant-observation and interviews, along with a membership network analysis, extends the sociological understanding of the Bohemian Grove into the 1990s. Using a list of 1,144 corporations, well beyond the 800 used in the studies for 1970 and 1980, the study found that 24 percent of these companies had at least one director who was a member or guest in 1991. For the top 100 corporations outside of California, the figure was 42 percent, compared to 64 percent in 1971.[15] The companies with three or more directors who were members of the Bohemian Club in 1991 are listed in Table 3.1.

As the case of the Bohemian Grove and its theatrical performances rather dramatically illustrates, clubs seem to have the same function within the upper class that the brotherhood has in tribal societies. With their restrictive membership policies, initiatory rituals, and great emphasis on tradition, clubs carry on the heritage of primitive secret societies. They create an attitude of prideful exclusiveness within their members that contributes greatly to an in-group feeling and a sense of fraternity within the upper class.

In concluding this discussion of the Bohemian Club and its retreat as one small example of the intersection of the upper class and corporate community, it needs to be stressed that the Bohemian Grove is not a place of power. No conspiracies are hatched there, nor anywhere else, for that matter. Instead, it is a place where people of power relax, make new acquaintances, and enjoy themselves. It is primarily a place of social bonding and the passing on of general values:

> The clubs are a repository of the values held by the upper-level prestige groups in the community and are a means by which these values are transferred to the business environment. The clubs are places in which the beliefs, problems, and values of the industrial organization are discussed and related to the other elements in the larger community. Clubs, therefore, are not only effective vehicles of informal communication, but also valuable centers where views are presented, ideas are modified, and new ideas emerge. Those in the interview sample were appreciative of this asset; in addition, they considered the club as a valuable place to combine social and business contacts.[16]

THE FEMININE HALF OF THE UPPER CLASS

During the late nineteenth and early twentieth centuries, women of the upper class carved out their own distinct roles within the context of male domination in business, finance, and law. They went to separate private schools, founded their own social clubs, and belonged to their own voluntary associations. As young women and party goers, they set the fashions for society. As older women and activists, they took charge of the nonprofit welfare and cultural institutions of the society, serving as fundraisers, philanthropists, and directors in a manner parallel to their male counterparts in business and politics. To prepare themselves for their leadership roles, they created the Junior League in 1901 to provide internships, role models, mutual support, and training in the management of meetings.

Due to the general social changes of the 1960s, and in particular the revival of the feminist movement, the socialization of wealthy young women has changed somewhat in recent decades. Most private schools are now coeducational. Their women graduates are encouraged to go to major four-year colleges rather than finishing schools. Women of the upper class are more likely to have careers; there are already two or three examples of women who have risen to the top of their family's business. They are also more likely to serve on corporate boards. Still, due to the emphasis on tradition, there may be even less gender equality in the upper class than there is in the professional stratum.

The most informative and intimate look at the adult lives of traditional upper-class women is provided in three different interview-and-observation studies, one on the East Coast, one in the Midwest, and one on the West Coast.[17] They reveal the women to be people of both power and subservience, taking decision-making roles in numerous cultural and civic organizations but also accepting traditional roles at home vis-à-vis their husbands and children. By asking the women to describe a typical day and to explain which activities are most important to them, these sociologists found that the role of community volunteer is a central preoccupation of upper-class women. It has significance as a family tradition and as an opportunity to fulfill an obligation to the community. One elderly woman involved for several decades in both the arts and human services said: "If you're privileged, you have a certain responsibility. This was part of my upbringing; it's a tradition, a pattern of life that my brothers and sisters [follow] too."[18]

The volunteer role is institutionalized in the training programs and activities of a variety of service organizations. This is especially the case with the Junior League, which is meant for women between 20 and 40 years of age, including some upwardly mobile professional women. "Voluntarism is crucial and the Junior League is the quintessence of volunteer work," explained one woman. "Everything the League does improves the situation but doesn't rock the boat. It fits into existing institutions."[19] Quite unexpectedly, many of the women serving as volunteers, fund-raisers, and board members for charitable and civic organizations view their work as a protection of the American way of life against the further encroachment of government into areas of social welfare. Some even see themselves as bulwarks against socialism. "There must always be people to do volunteer work," one commented. "If you have a society where no one is willing, then you may as well have communism, where it's all done by the government." Another stated: "It would mean that the government would take over, and it would all be regimented. If there are no volunteers, we would live in a completely managed society which is quite the opposite to our history of freedom." Another equated government support with socialism: "You'd have to go into government funds. That's socialism. The more we can keep independent and under private control, the better it is."[20]

Despite this emphasis on volunteer work, the women place high value on family life. They arrange their schedules to be home when children come home from school, and they stress that their primary concern is to provide a good home for their husbands. Several of them want to have greater decision-making power over their inherited wealth, but almost all of them want to be in the traditional roles of wife and mother, at least until their children are grown.

In recent years, thanks to the pressures on corporations from the feminist movement, upper-class women have expanded their roles to include corporate directorships, thereby providing another link between the upper class and the corporate community. One study of women in the corporate community reports that 26 percent of all women directors have upper-class backgrounds, which is very similar to overall findings for samples of predominantly male directors. The figure is even higher, 70 percent, for the 20 percent of directors who describe themselves as having been volunteers before joining corporate boards. Many of these women say their contacts with male corporate leaders on the boards of women's colleges and cultural organizations led to their selection as corporate directors.[21]

Women of the upper class are in a paradoxical position. They are subordinate to male members of their class, but they nonetheless exercise important class power in some institutional arenas. They may or may not be fully satisfied with their ambiguous power status, but they do bring an upper-class, antigovernment perspective to their exercise of power. There is thus class solidarity between men and women toward the rest of society. Commenting on the complex role of upper-class women, a feminist scholar draws the following stark picture:

> First they must do to class what gender has done to their work— render it invisible. Next, they must maintain the same class structure they have struggled to veil.[22]

DROPOUTS, FAILURES, AND CHANGE AGENTS

Not all men and women of the upper class fit the usual molds. A few are drop-outs, jet-setters, failures, or even critics of the upper class. Except for a few long-standing exceptions, however, the evidence also suggests that many of the young jet-setters and drop-outs return to more familiar pathways. Numerous anecdotal examples show that some members of the upper class even lead lives of failure, despite all the opportunities available to them. Although members of the upper class are trained for leadership and given every opportunity to develop feelings of self-confidence, there are some who fail in school, become involved with drugs and alcohol, or become mentally disturbed. Once again, however, this cannot be seen as evidence for a lack of cohesion in the upper class, for there are bound to be some problems for individuals in any group.

There are even a few members of the upper class who abandon its institutions and values to become part of the liberal-labor coalition or leftists. They participate actively in liberal or leftist causes as well as lend financial support. Several liberal and socialist magazines of the past and present have been supported by such people, including *The Nation* and *Mother Jones*. Some of the most visible recent examples of this tendency work through a national network of fifteen change-oriented foundations called the Funding Exchange. These foundations gave away over $50 million from the time they were founded in the 1970s to the 1990s. They receive money from wealthy individuals and then donate it to feminist, environmentalist, low-income, and minority-group activists. They also set up discussion groups for college-age members of the upper class who are working through issues relating to their class backgrounds and thinking about providing money for liberal causes. In the case of the Haymarket Foundation, the committee that makes the donations (about $400,000 per year) is composed primarily of activists from groups that have been supported by the foundation. This approach provides a way to overcome the usual power relations between donors and recipients.[23]

CONTINUITY AND UPWARD MOBILITY

Americans always have believed that anyone can rise from rags to riches if they try hard enough, but in fact a rise from the bottom to the top is very rare and often a matter of luck—being at the right place at the right time. In the late nineteenth century, a wealthy upper-class Bostonian with a Harvard education, Horatio Alger, became a best-selling author by writing short fictional books on young boys who had gone from penniless adversity to great wealth. In real life, the commentators of his day pointed to three or four actual examples. Subsequent research showed that most of the business leaders of that era did not fit the Horatio Alger myth. As one historian put it, Horatio Algers appeared more frequently in magazines and textbooks than they did in reality.[24]

Since 1982, the Horatio Alger story line has been taken up by *Forbes*, a business magazine that publishes an annual list of the allegedly 400 richest Americans. "Forget old money," says the article that introduces the 1996 list. "Forget silver spoons. Great fortunes are being created almost monthly in the U.S. today by young entrepreneurs who hadn't a dime when we created this list 14 years ago."[25] But the Horatio Alger story is no less rare today than it was in the 1890s. A study of all those on the *Forbes* lists for 1995 and 1996 showed that at least 56 percent of them came from millionaire families and that another 14 percent came from the top 10 percent of the income ladder.[26]

These figures are probably an underestimate because it is difficult to obtain accurate information on family origins from those who want to obscure their pasts. Even those in the upwardly mobile 30 percent often have excellent educations or other advantages. As for the immigrants on the *Forbes* list, they too sometimes come from wealthy families; contrary to the stereotype, not all immigrants to the United States arrive poor, at least not any more.[27]

To take one example, consider the social background of Wayne Huizenga, owner of the professional football and hockey teams in Miami, estimated to be worth $1.4 billion in 1996 through the creation of, first, Waste Management Company, and then Blockbuster Video. Huizenga is often depicted as starting out as a mere garbage collector. As *Current Biography* puts it: "The hero of a real-life Horatio Alger story, in his early twenties, Huizenga worked as a garbage-truck driver."[28] But he was born in a Chicago suburb, graduated from a private high school, and had a grandfather who owned a garbage-collection business in Chicago. His father was a real estate investor. True, Huizenga did start his own garbage company in southern Florida after not showing much aptitude for college, but he also merged it with companies in Chicago that were successors to his grandfather's firm, one of which was headed by a cousin by marriage. This is enterprising behavior, but it is not a Horatio Alger saga.

Forbes also talks about several people on its list as "college dropouts," but people who leave a prestigious institution like Harvard or Stanford to pursue a new opportunity where timing is everything hardly fit the image of a "college drop-out." For example, Bill Gates, the richest person in the United States, is often described as a college drop-out because he left Harvard early to found Microsoft before someone beat him to what was the next logical step in the marketing of computer software. However, he is also the son of a prominent corporate lawyer in Seattle and a graduate of the top private school in that city, and he did go to Harvard.

According to research studies, most upward social mobility in the United States involves relatively small changes for those above the lowest 20 percent and below the top 5 percent. The grandfather is a blue-collar worker, the father has a good white-collar job based on a B.A. degree, and one or two of the father's children are lawyers or physicians, but most of the father's grandchildren are back to being white-collar workers and middle-level executives. Upward social mobility of this type may be even less frequent for nonwhites. In addition, the best recent studies suggest that upward social mobility may be declining in recent years.[29]

As the findings on the rarity of great upward mobility suggest, the continuity of the upper class from generation to generation is very great. This finding conflicts with the oft-repeated folk wisdom that there is a large turnover at the top of the American social ladder. Once in the upper class, families tend to stay there even as they are joined in each generation by new families and by middle-class brides and grooms who marry into their families. One study demonstrating this point began with a list of twelve families who were among the top wealth-holders in Detroit for 1860, 1892, and 1902. After documenting their high social standing as well as their wealth, it traced their Detroit-based descendants into the late twentieth century. Nine of the twelve families still have members in the Detroit upper class; members from six families are directors of top corporations in the city. The study casts light on some of the reasons why the continuity is not even greater. One of the top wealth holders of 1860 had only one child, who in turn had no children. Another family persisted into a fourth generation of four great-granddaughters, all of whom married outside of Detroit.[30]

A study of listings in the *Social Register* for 1940, 1977, and 1995 reveals the continuing presence of families descended from the largest fortunes of the nineteenth and early twentieth centuries. Using a list of 87 families from one history of great American fortunes and 66 families from another such book, a sociologist found that 92 percent of the families in the first book were still represented in 1977, with the figure falling only to 87 percent in 1995. In similar fashion, 88 percent of the families in the second book were represented in 1977 and 83 percent in 1995. Over half of these families signaled their connection to the founder of the fortune by putting "the 4th," "the 5th," or "the 6th" after their names. Almost half were given the last name of their wealthy mothers as their first name, once again demonstrating the concern with continuity.[31]

The American upper class, then, is a mixture of old and new members. There is both continuity and social mobility, with the newer members being assimilated into the lifestyle of the class through participation in the schools, clubs, and other social institutions described earlier in this chapter. There may be some tensions between those newly arrived and those of established status, as novelists and journalists love to point out, but what they have in common soon outweighs their differences.

THE UPPER CLASS AND CORPORATE CONTROL

So far, this chapter has demonstrated the overlap between upper-class social institutions and top leadership in the corporate community. It is also possible to show how members of the upper class involve themselves in the ownership and control of specific corporations through family ownership, family offices, holding companies, and investment partnerships.

Family Ownership

Although information presented in the previous chapter shows it is wrong to think that very many companies ever were or are completely owned by just one family, family ownership nonetheless has been the focus of many investigations of corporate control. Although these investigations usually rely on public records that are not ideal for research purposes, they provide a good starting point. Three different studies provide detailed evidence on the extent of family involvement in the largest American corporations. The first uses both official documents and the informal—but often more informative—findings of the business press as its source of information. It concludes that 40 percent of the top 300 industrials were probably under family control in the 1960s, using the usual cut-off point of 5 percent of the stock as the criterion.[32] Analyzing the official records that became available in the 1970s, a team of researchers at Corporate Data Exchange provided detailed information on the major owners of most of the top 500 industrials for 1980, showing that significant individual and family ownership continues to exist for all but the very largest of corporations.[33] One individual or family is a top stockholder, with at least 5 percent of the stock, in 44 percent of the 423 profiled corporations that are not controlled by other corporations or foreign interests. The figures are much lower among the 50 largest, however, where only 17 percent of the 47 companies included in the study shows evidence of major family involvement. The small percentage of the very largest industrials under individual or family control concurs with findings in a third study, which focused on the 200 largest nonfinancial corporations for 1974–1975. For the 104 companies common to the two studies, there are only four disagreements in classifying the nature of their control structure, and some of those may be due to changes in ownership patterns between 1974 and 1980.[34]

The Family Office

A family office is an informal organization through which members of a family or group of families agree to pool some of their resources in order to hire people to provide them with advice on investments, charitable giving, and even political donations in some cases. Family offices often handle all financial transactions and legal matters as well. Their relevance here is in terms of their potential for maintaining control of corporations founded by an earlier generation of the family. Such offices contradict the belief that corporate control is necessarily lost due to the inheritance of stock by a large number of descendants.

They often serve as a unifying source for the family as well. They sometimes have employees who sit on boards of directors to represent the family.

The most detailed account of a family office is provided by a sociologist as part of a study of the Weyerhaeuser family of Saint Paul, Minnesota, and Tacoma, Washington, whose great wealth is concentrated in the lumber industry. By assembling a family genealogy chart that covers five generations, and then interviewing several members of the family, he determined that a family office, called Fiduciary Counselors, Inc. (FCI), aids the family in maintaining a central role in two major corporations. He demonstrates that there are members of the family on the boards of these companies whose last names are not Weyerhaeuser, and that the stock holdings managed by the family office are large enough to maintain control.

Fiduciary Counselors, Inc., also houses the offices of two Weyerhaeuser holding companies (meaning companies created only to own stock in operating companies). These holding companies are used to make investments for family members as a group and to own shares in new companies that are created by family members. Although the primary focus of the Weyerhaeuser family office is economic matters, the office serves other functions as well. It keeps the books for fifteen different charitable foundations of varying sizes and purposes through which family members give money, and it coordinates political donations by family members all over the country.[35]

Holding Companies

Holding companies, briefly defined in the previous paragraph, can serve the economic functions of a family office if the family is still small and tight-knit. They have the added advantage of being incorporated entities that can buy and sell stock in their own names. Because they are privately held, they need report only to tax authorities on their activities.

The second-richest person in the United States, Warren Buffett, the scion of third-generation wealth, operates through a holding company, Berkshire Hathaway. Along with his partners, he sits on the boards of several of the companies in which he invests. Table 3.2 lists the corporate directorships held by Buffett and his partners.[36]

Investment Partnerships

Some wealthy individuals and families operate through a slightly different financial arrangement, an investment partnership, which gives them more flexibility than the corporate form. Kohlberg, Kravis, Roberts, usually known as KKR, is the most visible example since the 1980s because it has been involved in many corporate takeovers. The

Table 3.2 Corporate Directorships Held by Warren Buffett and His Partners in Berkshire Hathaway

Warren Buffett	Walter Scott, Jr.
Coca-Cola	Burlington Resources
Geico	ConAgra
Gillette	First Bank Systems
Salomon	Kiewit
Washington Post	WorldCom
Howard Buffett	**Charles Munger**
Coca-Cola	Salomon

Source: Director listings in *Who Knows Who 1998.*

lead partner, Henry Kravis, who is sometimes listed as a self-made person because it is not generally known that his father was worth tens of millions of dollars, sits on eight corporate boards, including Safeway Stores and Gillette, companies that he and his partners acquired after 1986. His cousin and partner, George Roberts, joins him on seven of those boards and is on one other board as well. There can be little doubt about who controls these companies, or about the control of any other companies where investment partnerships or holding companies have representatives on the board of directors. The takeovers by KKR and similar firms show that firms allegedly controlled by their managers can be acquired by groups of rich investors whenever they so desire, unless of course they are resisted by a rival group of owners.[37]

The cumulative findings on the importance of family ownership, family offices, holding companies, and investment partnerships in large corporations suggest that a significant number of large corporations continue to be controlled by major owners. However, the very largest corporations in several sectors of the economy show no large ownership stake by individuals or families, whether through family offices, holding companies, or other devices. Their largest owners, in blocks of a few percent, are bank trust departments, investment companies, mutual funds, and pension funds. Moreover, interview studies suggest that bank trust departments and investment companies are no more likely than pension funds to take any role in influencing the management of the corporations in which they invest.[38]

While it may seem surprising at first glance that members of the upper class are least involved at the executive level in the very largest corporations, the reasons lie in issues of power and status, and have nothing to do with education or expertise. Members of the upper class usually are not interested in a career that requires years of experience in a corporate bureaucracy when there is no incentive for them to do so. They prefer to work in finance, corporate law, or their own family businesses, where they have greater autonomy and more opportunities to exercise power.

WHERE DO CORPORATE EXECUTIVES COME FROM?

There have been many studies of the class origins of the top executives in very large corporations. They most frequently focus on the occupation of the executive's father. These studies show that "between 40 percent and 70 percent of all large corporation directors and managers were raised in business families, which comprised only a tiny fraction of families of that era."[39] One study compared business leaders at thirty-year intervals over the century and found that the percentage whose fathers were businesspeople remained constant at 65 percent.[40] The most extensive study of corporate directors ever undertaken used parental occupation, listing in the *Social Register*, and attendance at a prestigious private school to estimate that 30 percent of several thousand directors came from the upper class (defined as the top 1 percent). Approximately 59 percent came from the middle class, which comprises about 21 percent of the population by this researcher's definition, and only 3 percent came from the remaining 78 percent of the population (8 percent of the sample was not classifiable).[41]

The overrepresentation of men and women from the upper class in large corporations is evidence for the power of the upper class on the *Who governs?* indicator of power. However, the fact remains that there are a great many high-level managers in corporations who come from middle-level origins and work their way up the corporate ladder. The number of such people may be exaggerated somewhat because relevant information on schools and clubs is not always available, but their role within the corporate community is a large one even by conservative estimates. Does this mean, perhaps, that professional managers remain distinct from upper-class owners and directors, suggesting there might be some degree of separation between the corporate community and the upper class?

THE ASSIMILATION
OF RISING CORPORATE EXECUTIVES

The evidence presented in this section shows how rising corporate executives are assimilated into the upper class and come to share its values, thereby cementing the relationship between the upper class and the corporate community rather than severing it. The aspirations of professional managers for themselves and for their offspring lead them into the upper class in behavior, values, and style of life.

Whatever the social origins of top managers, most of them are educated and trained in a small number of private universities and business schools. The results from several different studies reveal that "approximately one-third of those who oversee the nation's largest firms attended Harvard, Yale, or Princeton, and two-thirds studied at one of the twelve most heavily endowed schools."[42] It is in these schools that people of middle-class origins receive their introduction to the values of the upper class and the corporate community, mingling for the first time with men and women of the upper class, and sometimes with upper-class teachers and administrators who serve as role models. This modeling continues in the graduate schools of business that many of them attend before joining the corporation. Minority group members who are not from wealthy families show the same educational patterns as other upwardly mobile corporate executives in terms of attendance at these same schools.[43]

The conformist atmosphere within the corporations intensifies this socialization into upper-class styles and values. The great uncertainty and latitude for decision-making in positions at the top of complex organizations creates a situation in which trust among leaders is absolutely essential. That need for trust is what creates a pressure toward social conformity:

> It is the uncertainty quotient in managerial work, as it has come to be defined in the large modern corporations, that causes management to become so socially restricting; to develop tight inner circles excluding social strangers; to keep control in the hands of socially homogeneous peers; to stress conformity and insist upon a diffuse, unbounded loyalty; and to prefer ease of communication and thus social certainty over the strains of dealing with people who are "different."[44]

In this kind of an atmosphere, it quickly becomes apparent to new managers that they must demonstrate their loyalty to the senior management by working extra hours, tailoring their appearance to that of their superiors, and attempting to conform in their attitudes and behavior. They come to believe that they have to be part of the "old-boy network" in order to succeed in the company. Although there are competence criteria for the promotion of managers, they are vague enough or hard enough to apply that most managers become convinced that social factors are critical as well.

Executives who are successful in winning acceptance into the inner circle of their home corporations are invited by their superiors to join social institutions that assimilate them into the upper class. The first invitations are often to charitable and cultural organizations, where they serve as fund raisers and as organizers of special events. The wives of rising executives, whose social acceptability is thought to be a factor in managers' careers, experience their first extensive involvement with members of the upper class through these same organizations. Then, too, the social clubs discussed earlier in the chapter are important socializing agents for the rising executive.

Upwardly mobile executives also become intertwined with members of the upper class through the educational careers of their children. As the children go to day schools and boarding schools, the executives take part in evening and weekend events for parents, participate in fund-raising activities, and sometimes become directors or trustees in their own right. The fact that the children of successful managers become involved in upper-class institutions also can be seen in their patterns of college attendance. This is demonstrated very clearly in a study of upwardly mobile corporate presidents. Whereas only 29 percent of the presidents went to an Ivy League college, 70 percent of their sons and daughters did so.[45]

Rising executives are assimilated economically at the same time as they are assimilated socially. One of the most important of these assimilatory mechanisms is the stock option, explained in a footnote in Chapter 2. Stock-option plans, in conjunction with salaries and bonuses in the millions of dollars, allow some top executives to earn thousands of times more than the average wage earner each year. These high levels of remuneration enable upwardly mobile corporate leaders to become multimillionaires in their own right, and important leaders within the corporate community.

The assimilation of professional executives into the upper class also can be seen in the emphasis they put on profits, the most important of ownership objectives. This manifests itself most directly in the performance of the corporations they manage. Several studies that compare owner-controlled companies with companies that have professional managers at the top show no differences in their profitability.[46] Corporations differ in their profitability, but this fact does not seem to be due to a difference in values between upper-class owners and rising corporate executives.

By any indication, then, the presence of upwardly mobile executives does not contradict the notion that the upper class and the corporate community are closely related. In terms of their wealth, their social contacts, their values, and their aspirations for their children, successful managers become part of the upper class as they advance in the corporate hierarchy.

WEALTH AND POWER: WHO BENEFITS?

It is obvious that members of the upper class must have large amounts of wealth and income if they can afford the tuition at private schools, the fees at country clubs, and the very high expenses of an elegant social life. Exactly how much they have, however, is a difficult matter to determine because the Internal Revenue Service does not release information on individuals, and most people are not willing to volunteer details on this subject.

In considering the distribution of wealth and income in the United States, it must be stressed that the two distributions are different matters. The wealth distribution has to do with the concentration of ownership of marketable assets, which in most studies means real estate and financial assets (e.g., stocks, bonds, insurance, and bank accounts) minus liabilities. The income distribution, on the other hand, has to do with the percentage of wages, dividends, interest, and rents paid out each year to individuals or families at various income levels. In theory, those who own a great deal may or may not have high incomes, depending on the returns they receive from their wealth, but in reality those at the very top of the wealth distribution also tend to have the highest incomes, mostly from dividends and interest.

Numerous studies show that the wealth distribution is extremely concentrated. It was very stable over the course of the twentieth century, although there was a temporary decline in wealth concentration in the 1970s, in good part due to a decline in stock prices.[47] By the late 1980s, the wealth distribution was as concentrated as it had been in 1929, when the top 1 percent had 36.3 percent of all wealth.[48] In 1998, the last year for which figures from the Federal Reserve Board are available, the top 1 percent owned 38.1 percent of all marketable wealth and 47.3 percent of all financial wealth—that is, all marketable wealth minus the value of owner-occupied housing.

More generally, the top 1 percent of households "held half of all outstanding stock, financial securities, and trust equity, two-thirds of business equity, and 36 percent of investment real estate," and the top 10 percent had 90 percent of the stock, bonds, trusts, and business equity, and about 75 percent of nonhome real estate.[49] The percentage of yearly income received by the highest 1 percent of wealthholders also has increased since 1982, when it was 12.8 percent. By 1991, the figure was 15.7 percent, and in 1997 it was 16.6 percent.[50] Figures on inheritance tell much the same story. According to a study published by the Federal Reserve Bank of Cleveland, only 1.6 percent of Americans receive $100,000 or more in inheritance. Another 1.1 percent receive $50,000 to $100,000. On the other hand, 91.9 percent receive nothing.[51]

None of the studies on the wealth and income distributions include the names of individuals, so studies have to be done to demonstrate that people of wealth and high income are in fact members of the upper class. The most detailed study of this kind shows that nine of the ten wealthiest financiers at the turn of the twentieth century, and 75 percent of all families listed in a compendium of America's richest families, have descendants in the *Social Register*.[52] Supplementing these findings, another sociologist found that at least one-half of the ninety richest men of 1900 have descendants in the *Social Register*, and a study of ninety corporate directors worth $10 million or more in 1960 found that 74 percent meet criteria of upper-class membership.[53] However, the degree of overlap between great wealth and membership in the upper class has attracted little further research because the answer seems so obvious to most people.

There are newly rich people who are not yet assimilated into the upper class, and there are highly paid professionals, entertainers, and athletes who for a few years make more in a year than many members of the upper class. However, for the most part it is safe to conclude that the people of greatest wealth and highest income are part of—or are becoming part of—the upper class. Without a doubt, then, the .5 to 1 percent of the population that comprises the upper class includes most of the 1 percent who hold 38.1 percent of all marketable wealth, 47.3 percent of financial wealth, and 49.6 percent of the corporate stock.

In terms of the *Who benefits?* indicator of power, the upper class is far and away the most powerful group in the society. However, this indicator is only a starting point. It may not be convincing to some readers unless it is supplemented by information on how power is exercised to maintain this great concentration of wealth.

CLASS AWARENESS: A CAPITALIST MENTALITY

The institutions that establish the owners and high-level executives of corporations as a national upper class transcend the presence or absence of any given person or family. Families can rise and fall in the class structure, but the institutions of the upper class persist. Not everyone in this nationwide upper class knows everyone else, but everybody knows somebody who knows someone in other areas of the country, thanks to a common school experience, a summer at the same resort, membership in the same social club, or membership on the same board of directors. The upper class at any given historical moment consists of a complex network of overlapping social circles knit together by the members they have in common and by the numerous signs of equal social status that emerge from a similar lifestyle. Viewed from the standpoint of social psychology, the upper class is made up of innumerable face-to-face small groups that are constantly changing in their composition as people move from one social setting to another.

Involvement in these institutions usually instills a class awareness that includes feelings of superiority, pride, and justified privilege. Deep down, most members of the upper class think they are better than other people, and therefore fully deserving of their station in life. This class awareness is based in corporate ownership, but it is reinforced by the shared social identities and interpersonal ties created through participation in the social institutions of the upper class.

The fact that the upper class is based in the ownership and control of profit-producing investments in stocks, bonds, and real estate shows that it is a capitalist class as well as a social class. Its members are not concerned simply with the interests of one corporation or business sector, but with such matters as the investment climate, the rate of profit, and the overall political climate. That is, they have a capitalist mentality.

With the exception of those few who join the liberal-labor coalition or a leftist movement, members of the upper class also have a conservative outlook on issues that relate to the well-being of the corporate community as a whole. This tendency toward a general class perspective is utilized and reinforced within the policy-planning network discussed in the next chapter. The organizations in that network build upon the structural economic power explained in the previous chapter and the social cohesion demonstrated in this chapter in reaching consensus on policy matters, where the potential for misunderstanding and disagreement are great. Human beings are often distrustful or egotistical, and there can be differences in needs between corporations in different industries and of different sizes. Developing a common policy outlook is not automatic even for the corporate community and upper class. As they strive to make profits and defend their privileges in a constantly changing economy, they have to deal with a very large number of people who have little or nothing except a job and a house, or the opportunity to obtain educational credentials that might move them up the occupational ladder.

4

The Policy-Planning Network

Economic interests and social cohesion provide the foundation for the development of policy consensus, but they are not enough in and of themselves to lead to agreed-upon policies without research, consultation, and deliberation. The issues facing the corporate community are too complex and the economy is too big for new policies to arise naturally from common interests and social cohesion alone. That is why a set of nonprofit, nonpartisan organizations are a necessary feature of the corporate landscape. These organizations are the basis of a policy-planning process through which the corporate community articulates its general policy preferences, and then conveys them to the two major political parties, the White House, and Congress.

Members of the corporate community and upper class involve themselves in the policy-planning process in four basic ways. First, they finance the organizations at the center of these efforts. Second, they provide a variety of free services, such as legal and accounting help, for some of these organizations. Third, they serve as the directors and trustees of these organizations, setting their general direction and selecting the people who will manage the day-to-day operations. Finally, they take part in the daily activities of some of the groups in the network.

The policy-planning network explains how seemingly independent experts, who often provide new policy ideas, fit into the power equation. They do their work as employees and consultants of key organizations in the network, which gives them financial support, confers legitimacy on their efforts, and provides the occasions for them to present their ideas to decision-makers.*

Although the corporate community has a near monopoly on what is considered "respectable" or "legitimate" expertise by the mass media and government, this expertise does not go unchallenged. There also exists a small group of think tanks and advocacy groups financed by unions, direct mail appeals, and wealthy liberals. Some of these liberal policy organizations also receive part of their funding from major foundations controlled by moderate conservatives, to the great annoyance of ultraconservatives.

Moreover, as the annoyances expressed by the ultraconservatives reveal, the policy network is not totally homogeneous. Reflecting differences of opinion within the corporate community, the moderate and ultraconservative subgroups have long-standing disagreements, although those differences have been muted since the 1970s. The ultraconservative organizations are the ones most often identified with big business in the eyes of social scientists and the general public. In the past, they opposed the expansion of trade with Europe and Asia, and they still oppose any type of government regulation or occasional increases in the minimum wage. The fact that they are generally naysayers, who lost on several highly visible issues in the turmoil of the late 1960s and early 1970s, is one reason some social scientists and media commentators doubt that the corporate community is the dominant influence in shaping government policy.

No one factor has been shown by systematic studies to be the sole basis for the division into moderates and ultraconservatives within the corporate community. There is a tendency for the moderate organizations to be directed by executives from the very largest and most internationally oriented of corporations, but there are numerous exceptions to that generalization. Moreover, there are corporations that support policy organizations within both policy subgroups. Then, too, there are instances in which some top officers from a corporation will be in the moderate camp, and others will be in the ultraconservative camp. However, for all their differences, leaders within the two clusters of policy organizations have a tendency to search for compromise policies due to their common membership in the corporate community, their social bonds, and the numerous interlocks among all policy groups. When compromise is not possible, the final resolution of policy conflicts often takes place in legislative struggles in Congress.

---

*Independent experts are most often employed at universities and colleges. They rarely have a major impact on public policy except on highly technical issues in the natural sciences and engineering.

AN OVERVIEW OF THE POLICY-PLANNING NETWORK

The policy-planning process begins in corporate board rooms, social clubs, and informal discussions, where problems are identified as issues to be solved by new policies. It ends in government, where policies are enacted and implemented. In between, however, there is a complex network of people and institutions that plays an important role in sharpening the issues and weighing the alternatives. This network has three main components—foundations, think tanks, and policy-discussion groups.

Foundations are tax-free institutions created to give grants to both individuals and nonprofit organizations for activities that range from education, research, and the arts to support for the poor and the upkeep of exotic gardens and old mansions. They are an upper-class adaptation to inheritance and income taxes. They provide a means by which wealthy people and corporations can in effect decide how their tax payments will be spent, for they are based on money that otherwise would go to the government in taxes. From a small beginning at the turn of the twentieth century, they have become a very important factor in shaping developments in higher education and the arts, and they play a significant role in policy formation as well. The most influential of them historically are the Ford, Rockefeller, Carnegie, and Sloan foundations.

Think tanks are nonprofit organizations that provide settings for experts in various academic disciplines to devote their time to the study of policy alternatives, free from the teaching, committee meetings, and departmental duties that are part of the daily routine for most members of the academic community. Supported by foundation grants, corporate donations, and government contracts, think tanks are a major source of the new ideas discussed in the policy-planning network.

The policy-discussion organizations are nonpartisan groups that bring together corporate executives, lawyers, academic experts, university administrators, government officials, and media specialists to talk about such general problems as foreign aid, free trade, taxes, and environmental policies. Using discussion groups of varying sizes, these organizations provide informal and off-the-record meeting grounds in which differences of opinion on various issues can be aired and the arguments of specialists can be heard. In addition to their numerous small-group discussions, they encourage general dialogue by means of luncheon speeches, written reports, and position statements in journals and books. Taken as a whole, the several policy-discussion groups are akin to an open forum in which there is a constant debate concerning the major problems of the day.

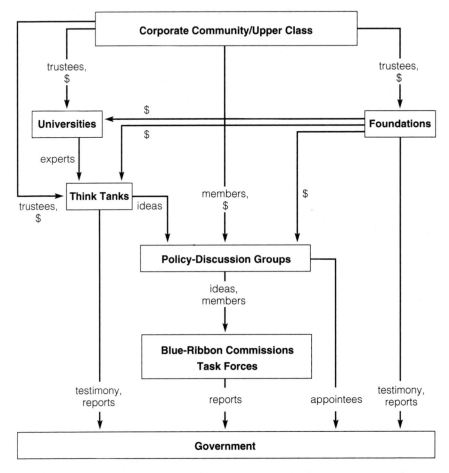

Figure 4.1 The Flow of Policy from the Corporate Community and Upper Class to Government through the Policy-Planning Network.

The three types of organizations making up the policy-planning network are interlocked with each other and the corporate community in terms of both common directors and funding. The evidence for this conclusion is presented throughout the chapter. Figure 4.1 presents an overview of the network, with linkages expressed in terms of (1) director interlocks, (2) money flows, and (3) the flow of ideas and plans. Anticipating the discussion of how the corporate community shapes government policy, which is presented in Chapter 7, the diagram shows some of the ways the output of the policy network reaches government.

No one type of organization is more important than the others. It is the network as a whole that shapes policy alternatives, with different organizations playing different roles on different issues. There is, however, one organization in the network, the Business Roundtable, that has the final say in attempting to influence government on the most important issues relating to economic policy. In so doing, it works closely with the Business Council, the Committee for Economic Development, and the U.S. Chamber of Commerce.

FOUNDATIONS

Among the nearly 6,300 foundations that exist in the United States, only a few hundred have the money and interest to involve themselves in funding programs that have a bearing on public policy. Foundations are of four basic types:

1. There are several thousand general-purpose foundations created by families to serve a wide variety of purposes. Most of the large general-purpose foundations are controlled by a cross section of leaders from the upper class and corporate community, but there are several ultraconservative foundations in this category that are tightly controlled by the original donors.

2. There are 862 corporate foundations that are funded by major corporations and directed by their officers. Their number and importance has increased greatly since the 1970s. Thirteen of them gave from $20 to $37.8 million in 1998 and are on the list of the top 100 foundation donors for that year.

3. There are 272 community foundations at the local level that are designed to aid charities, voluntary associations, and special projects in their home cities. They receive funds from a variety of sources, including other foundations, wealthy families, and corporations. They are directed by boards that include both corporate executives and community leaders.

4. Finally, there is a group of 189 foundations that use their money to finance a particular museum, garden project, or artistic exhibit. They are called *operating foundations* and are not of concern in terms of the policy-planning process. These operating foundations are often directed by the women of the upper class, as was discussed in the previous chapter.

Upper-class and corporate representation on the boards of the large general-purpose foundations most involved in policy-oriented grants has been documented in several studies. In one study of the 12 largest foundations, for example, it was found that half the trustees were members of the upper class.[1] A study of corporate connections into the policy network showed that 10 of these 12 foundations have at least one connection to the 201 largest corporations; most have many more than that.[2]

Foundations often become much more than sources of money when they set up special programs that are thought to be necessary by their trustees or staff. Then, they search out appropriate organizations to undertake the project, or else they create special commissions within the foundation itself. A few foundations have become so committed to a specific issue that they function as a policy-discussion organization. The Ford Foundation provides the best example of this point because it became involved in two of the main problems of the 1960s.

First, it became the equivalent of a policy group on the issue of urban unrest, creating a wide range of programs to deal with the problems generated by urban renewal and racial tensions in cities. One of these programs, called the Gray Areas Project, became the basis for the War on Poverty declared by the Johnson Administration in 1964. Once the War on Poverty was launched, the Ford Foundation invested tens of millions of dollars in support for minority-group and community-action organizations. These investments were seen at the time as a way of encouraging insurgent groups to take a nonviolent and electoral direction in addressing the problems they perceived. By the 1970s, when the social disruption had subsided, ultraconservatives began to criticize the Ford Foundation for its support of what they called liberal experiments. However, the foundation has persisted in this support, which is seen by moderate conservatives in the corporate community as a sensible way to incorporate minority groups into the larger society. Table 4.1 provides a list of the advocacy groups for minorities and women and civil-liberties groups that received large grants from the Ford Foundation in 1998.

Ford also played a major role in creating and sustaining the mainstream organizations of the environmental movement. Its conference on resource management in 1953, and subsequent start-up funding, led to the founding of the first and most prominent environmental think tank, Resources for the Future. This organization broke new ground by incorporating market economics into conservation work. Economists at Resources for the Future and other think tanks showed that resource substitution could be managed through the price system and that it was a myth to claim there is a trade-off between jobs and environmental regulation. They also pointed out that there was money to be made in cleaning up the air and water. Their work reassured corporate moderates that most environmental initiatives were completely

Table 4.1 Donations by the Ford Foundation to Advocacy Groups For Minorities and Women

Mexican-American Legal Defense and Education Fund	$2,700,000
Ms. Foundation	$1,310,000
American Civil Liberties Union (for race, poverty, and immigration rights projects)	$1,187,000
NAACP Legal Defense and Education Fund	$1,000,000
Native American Rights Fund	$1,000,000
National Council of La Raza	$950,000
Catholic Legal Immigration Network	$600,000
National Organization of Women Legal Defense and Education Fund	$600,000
National Asian Pacific American Legal Consortium	$550,000
NAACP Special Contribution Fund	$500,000
Indian Law Resources Center	$375,000
Puerto Rican Legal Defense and Education Fund	$300,000
National Council of Negro Women	$245,000
Total	$11,317,000

Note: The Ford Foundation gave 135 grants in the area of civil rights in 1998.

Source: *The Foundation Grants Index 2000* (New York: Foundation Center, 2000).

compatible with corporate capitalism, contrary to the angry outcries of ultraconservatives and the hopes of leftists.[3]

In the early 1960s, the Ford Foundation spent $7 million over a three-year period developing ecology programs at 17 universities around the country, thereby providing the informational base and personnel infrastructure for efforts to control pesticides and industrial waste. At the same time, the foundation put large sums into the land-purchase programs of The Nature Conservancy and the National Audubon Society. It also encouraged environmental education and citizen action through grants to municipal conservation commissions and the nationwide Conservation Foundation, the latter founded by the Rockefeller family as a combined think tank and policy-discussion group.[4] The new militant wing of the environmental movement soon moved beyond the purview envisioned by the moderate conservatives, but the fact remains that much of the early grassroots movement was encouraged and legitimated by major foundations.

The Ford Foundation aided environmentalists in another way in the 1970s by backing several new environmental law firms that used the legal system to force corporations and municipal governments to clean up the water, air, and soil. Leaders at the foundation actually created one of these organizations, the Natural Resources Defense Council, by bringing together several Wall Street corporate lawyers with a group of young Yale Law School graduates who wanted to devote their careers to environmental law. Ford then gave the new organization $2.6 million between 1970 and 1977. Between 1971 and 1977, it also gave $1.6 million to the Center for Law in the Public Interest in Los Angeles, $994,000 to the Environmental Defense Fund, and $603,000 to the Sierra Club Legal Defense Fund.[5]

Appointees to the Nixon Administration from the mainstream environmental groups helped secure tax-exempt status for the environmental law firms. They then presided over the creation of the Council on Environmental Quality and the Environmental Protection Agency. Indeed, the origins of these agencies provides an ideal example of how moderate conservatives create policies that are later seen as setbacks for the corporate community. At the same time, these organizations are often criticized by strong environmentalists as being too cautious and for "selling out" via compromises on key issues.[6]

Although the Ford Foundation gave 155 environmental grants in 1998, mostly to organizations in other nations, its support for American environmental groups has been more modest now that these organizations are firmly established. However, the slack has been picked up by several dozen other major foundations, including several corporate foundations. Table 4.2 shows foundation grants for 1998 to the Natural Resources Defense Council and to Environmental Defense (formerly the Environmental Defense Fund). Table 4.3 displays grants to several major environmental groups for 1996 from 137 corporate foundations.

Ford's support for disadvantaged minority communities, women, and the environmental movement led to the claim that it became a liberal organization in the 1960s, despite its corporate-dominated board of trustees, including the chairman of Ford Motor Company, Henry Ford II. However, this conclusion confuses liberalism with a sophisticated conservatism that does not bend in other areas, as seen in the foundation's support for opposition to unionization efforts. In 1967, it entered into an emerging conflict over public employee unions by financing a think-tank study that was very negative toward unions. Then, in 1970, it provided $450,000 to three associations of government managers—the U.S. Conference of Mayors, the National League of Cities, and the National Association of Counties—to establish the Labor-Management Relations Service, an organization intended to help government managers cope with efforts at union organizing. One year later, this organization set up the National Public Employer

Table 4.2 Contributions by Foundations in the Top 100 to the Natural
Resources Defense Council and Environmental Defense

Ranking and Name	NRDC	ED
2. Ford Foundation	$75,000	$100,000
3. Packard Foundation		$850,000
7. Pew Charitable Trusts	$3,043,000	$1,200,000
8. John and Catherine McArthur Foundation	$1,200,000	$1,200,000
13. Starr Foundation	$50,000	$1,000,000
16. Charles Stewart Mott Foundation	$100,000	$220,000
22. New York Community Trust	$400,000	$475,000
29. Doris Duke Charitable Foundation	$325,000	$500,000
32. Whitehead Foundation	$10,000	
35. Sloan Foundation		$30,000
45. Howard Heinz Endowment		$750,000
47. Joyce Foundation	$450,000	
53. George Gund Foundation	$30,000	
67. Boston Foundation	$10,000	
70. San Francisco Foundation	$245,000	
72. Park Foundation	$50,000	
89. Rockefeller Brothers Fund	$180,000	
Thirty-five Other Foundation Grants for NRDC	$2,810,500	
Twenty-one Other Foundation Grants for ED		$2,409,100
Total	$8,978,500	$7,534,100

Source: Foundation Grants Index 2000 (New York: Foundation Center, 2000).

Labor Relations Association, aided in good part by Ford and other
foundation monies. Publications from these two organizations provide advice on defeating organizing drives and surviving strikes. They
suggest contracting out public services to private businesses to avoid
unions and decrease wage costs.[7] This opposition to public employee
unions is consistent with the distance that all major foundations have
kept from the labor movement.[8]

Systematic studies of the degree to which public employees are
unionized in each state suggest that these efforts to help government
managers were successful. Less than half of the fifty states allow full
collective bargaining for all public employee groups, and nearly all
states forbid public employees to strike. The relative strength of the

Table 4.3 Donations to Major Environmental Groups by 137 Corporate Foundations

Organization	Amount
Nature Conservancy	$2,059,500
World Wildlife Fund	$620,495
Conservation International	$456,500
National Parks Foundation	$363,000
Resources for the Future	$323,500
Conservation Fund	$236,000
Tides Foundation	$148,500
Earthwatch Institute	$138,500
National Audubon Society	$129,715
Environmental Law Institute	$122,000
Total	$4,597,710

Source: Patterns of Corporate Philanthropy (Washington: Capital Research Center, 1999) p. 22.

corporate-conservative and liberal-labor coalitions in each state is the main factor in determining the degree to which state employees are successful in their efforts to unionize. Union density in the public sector, meaning the percent of public employees who are in unions, rose from 10.8 percent in 1960 to a peak of 40.2 percent in 1976, and has stabilized at about 36 to 37 percent since that time.[9]

Foundations, then, are an integral part of the policy-planning process, as both sources of funds and program initiators. Contrary to the usual perceptions, they are not merely donors of money for charity and value-free academic research. They are extensions of the corporate community in their origins, leadership, and goals.

THINK TANKS

The deepest and most critical thinking within the policy-planning network takes place in various think tanks. New initiatives that survive criticism by other experts are brought to the discussion groups for modification and assimilation by the corporate leaders. Among the dozens of think tanks, some highly specialized in one or two topics, the most important are the Brookings Institution, the American Enterprise Institute, the Urban Institute, the National Bureau of Economic Research, and the Rand Corporation. Their efforts are sometimes augmented by institutes and centers connected to universities, especially in the area of foreign relations, but these institutes are one step removed from the policy-planning network.*

Three highly visible think tanks—the Brookings Institution, the American Enterprise Institute, and the Heritage Foundation—vie for attention and influence in Washington. The Brookings Institution, the oldest and generally most respected of the three, was founded in 1927 from three institutes that go back as far as 1916. Virtually all of its early money came from foundations, although by the 1930s it was earning income from a small endowment provided by the Rockefeller Foundation and other sources. The Brookings Institution is sometimes said to be a liberal think tank, but that is a misperception generated in good part by ultraconservatives. The fact that Keynesian economists from Brookings advised the Kennedy and Johnson administrations also contributed to this stereotype. In fact, the Brookings Institution always has been in the mainstream or on the right wing. Although some of its economists were important advisors to the Democrats in the 1960s, by 1975 these same economists were criticizing government initiatives in ways that later were attributed to the employees of their main rival, the American Enterprise Institute.[10]

The American Enterprise Institute (AEI), formed in 1943 as an adjunct to the U.S. Chamber of Commerce, had little money and no influence until the early 1970s, when a former Chamber employee began selling the need for a new think tank to corporate executives by exaggerating the liberal inclinations of the Brookings Institution. His efforts received a large boost in 1972 when the Ford Foundation gave him a $300,000 grant. This gift was viewed as a turning point by the institute's staff because of the legitimacy a Ford grant conferred for future fundraising. The institute went from a budget of $1.1 million in 1971 to over $10 million in the 1980s.[11]

---

*In a very general sense, universities and their affiliated research institutes are part of the power equation. They educate future leaders and train the experts who work for the think tanks. It is also the case that the trustees of the top private universities, and many large state universities for that matter, are disproportionately from the corporate community and upper class, as demonstrated by numerous investigations stretching back to the early twentieth century. Nevertheless, universities as a whole are not part of the institutional infrastructure of the policy-planning network. The faculty at most universities are too diverse in their intellectual and political orientations to be considered part of the power structure, unless they also are employed by corporations or organizations in the policy-planning network. Nor are all students who graduate from high-status universities uniformly destined to join the corporate community or policy-planning network. As previously mentioned, a small minority joins the liberal-labor coalition or a left-wing group.

The AEI's fundraising efforts also were aided when appointees from the Nixon Administration joined it as honorary fellows, and then former president Gerald Ford became an honorary fellow in 1977. Several prominent economists also were hired. Given this line-up of highly visible conservatives, it is not surprising that the AEI is often given credit for the right turn in Washington policy circles in the 1970s, but in fact the institute came to prominence after the turn had begun, as shown in a close textual analysis of Brookings and AEI recommendations.[12] By the early 1980s, however, the AEI did play a very important role in providing ideas and staff members to the Reagan and Bush administrations. Reflecting its closeness to the Brookings Institution on policy issues, the two think tanks now cosponsor a Joint Center for Regulatory Studies.[13]

The Heritage Foundation, created in 1974, is the most recent and famous of the Washington think tanks. It is wrongly thought to reflect current wisdom in the corporate community, when it is actually the product of a few highly conservative men of great inherited wealth. The most important of these ultraconservatives are members of the Coors family, owners of the beer company that bears their name.[14] Close behind them is Richard Mellon Scaife, who is discussed in a later section of this chapter.

Unlike the AEI, the Heritage Foundation makes no effort to hire established experts or build a record of respectability within the academic or policy communities. Instead, it hires young ultraconservatives who are willing to attack all government programs and impugn the motives of all government officials as bureaucratic empire builders. While this approach doesn't endear the Heritage Foundation to its counterparts in Washington, it did lead to staff positions in the Reagan and Bush administrations, which needed people to carry out their antigovernment objectives.

The relationship of these three think tanks to the corporate community can be seen through their boards of directors. Brookings and the AEI have similar interlock patterns. Twenty-five of the Brookings Institution's thirty-three directors (86 percent) hold fifty corporate directorships at 48 corporations; seventeen of AEI's twenty-six directors (65 percent) have forty directorships at 37 corporations. Moreover, there are 7 corporations that have directors on the boards of both think tanks: Alcoa, American Presidents Lines, AT&T, Coca-Cola, CSX, Dow Chemical, and Levi Strauss. The Heritage Foundation, on the other hand, has no directors who are also directors of any corporations included in *Who Knows Who 1997*. The only current interlocks for the Heritage Foundation are with 5 ultraconservative foundations that provide much of its funding.

THE POLICY-DISCUSSION GROUPS

The policy groups serve several important functions for the corporate community.

1. They provide a setting in which corporate leaders can familiarize themselves with general policy issues by listening to and questioning the experts from think tanks and university research institutes.

2. They provide a forum where conflicts can be discussed, usually with the help of moderate conservative and ultraconservative experts, along with an occasional liberal on some issues.

3. They provide an informal training ground for new leadership. It is within these organizations that corporate leaders can determine in an informal fashion which of their peers are best suited for service in government and as spokespersons to other groups.

4. They provide an informal recruiting ground for determining which academic experts may be best suited for government service, either as faceless staff aides to the corporate leaders who take government positions or as high-level appointees in their own right.

In addition, the policy groups have three functions in relation to the rest of society:

1. These groups legitimate their members as serious and expert persons capable of government service. This image is created because group members are portrayed as giving of their own time to take part in highly selective organizations that are nonpartisan and nonprofit in nature.

2. They convey the concerns, goals, and expectations of the corporate community to those young experts and professors who aspire to foundation grants, invitations to work at think tanks, or consultative roles with government agencies.

3. Through such avenues as books, journals, policy statements, press releases, and speakers, these groups influence the climate of opinion in both Washington and the country at large. This point is developed when the opinion-shaping process is discussed in the next chapter.

The most extensive study of the relationship of policy discussion groups to foundations and think tanks started with a sample of 77 large foundations, which includes the 26 with over $100 million in assets at the time. It found 20 foundations that give over 5 percent of their total grants, or over $200,000, to public policy grants. These 20 foundations in turn lead to a group of 31 think tanks and discussion groups that receive grants from 3 or more of these foundations. The extent of the policy-planning network revolving around these core organizations is even greater than any previous studies had led social scientists to expect.[15]

Of the 225 trustees who serve on the 20 foundations, 124 are also trustees of another 120 foundations. Ten of the 20 foundations have trustee interlocks with 18 of the 31 policy-planning organizations and think tanks. The Rockefeller Foundation has the largest number of trustee interlocks with other foundations (34), followed by the Sloan Foundation, the Carnegie Corporation, the Ford Foundation, and Rockefeller Brothers Fund. The Rockefeller Foundation also has the largest number of trustee connections to the policy groups it finances (14), followed once again by the Sloan, Carnegie, Ford, and Rockefeller Brothers foundations. Moreover, all five of these foundations tend to be involved with the same policy groups. These foundations, then, are part of the moderate-conservative portion of the network.

This analysis also shows that a set of policy groups and think tanks identified with ultraconservative programs—the American Enterprise Institute, the Hudson Institute, the Hoover Institution, the Foundation for Economic Education, and Freedoms Foundation—are linked to another set of foundations, such as the Lilly Endowment, Olin Foundation, and Smith Richardson Foundation. Unlike the large foundations in the moderate part of the network, all of the very conservative foundations are under the direct control of the original donating family. Yet another study uses tax returns to reveal that 12 foundations provide half the funding for the American Enterprise Institute as well as 85 percent or more of the funding for the other prominent ultraconservative think tanks.[16] Corporate foundations also support some of these groups, but they give donations to the moderate-conservative groups as well. Table 4.4 lists the donations in 1996 to key think tanks and policy-discussion groups by 137 large corporate foundations.

The tremendous impact of a few extremely wealthy ultraconservatives can be seen in the funding career of the aforementioned Richard Mellon Scaife, an adopted son and heir to a big part of an oil and banking fortune in Pittsburgh. Based on a computerized record of all his donations since the early 1960s, the *Washington Post* estimates that he and his foundations have given about $620 million in current

Table 4.4 Donations to Think Tanks and Policy-Planning Organizations by 137 Corporate Foundations

Organization	Amount
American Enterprise Institute*	$1,595,500
Center for Strategic and International Studies*	$918,000
U.S. Chamber of Commerce*	$871,612
Committee for Economic Development**	$759,257
Brookings Institution**	$694,500
Institute for International Economics**	$452,000
Economic Strategy Institute	$390,000
Council on Foreign Relations**	$373,000
Heritage Foundation*	$341,000
Hudson Institute*	$300,765
Rand Corporation	$255,000
Cato Institute*	$241,000
Aspen Institute**	$195,500
American Assembly**	$176,000
Hoover Institution*	$128,500
Urban Institute**	$108,500
Total	$7,800,134

* ultraconservative organization
** moderate-conservative organization

Source: *Patterns of Corporate Philanthropy* (Washington: Capital Research Center, 1999).

dollars.[17] He also gives large donations to conservative political candidates and the Republican Party. A similar picture of combined policy and advocacy donations could be drawn for several other extremely wealthy individuals as well.[18]

A network analysis shows that the ultraconservative groups became more central to the overall policy network between 1973 and 1990. Using director overlaps for 12 think tanks and policy groups for 1973, 1980, and 1990, the study finds that the network became much more tightly interlocked (more dense) between 1973 and 1980, and that the most central discussion groups developed more ties with the ultraconservative think tanks. The density of the network declined slightly in 1990, with some ultraconservative think tanks moving to

Table 4.5 Centrality Scores and Bohemian Grove Participation for 12 Think Tanks and Policy-Discussion Groups

	Centrality Scores				
Organization	1973	1980	1990	Total*	Bohemian %, 1991
Business Roundtable	.59	.78	.66	2.03	20
Business Council	.59	.61	.72	1.92	26
Conference Board	.59	.64	.57	1.80	6
Committee for Economic Development	.56	.49	.59	1.64	5
Brookings Institution	.41	.56	.42	1.39	6
American Enterprise Institute	.26	.57	.55	1.38	19
Council on Foreign Relations	.32	.44	.62	1.35	8
Trilateral Commission	.34	.41	.20	.95	18
Hoover Institution	.47	.28	.19	.94	37
U.S. Chamber of Commerce	.14	.37	.28	.79	0
Heritage Foundation	.00	.28	.04	.32	0
National Association of Manufacturers	.08	.14	.07	.29	4
Average of all groups	.32	.46	.41	1.19	

Source: Val Burris, "Elite Policy-Planning Networks in the United States," *Research in Politics and Society,* 4 (1992): 126; Peter Phillips, *A Relative Advantage: Sociology of the San Francisco Bohemian Club.* Ph.D. Dissertation, University of California, Davis, 1994, p. 123.

Note: *The total of the three centrality scores provides a rough way to rank the 12 organizations overall, even though there are some fluctuations from year to year.

the periphery again, but the network is still much more dense than it was in 1973. Over 90 percent of the policy-group directors who sit on the boards of two or more organizations are corporate executives, mostly from very large corporations. About half attended high-status universities as undergraduates, and half are in upper-class social clubs, although only a small percentage of them are from upper-class families originally.[19] Table 4.5 presents the centrality scores for each of the organizations, along with the percentage of its directors at the Bohemian Grove in 1991.

   It is now time to look at some of the policy-discussion groups in more detail.

The Council on Foreign Relations

The Council on Foreign Relations (CFR) is the largest of the policy organizations. Established in 1921 by bankers, lawyers, and academicians interested in fostering the larger role the United States would play in world affairs as a result of World War I, the CFR's importance in the conduct of foreign affairs was well established by the 1930s. Before 1970, the members were primarily financiers, executives, and lawyers, with a strong minority of journalists, academic experts, and government officials. After that time, there was an effort to respond to criticism by including a larger number of government officials, especially foreign-service officers, politicians, and aides to congressional committees concerned with foreign policy. By 2000, the council had nearly 3,900 members, most of whom do little more than receive reports and attend large banquets. Although originally strictly a discussion group, the CFR now has a Studies Department that makes it the largest think tank in the area of foreign policy as well as the leading center for discussion groups.

Several different studies demonstrate the organization's connections to the upper class and corporate community. A sample of 210 New York members found that 39 percent are listed in the *Social Register,* and a random sampling of the full membership found 33 percent in that directory.[20] In both studies, directors are even more likely than regular members to be members of the upper class. Overlaps with the corporate community are equally pervasive. Twenty-two percent of the 1969 members served on the board of at least one of *Fortune*'s top 500 industrials, for example. In a study of the directors of 201 large corporations, it was found that 125 of these companies have 293 positional interlocks with the CFR. Twenty-three of the very largest banks and corporations have four or more directors who are members.[21]

The full extent of council overlap with the corporate community and government became clear in a study for this book of its entire membership list. The analysis determined that about one in every five members is an officer or director of a business listed in *Poor's Register of Corporations, Directors, and Executives.* Membership is once again found to be greatest for the biggest industrial corporations and banks. Overall, 37 percent of the 500 top industrials have at least one officer or director who is a member, with the figure rising to 70 percent for the top 100 and 92 percent for the top 25. Twenty-one of the top 25 banks have members, as do 16 of the largest 25 insurance companies. However, only the top 10 among utilities, transporters, and retailers are well represented.

The success of the council's effort to include more government officials in the enlarged council is reflected in this study. Two hundred

Table 4.6 Major Companies with One or More Directors Who Are Also Directors of the Council on Foreign Relations

American Insurance Group (3)	Federal Express
Alcoa	Goldman Sachs
Ameritech	IBM
Boeing	Lockheed
Bristol-Myers Squibb	Lucent (2)
Chevron	Qualcom
Chubb Insurance	Sara Lee
Citigroup (2)	Time Warner
Delta	Times Mirror
Disney	TRW
Eastman Kodak	Xerox (2)

Source: List of officers and directors for the Council on Foreign Relations, 1999–2000, and Jeanette Glynn, *Who Knows Who 1998* (Detroit: Gale Research: 1998).

and fifty members are listed in the index of the *Governmental Manual.* About half are politicians and career government officials; the other half are appointees to the government who come from business, law, and the academic community. In addition, another 184 members are serving as unpaid members of federal advisory committees. As shown in Table 4.6, the directors of the council for 1999 to 2000 have numerous interlocks with the corporate community.

The organization itself is far too large for its members to issue policy proclamations as a group. Moreover, its usefulness as a neutral discussion ground would be diminished if it tried to do so. As things now stand, however, its leaders can help to mediate disputes that break out in the foreign-policy establishment and can serve in both Republican and Democratic administrations. In fact, its board of directors virtually moved into the State Department and other government agencies after Clinton was elected in 1992, a point that is demonstrated in Chapter 7.

The CFR receives its general funding from wealthy individuals, corporations, and subscriptions to its influential periodical, *Foreign Affairs.* For special projects, such as an effort to rethink U.S.–Russian relationships, it often relies upon major foundations for support. It conducts an active program of luncheon and dinner speeches at its New York clubhouse, featuring government officials and national leaders from all over the world. It also encourages dialogue and disseminates information through books, pamphlets, and articles in *Foreign Affairs*. The most important aspects of the CFR program, however, are its discussion groups and study groups. These small gatherings of about fifteen to twenty-five people bring together business executives, government officials, scholars, and military officers for detailed consideration of specific topics in the area of foreign affairs. Discussion groups, which meet about once a month, are charged with exploring problems in a general way, trying to define issues and identify alternatives.

Discussion groups often lead to study groups. Study groups revolve around the work of a visiting research fellow (financed by a foundation grant) or a regular staff member. The group leader and other experts present monthly papers that are discussed and criticized by the rest of the group. The goal of such study groups is a detailed statement of the problem by the scholar leading the discussion. Any book that eventuates from the group is understood to express the views of its academic author, not of the council or the members of the study group, but the books are nonetheless published with the sponsorship of the CFR. The names of the people participating in the study group are listed at the beginning of the book.

The CFR's most successful set of study groups created the framework for the post–World War II international economy. Beginning in 1939 with financial support from the Rockefeller Foundation, its War-Peace Studies developed the postwar definition of the national interest through a comprehensive set of discussion groups. These groups brought together approximately 100 top bankers, lawyers, executives, economists, and military experts in 362 meetings over a five-year period. The academic experts within the study groups met regularly with officials of the State Department. In 1942, the experts became part of the department's new postwar planning process as twice-a-week consultants, while at the same time continuing work on the War-Peace project. As all accounts agree, the State Department had little or no planning capability of its own at the time.

Although the study groups sent hundreds of reports to the State Department, the most important one within the War-Peace Studies defined the minimum geographical area that was needed for the American economy to make full utilization of its resources and at the same time maintain harmony with Western Europe and Japan. This geographical area, which came to be known as the *Grand Area*, included Latin America, Europe, the colonies of the British Empire, and all of Southeast Asia. Southeast Asia was necessary as a source of raw materials for Great Britain and Japan, and as a consumer of Japanese products. The American national interest was then defined in terms of the integration and defense of the Grand Area, which led to plans for the

United Nations, the International Monetary Fund, and the World Bank, and eventually to the decision to defend Vietnam from a communist takeover at all costs. The goal was to avoid both another Great Depression and increased government control of what was then seen as a very sluggish economy.[22]

The Committee for Economic Development

The Committee for Economic Development (CED) was established in the early 1940s to help plan for the postwar world. The corporate leaders instrumental in creating this new study group had two major concerns at the time: (1) There might be another depression after the war; and (2) if they did not have a viable economic plan for the postwar era, the liberal-labor coalition might present plans that would not be acceptable to the corporate community. The goal of the CED was to avoid any identification with special-interest pleading for business and to concern itself with the nation as a whole: "The Committee would avoid promoting the special interests of business itself as such and would likewise refrain from speaking for any other special interests. The CED was to be a businessman's organization that would speak in the national interest."[23]

The organization consisted of 200 corporate leaders in its early years. Later it added a small number of university presidents. In addition, leading economists and public administration experts have served as advisers and conducted research for it; many of them have gone on to serve in advisory roles in both Republican and Democratic administrations. Although there is an overlap in membership with the larger Council on Foreign Relations (25 percent of its 257 trustees are in CFR; 4 of CFR's 32 directors are CED trustees), the committee has a different mix of members. Unlike the CFR, it has few bankers and no corporate lawyers, journalists, or academic experts among its trustees.

With the exception of a strong antiunion stance that is standard for all corporate policy groups, the Committee for Economic Development was the model of a moderate-conservative group until corporate leaders changed its orientation in the mid-1970s. For example, it crafted a compromise on legislation drafted by liberals in 1944 and 1945 calling for policies that would generate full employment, advocate higher taxes to pay for the Vietnam War, and support modest improvements in government programs for income maintenance and health care in the early 1970s.

Like the CFR, the CED works through study groups that are aided by academic experts. The study groups have considered every conceivable issue from farm policy to government reorganization to campaign finance laws, but the greatest emphasis is on economic issues of both a domestic and an international nature. Unlike the CFR, the results of committee study groups are released as official policy statements of the organization. They contain footnotes in which trustees register any disagreements they may have with the overall recommendations. These statements are of great value to social scientists for studying the range of policy orientations in the corporate community.

Reflecting a rightward turn by moderate conservatives in the power elite in the 1970s, there were major changes in the orientation of the CED between 1974 and 1976. These changes provide an ideal example of how a new policy direction on the part of leading trustees can bring about shifts within a policy group and quickly end any role for liberal experts.* This shift in orientation was related to the liberal-labor pressure for greater government intervention in the economy, due to the inflationary crisis of the period. However, the specific triggers to changes in the CED were internal to the organization. First, the economist serving as president at the time made the mistake of signing a public statement, along with labor leaders and liberal economists, suggesting a small step toward greater government planning. Second, a CED study group on controlling inflation, advised in part by liberal economists, was moving in the direction of advocating wage and price controls by government.

Trustees from several of the largest companies were extremely upset by what they interpreted as a trend toward greater acceptance of government controls. They reacted on a number of levels. First, several of their companies lowered their financial contributions or threatened to withdraw support altogether for the CED. Since large companies make the biggest contribution to the organization's budget, these threats were of great concern to the president and his staff.

Second, the chairman of the trustees, a senior executive at Exxon, appointed top executive officers from General Motors, Cutter-Hammer, and Itek as a three-person committee to make a study of the internal structure of the organization. One result of this study was the retirement of the president one year earlier than expected and the president's replacement by a conservative monetary economist from the Federal Reserve Bank of Minneapolis. The new president immediately wrote to all trustees asking for their advice on future policy directions, pledging greater responsiveness to the trustees. He also brought in several new staff members, one of whom said in an interview in 1995 that it was their job to neutralize liberal staff members.

---

*The following account is based on a series of interviews I conducted in 1990, 1992, and 1995 with retired CED trustees and employees, along with documents given to me on the condition of complete confidentiality.

Third, many of the trustees on the Research and Policy Committee, which oversees all study groups within the CED, decided to oppose the report on inflation and price controls. In all, there were fifteen pages of dissents attached to the report, most from a very conservative perspective, and seven trustees voted to reject publication. Fourth, the three economists primarily responsible for drafting the report—a university president, a prominent think-tank representative, and a CED staff member—were criticized in letters to the CED president for having too much influence in shaping the recommendations. The CED leader from Exxon later characterized the ill-fated statement as a "poor compromise between the views of trustees and a stubborn chairman and project director." Fifth, some trustees were personally hostile to the economists who were said to be too liberal. The think-tank economist was even accused of being a Communist.

The dramatic difference between the CED at the beginning and end of the 1970s is demonstrated by a comparison of policy statements issued in 1971 and 1979. In the first report, the emphasis was on the social responsibility of corporations and the need for corporations to work in partnership with government on social problems. The report at the end of the decade stressed the need to redefine the role of government in a market system. The CED now ignored all the social issues it had addressed before 1974. This change occurred even though 43 percent of the 40 members of the Research and Policy Committee in 1979 were on that committee and endorsed the more liberal policy statement in 1971.[24] This is strong evidence that the moderate conservatives had come to agree with ultraconservatives on many issues.

The organization's internal critics also claimed that it was ineffective in its attempts to influence the policy climate in Washington and that it overlapped with other policy groups in any case. Ironically, the CED's Washington liaison, who was not supposed to lobby because of the organization's tax-exempt status, was one of the key links between business and the Republicans in Congress at the time. He went to work in the Reagan Administration in 1980, eventually ending up as the president's White House chief-of-staff. Although the outgoing president wrote a lengthy memo documenting CED's behind-the-scenes effectiveness, the new president was instructed to find a new niche for the organization in relation to other organizations, especially the Business Roundtable. The success of the Business Roundtable led to a repositioning of CED by corporate executives who were top officers in both CED and the Business Roundtable. As one of these officers wrote in a letter to several trustees in the summer of 1978, after a meeting with a small group of CEOs from leading corporations:

The meeting was especially helpful in sharpening our sense of CED's special role within the spectrum of major national business-related organizations. The group was encouraged to learn of new efforts by CED to coordinate its work with that of the Business Roundtable, the Conference Board, the American Enterprise Institute, and others, thus minimizing duplication and overlap. CED can be especially effective, it was felt, in synthesizing the ideas of scholars and converting them into practical principles that can provide guidance for public policy on a selected number of key issues.

None of this upheaval was visible to outside observers, which underscores the importance of historical studies in understanding how the policy network functions. The only article mentioning the CED's problems appeared in the *Wall Street Journal* in December 1976. It quoted one trustee, an executive from Mobil Oil, claiming that "in the early days, the trustees were men who saw a need for some more government intervention, but now some of the trustees believe the intervention has gone far enough." An academic economist who once advised the CED said it had "lost its purpose" and "doesn't have the sense to go out of business."[25] It would have been hard to know what to make of such charges at the time without extensive interviewing or access to the kind of internal files that usually only become available many years later.

When the fate of the liberal experts in this example is coupled with the importance of foundation grants and appointments to think tanks for experts, along with their need to be relevant and useful in the eyes of corporations and government, there is little reason to believe that experts are free to say and recommend whatever they wish. To the contrary, they work within the constraints of what is acceptable to the corporate leaders who finance and direct the organizations of the policy-planning network. What is acceptable can vary from time to time, depending on the circumstances, but that does not mean there are no constraints. In this case, the shift to the right by the moderates led to the removal of liberal experts.

The Business Council

The Business Council is a unique organization in the policy-planning network because of its close formal contact with government. It was created during the 1930s as a quasi-governmental advisory group. It still holds regular consultative meetings with government officials, even though it became an independent organization in 1962. Since the 1960s, most of its private meetings with government officials have been held in the relaxed and friendly atmosphere of an expensive resort hotel in Hot Springs, Virginia, 60 miles from Washington. During the meetings Business Council members hear speeches by government officials, conduct panels on issues of the day, receive reports from their staff, and talk informally with each other and the government officials in attendance. Business sessions are alternated with social events, including golf tournaments, tennis matches, and banquet-style dinners for members, guests, and spouses. The expenses for the meetings, reports, and social events are paid by the corporate leaders.[26]

The members are, with few exceptions, the chairmen or presidents of the largest corporations in the country. The centrality of the Business Council within the corporate community can be seen in a tabulation of all the directorships listed by the 154 Business Council members included in one of the biannual editions of *Who's Who in America*. This self-report information shows that these men hold 730 directorships in 435 banks and corporations, as well as 49 foundation trusteeships in 36 different foundations and 125 trusteeships with 84 universities. The 435 corporations are at the heart of the corporate community; 176 of them are among the 800 largest corporations.[27]

The Business Roundtable

The Business Roundtable is at the heart of both the corporate community and the policy-planning network. Its 79 directors for 1997 have 206 directorships with 134 corporations, 32 of which are in the top 50 in size. Thirty-six of the 79 Business Roundtable directors are in the Business Council as well. The Roundtable's interlocks with other policy groups and with think tanks are presented in Figure 4.2.

In effect, the Business Roundtable is the lobbying extension of the Business Council. Whereas the Business Council prefers to remain in the background and talk informally with members of the executive branch, the Business Roundtable has an activist profile. It sends its leaders to lobby members of Congress as readily as it meets privately with the president and cabinet leaders. Indeed, it was formed in part because corporate leaders came to the conclusion that the Business Council was not effective enough in pressing the corporate viewpoint on government. There was also a fear that the corporate community was relying too heavily on specific trade associations and hired lobbyists in approaching Congress. The founders of the Business Roundtable hoped that direct lobbying of legislators by chief executives would have more impact.[28]

The 150 companies in the Business Roundtable pay from $10,000 to $35,000 per year in dues, depending on their size. This provides a budget of over $3 million a year. Decisions on where the Roundtable will direct its efforts are determined by a policy committee that meets every two months to discuss current policy issues, cre-

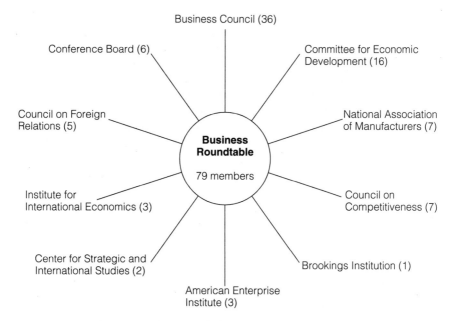

Figure 4.2   The Network around the Business Roundtable. *Source:* Updated from Val Burris, "Elite Policy-Planning Networks in the United States," *Research in Politics and Society,* vol. 4, 1992, p. 124.

ate task forces to examine selected issues, and review position papers prepared by task forces. Task forces are asked to avoid focusing on problems in any one industry and to concentrate instead on issues that have a broad impact on business. With a staff of less than a dozen people, the Business Roundtable does not have the capability to develop its own information. However, this presents no problem because the organization has been designed so that task force members will utilize the resources of their own companies as well as the information developed in other parts of the policy network.

After working more informally and behind the scenes to bring about the antiunion changes at the National Labor Relations Board described in Chapter 2, the Business Roundtable began its public efforts by coordinating the successful lobbying campaign against a consumer-labor proposal for a new governmental Agency for Consumer Advocacy in the mid-1970s.[29] It created the Clean Air Working Group that battled the environmental-labor coalition to a standstill from 1980 to 1990 on a proposed tightening of the Clean Air Act, agreeing to amendments only after several standards were relaxed or delayed and a plan to trade pollution credits in marketlike fashion was accepted by environmentalists.[30] On the other hand, it helped rein in the ultraconservatives in the Reagan Administration by calling for tax increases in 1982 and 1983 that began to reduce the huge deficits the administration's earlier tax cuts had created. In 1985, it called for cuts in defense spending as well.[31] Along with other business organizations, it quietly opposed the attack on affirmative action by the ultraconservatives in the Reagan Administration, pointing out that the policy had proven to be very useful for corporate America.[32] It even supported a mild extension of the Civil Rights Act in 1991, putting it at odds with the U.S. Chamber of Commerce.[33]

More recently, it joined with the U.S. Chamber of Commerce and the National Federation of Independent Business in defeating the Clinton program for national health care reform in 1994.[34] Then, it organized the grassroots pressure and forceful lobbying for the corporate community's victories in 1994 on the North American Free Trade Agreement and in 2000 on permanent normal trading status for China. Both of these initiatives were strongly resisted by organized labor, environmentalists, and many of their liberal allies.[35]

THE LIBERAL-LABOR POLICY NETWORK

There is also a small liberal-labor policy network. It suggests new ideas and perspectives to liberal political organizations, unions, and the government in an attempt to challenge the corporate community. Because the organizations in it are small in comparison to the corporate-backed organizations, they also serve as advocacy groups as well as think tanks.

Several organizations in the liberal-labor network receive some of their financial support from labor unions, but the sums are seldom more than a few hundred thousand dollars per year. However, it is difficult to know the exact figures because the donations come from different unions, and the AFL-CIO is not enthusiastic about the idea of compiling the totals. The liberal policy groups also receive grants from a small number of liberal foundations, and grants for specific projects from a few mainstream foundations, especially Ford, Rockefeller, and Carnegie. Even with grants from the mainstream foundations and backing from labor unions, the liberal-labor policy organizations usually do not come close to matching the budgets of their moderately conservative and ultraconservative opponents. Most liberal groups have budgets of from $2 million to $6 million a year, less than one-fourth the figures for the Brookings Institution, the American Enterprise Institute, and the Heritage Foundation, which have budgets in the range of $20 to $30 million a year.

As previously noted, the liberal-labor coalition has excellent media connections, in part because some of its members are prominent journalists. Although its reports are not featured as often as those of its conservative rivals, it nonetheless has the ability to obtain wide coverage for stories critical of corporate policy proposals. This media visibility is further enhanced by claims about liberal-labor power in ultraconservative fundraising pitches. The successes and failures of the liberal-labor policy network are examined in Chapters 6 and 7.

THE POWER ELITE

In concert with the large banks and corporations in the corporate community, the foundations, think tanks, and policy-discussion groups in the policy-planning network provide the organizational basis for the exercise of power on behalf of the owners of all large income-producing properties. The leaders of these organizations are therefore the institutionalized leadership group for those who have an economic stake in preserving the governmental rules and regulations that maintain the current wealth and income distributions.

This leadership group is called *the power elite*. The power elite is composed of members of the upper class who have taken on leadership roles in the corporate community and the policy network, along with high-level employees in corporations and policy-network organizations. More formally, the power elite consists of those people who serve as directors or trustees in profit and nonprofit institutions controlled by the corporate community through stock ownership, financial support, or involvement on the board of directors. This precise definition includes the top-level employees who are asked to join the boards of the organizations that employ them. The definition is useful for research purposes in tracing corporate involvement in voluntary associations, the media, political parties, and government.*

The concept of a power elite makes it possible to integrate class and organizational insights in order to create a more complete theory of power in America. Once again, as in the case of corporations, the key point is that any differences between class and organizational perspectives on issues are worked out in meetings of the boards of directors, where wealthy owners and CEO's from major corporations meet

---

*Although the power elite is a leadership group, the phrase is usually used with a plural verb in this book to emphasize that the power elite are also a collection of individuals who have some internal policy disagreements, as well as personal ambitions and rivalries that receive detailed media attention and often overshadow the general policy consensus.

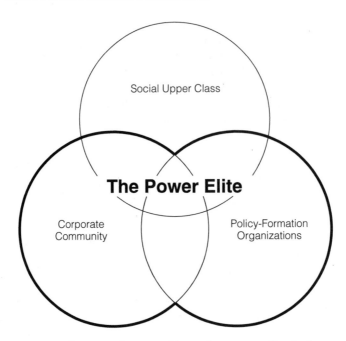

Figure 4.3   A multinetwork view of how the power elite is drawn from three overlapping networks of people and institutions: the corporate community, the social upper class, and the policy-formation network. The power elite is defined by the thick lines.

with the top employees of the policy-network organizations. This intertwining of class and organizational theories is discussed further in the last chapter, when the main alternative theories are compared with the one that is unfolding in this book.

In theory, the corporate community, the upper class, and the policy-planning network, which together provide the organizational basis and social cohesion for the power elite, can be imagined in terms of the three intersecting circles presented in Figure 4.3. A person can be a member of one of the three, or two of the three, or all three. There can be upper-class people who are only socialites, and therefore play no part in the exercise of power, even though they are wealthy. There also can be corporate leaders who are neither upper class nor involved in policy planning, focusing exclusively on their roles in the corporate community. And there can be policy experts who are neither upper class nor members of the corporate community, spending all their time doing research and writing reports. More broadly, not all members of the upper class are involved in governing, and not all members of the power elite are well-born and wealthy.

As a practical matter, however, the interrelations among these three sectors are closer than the image of three intersecting circles would indicate. A majority of the male members of the upper class between 45 and 65 are part of the corporate community as financiers, active investors, corporate lawyers, officers of privately held companies, or titled executives, although not necessarily as directors in top corporations. Then, too, some members of the policy network become involved in the corporate community as consultants and advisers even though they do not rise to the level of corporate directors. In other words, the corporate community becomes the common sector that encompasses many of the older males within the three overlapping circles.

Although this chapter provides evidence for the existence of a network of policy-planning organizations that is an extension of the corporate community in its financing and leadership, it does not claim there is a completely unified power elite policy outlook that is easily agreed upon. Instead, it shows that the upper class and corporate community have created a complex and only partially coordinated set of institutions and organizations. They often disagree among themselves about what policies are most compatible with the primary objectives of the corporate community. Nonetheless, the emphasis has to be on the considerable similarity in viewpoint among institutions that range from moderately conservative to highly conservative in their policy suggestions. Moreover, even though they are not able to agree completely among themselves, they have accomplished an equally important task: They have been able to marginalize the few experts with a more liberal point of view.

This chapter thus provides evidence for another form of power exercised by the corporate community and upper class through the power elite—expertise. Expert power is an important complement to the structural power and social cohesion discussed in the two previous chapters. Since government officials with only small policy-planning staffs must often turn to foundations, policy groups, and think tanks for new ideas, it is once again a form of power that can be exercised without any direct involvement in government.

Structural power and expertise are formidable quite independent of any participation in politics and government, but they are not enough to make owners and top executives the most powerful class. Since government is the main avenue through which some redistribution of the country's wealth and income could be brought about in a democratic way, it is the institution within which the liberal-labor coalition and its policy network press for new rights and benefits. In addition, it can pass laws that help or hinder profit-making, and it can collect and utilize tax funds in such a way as to stimulate or discourage economic growth. Then too, it is the place in the social system that legitimates new policies through the actions of elected officials.

Given the great stakes involved, there is too much uncertainty in the relationship between the corporate community and the government for the power elite to rely solely on structural economic power and expertise to insure that their interests are realized. They therefore work very hard to shape public opinion, influence elections, and determine government policy on the issues of concern to them.

5

The Role of Public Opinion

Due to the constitutional protections surrounding free speech and the right of assembly, there is the potential for public opinion to have great influence on government policies. Citizens can organize groups to express their preferences to elected officials on specific policy issues. Members of the power elite are very aware that the opinions of ordinary citizens might therefore lead to policies they do not like. In fact, the opinions of the majority have differed from those of the power elite on several economic issues for many generations, so they do everything they can to shape public opinion and guarantee the success of the policies they favor.

To the degree that something as general and nebulous as public opinion can be known in a country with 3.5 million square miles and over 280 million people, it is largely through public opinion surveys. Such surveys, however, present only a rough idea of what people in general actually think because the results are highly sensitive to a number of factors, especially the order of questions and the way they are worded. The lack of any social context when a question is asked over the telephone also makes the replies to many questions suspect. Thus, it is very difficult to know what the public's opinion is on an issue if polls have to be relied upon.

Ironically, polls are probably most valuable to members of the power elite, who analyze them to determine the words, phrases, and images to use in packaging the policies they wish to implement.[1] Polls may even be used to create the impression that the public favors one or another policy, when in fact there is no solidified public opinion on the issue. In addition, as one public opinion expert argues, "The rigid, structured nature of polling may narrow the range of public discourse by defining the boundaries for public debate, and by influencing the ways that journalists report on politics."[2] Polls produce their best results on a question of interest to politicians: how are people likely to vote in an upcoming election.

Setting aside the weaknesses of polling, and its uses for the power elite, the results of several decades of such surveys present a seeming paradox. On the one hand, the answers to questions repeated over the years on issues on which people have direct experience suggest that public opinion is rational and sensible within the context of people's lives and the quality of the information available to them. For example, more people accept the idea of women working outside the home as they see more women in the workplace. More white people came to have positive opinions concerning African-Americans as they learned more about the Civil Rights Movement.[3] On the other hand, polls asking about the stands taken by elected officials or the respondents' views on specific issues being considered in Congress suggest that most people pay little attention to politics, have a limited understanding of the options being considered, and do not develop opinions on impending legislation even when it has received much attention in the media. These findings suggest it is unlikely that public opinion is focused enough on any specific issue to have any independent effect.[4]

In terms of understanding how the power elite shape government policies, there are three questions that need to be answered in regard to the possible influence of public opinion.

1. Do the power elite have the capacity to shape public opinion on issues of concern to them, thereby making any correlation between public opinion and public policy irrelevant for claims about the influence of public opinion?

2. To the degree that public opinion on some issues is independent of the shaping efforts of the power elite, is there any evidence that those opinions have an impact on policy?

3. Are there issues on which the power elite expend little or no effort to shape public opinion, rendering public influence on those issues irrelevant to the question of corporate power?

The exploration of these three questions begins with an analysis of the general way in which the power elite operates in the arena of public opinion.

THE OPINION-SHAPING PROCESS

Many of the foundations, policy-planning groups, and think tanks in the policy-planning network also operate as part of the opinion-shaping process. In this process, however, they are joined by two other very weighty forces, large public relations firms and the public affairs departments of the major corporations. Both have expert staffs and the ability to complement their efforts with financial donations from the corporate foundations discussed in the previous chapter. These core organizations are connected to a diffuse dissemination network that includes local advertising agencies, corporate-financed advertising councils, special committees to influence single issues, and the mass media. In contrast to the policy-planning process, where a relatively small number of organizations do most of the work, there are hundreds of organizations within the opinion-shaping process that specialize in public relations and education on virtually every issue. Thus, at its point of direct contact with the general public, the opinion-molding process is extremely diverse and diffuse. A general picture of the opinion-shaping network is provided in Figure 5.1.

The policy discussion groups do not enter into the opinion-shaping process directly, except through releasing their reports to newspapers and magazines. Instead, their leaders set up special committees to work for changes in public opinion on specific issues. Sometimes, it is not possible to illustrate this close connection until historical archives are available. For example, three of the most important opinion-shaping committees of the post–World War II era denied any connection to the Council on Foreign Relations, but papers and correspondence related to the organization reveal otherwise.[5]

To create an atmosphere in which policy changes are more readily accepted by the general public, these committees attempt to picture the situation as one of great crisis. For example, this is what the Committee on the Present Danger did in the mid-1970s in order to gain public support for increased defense spending, claiming that government estimates of Soviet defense spending and military capability were far too low. Both claims proved to be patently false.[6] Similarly, the perception of a health-care crisis in the late 1980s was in good part the product of corporate concern about the rising costs of their health benefit plans.[7]

One of the most important goals of the opinion-shaping network is to influence public schools, churches, and voluntary associations by establishing a supportive working relationship with them. To that end, organizations within the network have developed numerous links to these institutions, offering them movies, television programs, books, pamphlets, speakers, advice, and financial support. However,

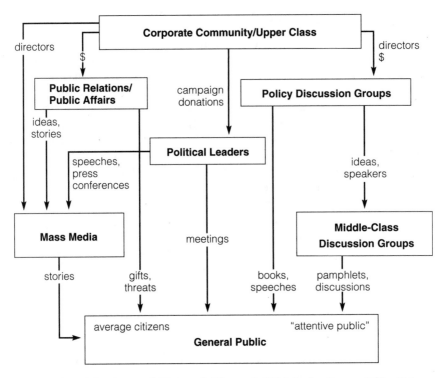

Figure 5.1   The General Network Through Which the Power Elite Tries to Shape Public Opinion

the schools, churches, and voluntary associations are not part of the network. Rather, they are independent settings within which the power elite must constantly contend with spokespersons from the liberal-labor coalition and the New Christian Right. To assume otherwise would be to overlook the social and occupational affiliations of the members, along with the diversity of opinion that often exists in these institutions of the middle and lower levels of the social hierarchy.

To prevent the development of attitudes and opinions that might interfere with the acceptance of policies created in the policy-planning process, leaders within the opinion-molding process also attempt to build upon and reinforce the underlying principles of the American belief system. Academically speaking, these underlying principles are called laissez-faire liberalism, and they have their roots in the work of several European philosophers and the American Founding Fathers. These principles emphasize individualism, free enterprise, competition, equality of opportunity, and a minimum of reliance upon government in carrying out the affairs of society. Slowly articulated during the centuries-long rise of the capitalist system in Europe, they arrived in America in nearly finished form. They had no serious rivals in a small new nation that did not have a feudal past or an established state church.[8]

Although this individualistic belief system remains pervasive, it is only an independent factor in shaping the opinions and behaviors of Americans because rival power groups like the liberal-labor coalition have not been able to challenge its acceptance. American cultural beliefs that seem timeless are in fact sustained by the pervasiveness of organizations created and funded by the power elite. Such beliefs, in other words, are "institutionalized," turned into taken-for-granted habits and customs, which are constantly reinforced by how organizations function. They reach this status because liberals and union leaders do not have the organizational basis from which to present a more communal or cooperative viewpoint.

These unchallenged values are known to most citizens as plain "Americanism." They are seen as part of human nature or the product of good common sense. If Americans can be convinced that some policy or action is justified in terms of this emotion-laden and unquestioned body of beliefs, they are more likely to accept it. Thus, the organizations that make up the opinion-shaping network strive to become the arbitrators of which policies and opinions are in keeping with good Americanism, and which are "un-American." These organizations struggle against the liberal-labor coalition and the New Christian Right to define what policies are in the national interest, and to identify those policies with Americanism.

The efforts of the opinion-shaping network sometimes reach a more subtle level as well. Even though many people do not accept the overt messages presented in ads, speeches, and booklets, they often accept the implicit message that their problems lie in their own personal inadequacies. An individualistic ideology, with its strong emphasis on personal effort and responsibility, not only rewards the successful, but blames the victims.* Educational failure and other social problems, which are best understood in terms of the ways in which a class system encourages some people and discourages others, are turned into reproaches of the victims for their alleged failure to correct personal defects and take advantage of the opportunities offered to them.[9] A classic study based on in-depth interviews explains how an individualistic ideology leaves many working people with a

---

*An *ideology* is the complex set of rationales and rationalizations through which a group, class, or nation interprets the world and justifies its actions. An ideology usually is fervently believed by those who espouse it.

paralyzing self-blame for their alleged failures even though they know the social system is not fair to them:

> Workingmen intellectually reject the idea that endless opportunity exists for the competent. And yet, the institutions of class force them to apply the idea to themselves: If I don't escape being part of the woodwork, it's because I didn't develop my powers enough. Thus, talk about how arbitrary a class society's reward system is will be greeted with general agreement—with the proviso that in my own case I should have made more of myself.[10]

This self-blame is important in understanding the reluctant acquiescence of wage earners in an unjust system:

> Once that proviso (that in my own case I should have made more of myself) is added, challenging class institutions becomes saddled with the agonizing question, Who am I to make the challenge? To speak of American workers as having been "bought off" by the system or adopting the same conservative values as middle-class suburban managers and professionals is to miss all the complexity of their silence and to have no way of accounting for the intensity of pent-up feeling that pours out when working people do challenge higher authority.[11]

The system is not fair, but that's the way things are: The average American seems to have a radical critique and a conservative agenda, and the result is a focus on the pleasures of everyday life and a grumbling acceptance of the political status quo.

Public Relations/Public Affairs

Public relations is a multibillion dollar industry created by the power elite in the 1920s for the sole purpose of shaping public opinion. There are hundreds of important independent firms, but much of the major work is done by a few large ones. The biggest, Burson-Marsteller, with 63 offices in 32 countries and clients ranging from General Electric to Philip Morris to the National Restaurant Association, had a fee income of $33.9 million in 1998. Most public relations firms are in turn owned by even larger advertising companies. Burson-Marsteller, for example, is owned by Young & Rubicam, which had billings of over $8 billion in the same year.

Public-relations firms usually do not run general campaigns aimed to shape overall public opinion. Instead, they are hired to work on very specific issues and are asked to focus on relatively narrow target audiences. For example, Burson-Marsteller created the National

Smokers Alliance in the early 1990s for the tobacco industry, sending its paid canvassers into bars to find members and potential activists. The second-largest PR firm, Shandwick, helped plan Earth Day in 1995; its client list includes Procter & Gamble, Monsanto Chemicals, and the Western Livestock Producers Alliance. Another firm, National Grassroots and Communications, specializes in creating local organizations to oppose neighborhood activists.[12] Still another, Nichols-Dezenhall Communications Management Group, concentrates on helping corporations by "aggressively exposing and discrediting" their critics.[13]

Public relations sometimes operates through the mass media, so it is not surprising that one-third of its 150,000 practitioners are former journalists, and that about half of current journalism school graduates go into one form of public relations work or another. Some public relations experts with journalism backgrounds put their contacts to work by trying to keep corporate critics from appearing in the media. One company keeps files on practicing journalists for possible use in questioning their creditability. Public relations experts use their skills to monitor the activities of groups critical of specific industries, everyone from animal-rights groups opposed to the use of animals in testing cosmetic products to antilogging groups. Some of the actions taken against these groups, which include infiltration of meetings and copying materials in files, add up to spying.[14]

Public affairs, on the other hand, is a generally more benign form of public relations, practiced by departments within the large corporations themselves. Here, the emphasis is on polishing the image of corporations rather than criticizing journalists and opposition groups. These departments are more frequently staffed by women and minorities than other corporate departments, in order to provide the company with a human face more reflective of the larger community. In one large corporation, the employees in public affairs refer to their department as the "velvet ghetto" because the job is a pleasant one with an excellent salary and expense account, but one that rarely leads to positions at the top of the corporation.[15]

The first task of employees in public affairs departments is to gather newspaper stories and radio-TV transcripts in order to monitor what is being said about their own corporation at the local level. They then try to counter any negative commentary by placing favorable stories in local newspapers and giving speeches to local organizations. They also join with members of other public affairs departments in an effort to shape public opinion in the interests of corporations in general. The general goal of public affairs personnel is "looking good and doing good."[16]

Table 5.1 Donations to Advocacy Organizations by 137 Corporate
Foundations in 1996

Organization	Amount
Urban League	$3,299,957
Enterprise Foundation*	$1,652,000
NAACP**	$1,610,460
National Council for Negro Women	$697,567
Children's Defense Fund	$678,750
Anti-Defamation League	$636,770
Catalyst ***	$425,500
National Council of La Raza	$372,900
Ms. Foundation	$285,500
U.S. Catholic Conference	$276,150
African-American Institute	$232,000
Planned Parenthood	$230,225
American Jewish Committee	$139,000
Mexican American Legal Defense and Education Fund	$125,000
National Asian Pacific American Legal Consortium	$112,500
Total	$10,774,279

* This organization, created with funds from a wealthy developer, supports low-income
housing and community development projects.
** National Association for the Advancement of Colored People.
*** Catalyst supports women in management and studies the ascent of women to top
management positions and seats on boards of directors.

Source: *Patterns of Corporate Philanthropy* (Washington: Capital Research Center,
1999), p. 22.

The efforts of the public affairs departments are in good measure
based on the large financial gifts they are able to provide to middle-
class charitable and civic organizations through the corporation's
foundation. Their donations topped $6.1 billion in 1994, 33 percent of
which went to education, 25 percent to health and charitable services,
12 percent to civic and community affairs, and 11 percent to culture
and the arts.[17] The emphasis on improving the image of the corporation and cultivating good will is seen most directly in the fact that it is
cigarette companies and corporations with poor environmental repu-
tations that give the most money to sporting events, the arts, and the
Public Broadcasting System.[18] Table 5.1 presents donations by corpo-

rate foundations to leading advocacy organizations for minorities, women, children, and religious groups in 1996.

In the case of some of the largest charitable groups and civic associations, directors and executives from the top corporations may agree to serve on the boards of directors as well as giving financial support. They thereby join with women of the upper class in bringing the power-elite perspective to some of the organizations that serve the largest numbers of middle-level Americans. In a study of director interlocks between the 100 largest industrial corporations and national nonprofit groups, there were 37 links with the United Way, 14 with the Boys and Girls Clubs of America, and 14 with the Boy Scouts of America.[19]

Despite all these efforts, public opinion toward corporations in general became much more negative from the late 1960s to the mid-1970s in the face of criticism by activists, who blamed the corporate community for the Vietnam War and environmental degradation. Corporations redoubled their public relations efforts at that point. Coincidentally or not, confidence in them began to go up again, but the very fact that it would decline in the first place shows the limits of public relations when it comes to shaping general attitudes toward the corporate community.[20] However, the critical point in terms of power is that very few average citizens can be mobilized to protest against any one corporation or industry on a specific issue. In this sense, establishing a positive image for specific corporations through gifts and financial donations is very useful.

The Advertising Council

Although it is not feasible to discuss very many of the numerous small organizations that attempt to shape public opinion, the Advertising Council, usually called the Ad Council, provides a good example of how they operate. In effect, it sells the free-enterprise system through public-interest advertising on a wide range of issues. In 1999, its outgoing president claimed that "over the decades the Ad Council has fought totalitarianism and racism, saved lives, healed the environment and made life measurably better for all Americans."[21] Whether that high praise is true or not, the Ad Council is a case study in how individualism and Americanism are called into service on behalf of the power elite.

The Ad Council began its institutional life as the War Advertising Council during World War II, founded as a means to support the war effort through advertising in the mass media. Its work was judged so successful in promoting a positive image for the corporate community that it was continued in the postwar period as an agency to support the Red Cross, United Way, conservation, drug education, and other campaigns that its corporate-dominated board and advisory committees believe to be in the public interest. With an annual budget of only a few million dollars, the council nonetheless places over $1.2 billion worth of free advertising each year through radio, television, magazines, newspapers, billboards, and public transportation.[22] After the council leaders decide on what campaigns to endorse, the specifics of the program are given to a Madison Avenue advertising agency, which does the work without charge.

Most council campaigns seem relatively innocuous and in a public interest that nobody would dispute. Its best-known figures, Smokey Bear and McGruff the Crime Dog, were created for the campaigns against forest fires and urban crime. However, as one media analyst demonstrates in a detailed study of these campaigns, many of them have a strong slant in favor of corporations. The council's environmental ads, for example, suggest that "people start pollution, people can stop it," thereby putting the responsibility on individuals rather than on a system of production that allows corporations to avoid the costs of disposing of their waste products by dumping them into the air or water. A special subcommittee of the council's Industry Advisory Committee gave very explicit instructions about how this particular ad campaign should be formulated: "The committee emphasized that the advertisements should stress that each of us must be made to recognize that each of us contributes to pollution, and therefore everyone bears the responsibility."[23] Thus, the Keep America Beautiful campaign is geared to show corporate concern about the environment while at the same time deflecting criticism of the corporate role in pollution by falling back on the individualism of the American creed.

The effectiveness of such campaigns is open to question. It is not clear that they have a direct influence on very many opinions. Studies by social scientists suggest that advertising campaigns of a propagandistic nature work best "when used to reinforce an already existing notion or to establish a logical or emotional connection between a new idea and a social norm."[24] But even when an ad campaign can be judged a failure in this limited role, it has filled a vacuum that might have been used by a competing group. This is especially the case with television, where the council is able to capture a significant percentage of the public-service advertising time that television networks provide. Thus, the council has the direct effect of reinforcing existing values while simultaneously preventing groups with a different viewpoint from presenting their interpretation of events.

The Ad Council is typical of a wide variety of opinion-shaping organizations that function in specific areas from labor relations, where the National Right to Work Committee battles union organizers, to something as far removed as the arts, where the Business Committee for the Arts encourages the artistic endeavors of low-income children as a way to boost the morale of those trapped in the inner city. Those functions are basically three in number:

1. They provide think-tank forums where academics, journalists, and other cultural experts can brainstorm with corporate leaders about the problems of shaping public opinion.

2. They help to create a more sophisticated corporate consciousness through forums, booklets, speeches, and awards.

3. They disseminate their version of the national interest and good Americanism to the general public on issues of concern to the power elite.

SHAPING OPINION ON FOREIGN POLICY

The opinion-shaping network achieves its clearest expression and greatest success in the area of foreign policy, where most people have little information or interest, and are predisposed to agree with top leaders out of patriotism and a fear of whatever is strange or foreign. "Especially in the realm of foreign policy," two experts on public opinion conclude, "where information can be centrally controlled, it seems especially likely that public opinion is often led." They say that this leading is done by "public officials and other influential groups and individuals."[25] Because so few people take a serious interest in foreign-policy issues, the major efforts in opinion-shaping are aimed toward a small stratum of highly interested and concerned citizens of college-educated backgrounds.

The most prominent organization involved in shaping upper-middle-class public opinion on foreign affairs is the Foreign Policy Association (FPA), based in New York. About one-third of its seventy-six–person governing council are also members of the Council on Foreign Relations. Although the FPA does some research and discussion work, its primary focus is on molding opinion outside the power elite, a division of labor with the Council on Foreign Relations that is well understood within foreign-policy circles. The FPA's major effort is an intensive program to provide literature and create discussion groups in middle-class organizations and on college campuses, working closely with local World Affairs councils. Its general activities are backed by several dozen private and corporate foundations. In 1999, for example, it received over $100,000 from the American International Insurance Group, the Freeman Foundation, and the Starr Foundation, over $75,000 from Alliance Capital Management and Exxon, over $30,000 from Bankers Trust, Chase Manhattan Bank, Seagram, and Texaco, and from $5,000 to $30,000 from four dozen other corporate foundations.

Although the efforts of the foreign-policy groups are important in shaping opinions among the most attentive publics, the actions of the president and his top foreign-policy officials are the strongest influences on general public opinion. Public opinion polls conducted before and after an escalation in the war in Vietnam still provide one of the most dramatic examples of this point. Before the bombing of Hanoi and Haiphong began in late spring 1966, the public was split fifty-fifty over the question of bombing, but when asked in July 1966, after the bombing began, if "the administration is more right or more wrong in bombing Hanoi and Haiphong," 85 percent were in favor. Similarly, 53 percent of the public approved of the 1983 invasion of the Caribbean Island of Grenada when they first heard about it, but 64 percent did so after President Reagan gave a nationwide television address to explain the decision. College-educated adults and people in younger age groups are most likely to show this change in opinion shortly after a presidential initiative.[26] However, there are limits to the shaping of public opinion on foreign policy when social stability is threatened and there is potential for social protest. For example, opposition to both the Korean and Vietnam Wars grew consistently as the number of American casualties continued to mount, and demonstrations and teach-ins at universities in the mid-1960s helped consolidate a large minority against the Vietnam War by 1967 and probably played a role in halting the escalation of the ground war. A strong nuclear disarmament movement also developed in the early 1980s when it seemed like the Reagan Administration was going to destabilize the nuclear balance.[27]

TRYING TO SHAPE OPINION ON ECONOMIC POLICY

Corporate leaders find the generally liberal opinions held by a majority of people on economic issues to be very annoying and potentially troublesome. They blame them in part on a lack of economic understanding. They label this alleged lack of understanding *economic illiteracy*, a term that implies that people have no right to their opinions because of their educational deficiencies. They claim these negative attitudes would change if people had the facts about the functioning of corporations and the economy, and they have spent tens of millions of dollars trying to present the facts as they see them. However, attempts to shape public opinion on domestic economic issues, where people feel directly involved and have their own experiences upon which to rely, are usually less successful than in the area of foreign policy.

Table 5.2 Donations to the National Council for Economic Education by Corporate Foundations in 1998

Corporate Foundation	Amount
Ameritech	$150,000
International Paper	$132,000
AT&T	$75,000
Northwestern Mutual Life	$50,000
Procter & Gamble	$25,000
State Farm Insurance	$25,000
American Express	$25,000
Coca-Cola	$20,000
GTE	$15,000
Amoco	$15,000
Exxon	$15,000
Warner-Lambert	$14,000
Goldman Sachs	$10,000
Alcoa	$10,000
Mobil	$10,000
General Mills	$10,000
Bristol Myers Squibb	$10,000
Total	$611,000

Source: The Foundation Grants Index 2000 (New York: The Foundation Center).

These points can be demonstrated by a look at the central organization in the field of economic education, the National Council on Economic Education (NCEE). It is only one of many organizations that attempt to shape public opinion on domestic economic issues, but its efforts are typical in many ways. Founded in 1949 by leaders within the Committee for Economic Development, who wanted to counter the strident ultraconservative economic educational efforts of the National Association of Manufacturers, the NCEE received much of its early funding from the Ford Foundation.[28] Most of its financial support now comes from corporations and corporate foundations. Table 5.2 lists its corporate foundation support for 1998.

The NCEE's twenty-nine–person board reflects the fact that it is part of the opinion-shaping network. It includes Harold Burson, the founder of Burson-Marsteller; vice presidents from Ameritech and General Mills; the chief economist from AT&T; a vice president from the American Farm Bureau Federation's insurance company; and four university professors. The board is unusual in that it has included leaders from the AFL-CIO since the outset. In 2000, for example, the union's directors of education and public policy were on the board.

The NCEE attempts to influence economic understanding by means of books, pamphlets, videos, and press releases. Its most important effort is aimed toward elementary and high schools through its "Economics America" program. This program provides schools with the curriculum plans and materials that are needed to introduce basic economic ideas at each grade level. To prepare teachers to carry out the curriculum, the NCEE has created a network of state councils and 260 university centers to coordinate the training of teachers in the nation's colleges and universities. The NCEE claims that:

> Each year the network trains about 120,000 teachers serving 8 million students. More than 2,600 school districts, teaching about 40 percent of the nation's students, conduct comprehensive programs in economic education with assistance from the network.[29]

As this brief overview shows, the NCEE's program begins in corporate board rooms and foundation offices, flows through affiliated councils and university centers, and ends up in teacher-training programs and public school curricula. In that regard, it is an ideal example of the several steps and organizations that are usually involved in attempts to shape public opinion on any domestic issue. And yet, despite all this effort, the level of "economic illiteracy," according to polls taken for the corporations, remained as high in the 1990s as it was in the 1940s. The average American receives a score of 39 percent; college graduates average 51 percent.[30] This inability to engineer wholehearted consent to the views of the power elite on economic issues reveals the limits of the opinion-shaping process in general. These limits are in good part created by the work experiences and general observations of average citizens, which lead them to be skeptical about many corporate claims. Then, too, the alternative analyses advocated by trade unionists, liberals, socialists, and middle-class ultraconservatives also have a counteracting influence.

Although the power elite is not able to alter the liberal views held by a majority of Americans on a wide range of economic issues, this does not necessarily mean that the liberal opinions have much influence. To the contrary, a large body of evidence suggests that the majority's opinion is often ignored. This point is made most clearly by the right turn taken by the Carter and Reagan administrations from 1978 to 1983, despite strong evidence that the public remained liberal on the issues under consideration: "Throughout that period the public consistently favored more spending on the environment, education, medical care, the cities, and other matters, and it never accepted the full Reagan agenda of 'deregulation.'"[31] An even more detailed analysis of survey data relating to the alleged rightward shift found little support for the claim except on issues of crime. It concludes Democratic and Republican leaders embraced conservatism in the 1970s, but that the American electorate did not follow their lead.[32]

It is usually possible to ignore public opinion on domestic economic issues for several intertwined reasons. First, the general public lacks an organizational base for making direct contact with legislators, which makes it very hard for people to formulate and express opinions on complex and detailed legislation. Second, as explained in Chapter 6, the two-party system makes it difficult to influence policy through the electoral process. Third, as shown in Chapter 7, liberal initiatives are blocked by a conservative voting bloc that is by and large invulnerable to liberal public opinion.

SOCIAL ISSUES

Several highly charged social issues receive great attention in the mass media and figure prominently in political campaigns: abortion, busing, the death penalty, gun control, school prayer, pornography, and protection against discrimination for gays and lesbians. Despite the time and energy that goes into these issues, they are not ones that are of concern to the power elite. There is no power elite position on any of them. Some individuals within the power elite may care passionately about one or more of them, but these issues are not the subject of discussion at the policy groups or of position papers from the mainstream think tanks because they have no direct bearing on the corporate community.

Nonetheless, these issues are often front and center in battles between the corporate-conservative and liberal-labor coalitions, because liberals seek changes on all of them and social conservatives resist such changes. Although the New Christian Right is deeply and genuinely concerned with moral issues as a matter of principle, such issues are seen by most conservatives as cross-cutting issues that can be used as wedges in trying to defeat liberal-labor candidates in the electoral arena. These issues are thought to be useful to conservatives because voters who agree with the liberal-labor coalition on economic issues often disagree with it on one or more social issues, providing an opportunity for conservatives to win their allegiance. Although a majority of Americans were liberal or tolerant on most of these issues by the 1980s, conservatives nonetheless stress them because they hope to gain support from a few percent of the most emotional opponents who might otherwise vote Democratic. If each of these issues can win over just 1–2 percent of voters, the cumulative effect can make a large difference in close elections. Social issues are therefore a key part of the corporate-conservative electoral strategy even though they are not issues of substantive concern to the power elite.

The importance of these wedge issues for conservatives is seen most clearly in the case of reactions to the civil and voting rights won by African-Americans and their liberal white allies in the mid-1960s. The resentments generated in most Southern whites by these gains for African-Americans were used by Republican presidential candidate Barry Goldwater in 1964 to capture the four traditionally Democratic states of South Carolina, Georgia, Alabama, and Mississippi, the only states he won besides his home state of Arizona. They were then used by the Democratic governor of Alabama, George Wallace, to win 13.5 percent of the vote nationwide in his third-party presidential race in 1968, thereby taking away enough angry white Democratic votes to give Richard Nixon a very narrow victory over his Democratic opponent. In 1972, President Nixon solidified these voters for the Republicans at the presidential level, especially in the South, paving the way for the Reagan-Bush era from 1980 to 1992. From the 1970s on, first busing and then affirmative action were used as wedge issues by Republicans, usually joined by abortion, school prayer, and gun control.[33]

THE ROLE OF THE MASS MEDIA

The mass media—newspapers, magazines, radio, and most especially, television—have a complex relationship to the upper class and corporate community. On the one hand, they are lucrative business enterprises, owned by members of the upper class and directed by members of the corporate community, with extensive connections to other large corporations. Moreover, the three major television networks are owned by even larger corporations: the Disney Corporation owns ABC, General Electric owns NBC, and Westinghouse owns CBS.[34] On the other hand, there are differences of opinion between corporate leaders and media professionals on some issues, as revealed in opinion surveys of top leaders from business, labor, media, and minority group organizations. These studies show that representatives of the mass media tend to be more liberal on foreign policy and domestic issues than corporate and conservative leaders, although not as liberal as the representatives of minority groups and liberal organizations. On questions of environment, which are very sensitive to corporate leaders, the media professionals hold much the same liberal views as people from labor, minority, and liberal organizations.[35]

The net result of these contradictory forces is an often tense relationship between media executives and the rest of the corporate community, with corporate leaders placing part of the blame on the mass media for any negative opinions about business held by the general public. This rift seemed especially large in the 1970s, leading the corporations and foundations to fund conferences and new journalism programs that would lead to new understandings. The corporations also began to run their own analyses and opinion pieces as advertisements on the editorial pages in major newspapers and liberal magazines, thereby presenting their viewpoints in their own words on a wide variety of issues. Since that time they have spent several hundred million dollars a year on such advocacy advertising.[36]

Many conservatives believe that reporters insert liberal biases into their coverage of events at the expense of the hapless owners and directors. One conservative analyst calls the media a "liberal establishment" whose leadership "has established itself as equal in power to the nation's corporate and governmental leadership," due to the fact that "television is the major source of information for the vast majority of Americans." He believes that the media leaders have a "liberal, reformist" agenda that they further by focusing on scandal, abuse, and corruption."[37]

Such claims are first of all contradicted by studies of the socialization of journalists, which show that they make every effort to present both sides of a story and keep their own opinions separate.[38] Moreover, the evidence shows that what appears in the media is most importantly shaped by forces outside of them. A political scientist who specializes in media studies concludes that the media is "to a considerable degree dependent on subject matter specialists, including government officials among others, in framing and reporting the news."[39] When the experts agree, or dissident experts are not included, there is more likely to be unanimity in public opinion on the issue.

These findings suggest that it is necessary to understand the politics of "expert communities" in order to explain any influence on public opinion by the mass media, which is where the policy-planning and opinion-shaping networks come into the picture. They supply the experts, including those corporate leaders who have been legitimated as statesmen on the basis of their long-time involvement in policy-discussion groups. As one small indication of this point, a Lexis-Nexis search for this book of a large newspaper index for January 1999 through October 2000 shows that the Brookings Institution is mentioned 753 times, followed by 706 mentions for the Heritage Foundation and 243 for the American Enterprise Institute. By way of contrast, the liberal Economic Policy Institute appears 161 times. The dependence of the media on government leaders and outside experts as sources greatly constrains any motivation liberal journalists in the media might have to inject their personal views.

The importance of outside experts and government officials in shaping what appears in the media is best seen in the case of defense spending, where public opinion moves in tandem with shifts in media coverage.[40] Since it is unlikely that liberal journalists advocated the vast increases in defense spending from 1978 to 1985, this finding supports the conclusion that government officials and experts are the main influences on media content on most issues of political importance. Indeed, the rise in defense spending fits nicely with the intense media scare campaign by the Committee on the Present Danger and related organizations.[41]

Studies of media content show that there is a great emphasis on bad news and sensationalism, with a special emphasis on crime and disasters. They are an overwhelming aspect of news coverage, especially local news, because they are believed to attract audiences. Moreover, some studies suggest that crime news may have the largest impact on public opinion of any type of news item. The more crime news that people watch, the more likely they may be to overestimate the actual amount of crime, overestimate African-American involvement in violent crime, favor more money for crime prevention, and favor the death penalty.[42] None of these outcomes could be claimed as fulfillment of a liberal agenda, so it is unlikely that such stories appear because of a liberal bias. If anything, they reflect the corporate-conservative coalition's constant outcry for the restoration of law and order.

In studying media influence, by far the greatest attention has been paid to television news. There is experimental evidence from social psychology studies suggesting that the placement of a story first on the evening news, or repeating it several times during the course of a week, leads people to think of those issues as more important, giving television an agenda-setting function.[43] However, there is also evidence that the news is often not watched even though the television is on, and that people don't remember much of what they do see. The declining audience for news programs has led to even more emphasis on human-interest stories, so the news is increasingly seen as a form of entertainment by television executives and viewers alike. Several studies suggest that most people actually retain more politically relevant information from what they read in newspapers and magazines. In addition, the potential effects of television seem to be counteracted by people's beliefs and membership identifications, their ability to screen out information that does not fit with their preconceptions, and their reliance on other people in developing their opinions.[44]

Even the growing number of large newspaper chains may not limit public discussion in the way some critics fear. Using survey responses from 409 journalists at 223 newspapers, a journalism profes-

sor found that their reporters and editors report high levels of autonomy and job satisfaction. Further, he found that a range of opinions
appears in the newspapers, including critical ones. In comparison to
small local newspapers, he also found that large newspapers and
newspaper chains are more likely to publish editorials and letters that
deal with local issues or are critical of mainstream groups and institutions.[45]

The limits of the mass media in shaping public opinion are most
recently demonstrated by the failure of the public to endorse the impeachment of President Bill Clinton, even though it was enthusiasti-
cally advocated by most of the Washington pundits who appeared on
television news and discussion programs. In addition, over 140 newspapers called for his resignation. However, to the surprise of media
leaders, a strong majority of Americans opposed impeachment despite
their highly negative opinion of the president's personal behavior.
They made their own distinction between job performance and personal morality. One polling expert believes that the campaign against
the president may have increased public resentment toward the
media. He also concludes that this event "proves just the opposite of
what most people believe: how little power the media elite have over
public opinion."[46]

When all is said and done, as a textbook by leaders in the field of
public opinion research states, the direct evidence from surveys for a
strong media influence on public opinion in general is surprisingly
weak.[47] Another authoritative text on public opinion, now in its fifth
edition, concludes its chapter on mass media effects on public opinion
by saying there is "no clear evidence that this relationship is more
than minimal, however, or that the direction of influence is entirely
from the media to the public."[48] Further, a detailed analysis of how
people in focus groups react to various media stories suggests that
"(a) people are not so passive, (b) people are not so dumb, and (c) people negotiate with media messages in complicated ways that vary from
issue to issue."[49]

If the studies on media concentration, the socialization of journalists, the sources of news, and the actual effects of the media on
public opinion are taken as a whole, it seems unlikely that the media
have the independent capacity to shape people's opinions on the issues
that have to do with power in America. The media can shape what
people think is important, but the news they stress reflects the biases
of those with access to them—corporate leaders, government officials,
and policy experts. Even here, there is ample evidence that the views
of liberal critics make frequent appearances in newspapers and magazines, and that corporations and establishment politicians are regularly criticized.[50]

The mass media reach more people than any other outlet for the pamphlets, speeches, and infomercials created by the opinion-forming network, but the people they reach are those who matter the least from the point of view of the opinion molders. Media often can amplify the message of the powerful and sometimes marginalize the concerns of the less powerful, but they are not the most central organization in the opinion-shaping network.

THE ROLE OF POLLS

Public opinion polls can be a way to gain useful information for the social sciences, but they are also a tool that can be used by political leaders and advocacy groups to influence public opinion. For example, interviews with former congressional and White House aides suggest that polling data about public opinion is used to decide how to present and package the votes the elected officials intend to make because of their strong policy preferences.[51] Then too, polls are sometimes constructed so that their results can be used to shape public opinion when they are reported to the public via the media. This is done by using loaded terms or political labels. For example, in a study asking the public about a law that did not really exist, public opinion differed by 20 to 30 percentage points depending on whether it was alleged to be of interest to Democratic or Republican leaders.[52] Poll results also change depending upon the choices that are included in the question. In a poll of the general public in early 1997, it was found that a majority favored an amendment to the constitution to balance the federal budget, but a majority opposed such an amendment if they were asked if they favored it even if it meant a cutback in Social Security.[53]

Public Agenda, a conservative advocacy group in favor of school vouchers, issued a report in 1999 claiming that most people knew very little about charter schools, but that 68 percent favored them once they were explained. The survey characterized charter schools as public schools with more control over their own budget, staff, and curriculum, and free from many existing regulations. Then, the Business Roundtable claimed in 2000 that one of its surveys showed that 75 percent of the public favors standardized tests for promoting children in school, but it left out the many negative reactions by respondents to questions about such tests, which could lead to another conclusion, that "nearly all Americans reject tests as the main basis for promotion."[54] Some of the questions used by the National Council on Economic Education to demonstrate "economic illiteracy" show a subtle advocacy bias. For example, its test asks what "the best measure of the economy's performance is," then counts as incorrect "the unemployment rate" and the "consumer price index," even though both are excellent measures from the average person's point of view. The correct answer is supposedly "gross domestic product," the money value of all goods and services produced within the country.

Polls also can be used to suggest that a public opinion exists on issues for which there is none. This does not mean people do not have general opinions, but that they often make it up as they go along when responding to specific questions about policy preferences. If questions about affirmative action or oil drilling are framed in one way, they yield one answer, but framed in another way they yield a different answer, especially for those without knowledge or firm opinions.[55] It therefore becomes relatively easy for advocacy groups to obtain whatever results they wish when they conduct a survey.

Results such as these suggest that the alleged public opinion on an issue is sometimes a myth, based on the results of questionable polls reported in newspapers. In those cases, the public opinion reported by the media is only another tool in the arguments between the liberal-labor and corporate-conservative coalitions. Although there is a sensible public opinion on many general issues of great import to average Americans, there are aspects of public opinion that seem to be as chaotic and contrived as careful research studies suggest.[56]

THE ENFORCEMENT OF PUBLIC OPINION

There are limits to the tolerance that exists within the power elite for the general public's disagreements about public issues, although these limits vary from era to era and are never fully clear until they are tested. There are thus costs for people who move outside the general consensus. The attempt to enforce the limits on disagreement are carried out in a variety of ways that begin with exclusion from events or dismissal from jobs. Those who disagree with the consensus are sometimes criticized in the media or branded as "extremists" or "un-Americans." Such punishments are relatively minor for those who are extremely committed to their viewpoint, but experiments on conformity in social psychology suggest that most people are very uncomfortable when they are in any way excluded or criticized by their peers. Similar studies show that most people also find it very hard to be in open disagreement with authority figures.[57]

The use of scorn, isolation, and other sanctions is seen most directly in the treatment of "whistleblowers," employees of corporations or government agencies who expose wrongdoing by their superiors. Contrary to the impression that they are rewarded as good citizens for stepping forward, they are treated as pariahs, relieved of their responsibilities by higher authority figures in the organization, and shunned by peers. Friends are afraid to associate with them. Their lives are often turned upside down. Many regret they took the action they did, even though they thought it was the honest or moral course to take.[58]

Those who become prominent public critics of some aspect of conventional wisdom receive similar harsh treatment, unless they can be isolated as oddball characters not worth attacking. Their motives are questioned and negative stories appear in the media, which attempt to demonstrate they are acting from irrational psychological motives. To take one famous example, when consumer activist Ralph Nader dared to testify before Congress in 1966 about the defects in one of the small cars manufactured by General Motors, the company hired a private detective agency to try to find personal gossip about him that could be used to discredit his testimony. At first, General Motors denied any involvement in these activities, then claimed that the investigation concerned Nader's possible connection to bogus car insurance claims. Later, the company apologized even while denying any harassment, but then the detective agency admitted that it had been hired to "get something somewhere on this guy . . . get him out of their hair . . . shut him up." There was no personal wrongdoing to be discovered, the company was heavily criticized in the media, and Nader collected damages when his lawsuit was settled out of court.[59]

Government officials sometimes resort to severe sanctions in an attempt to discredit liberal and radical leaders who influence public opinion and inspire public demonstrations. In the case of Martin Luther King, Jr., and many other civil rights activists, the government not only spied on them, but planted false information and issued false threats in order to disrupt their efforts. Such actions may not seem at first glance to be part of an opinion-shaping process, but they are, because they serve as a reminder that attempts to change opinions and laws can have serious negative consequences. Government violence and other illegal methods are seldom used on dissenters in times of domestic tranquillity, but they have been employed in times of social upheaval in the past when members of the power elite appointed to the government felt it necessary to do so. For example, the government official who authorized wire taps on Martin Luther King, Jr., in 1963 was Attorney General Robert F. Kennedy, the son of a multimillionaire and the brother of President John F. Kennedy.

WHEN PUBLIC OPINION CAN AND CANNOT BE IGNORED

Public opinion does not have the routine importance often attributed to it in civics books. It is shaped on foreign and defense issues, ignored on domestic economic issues, and irrelevant to the power elite on social issues, except as a way to gain votes. Although people have sensible opinions within the context and time constraints of their everyday lives, it is unlikely that any focused public opinion exists on most of the complicated legislative issues of concern to the corporate community. The power elite and politicians therefore enjoy a great deal of leeway on most policy questions.

Public opinion usually can be ignored because people's beliefs do not lead them into opposition or disruption if they have stable roles to fulfill in the society or see no clear organizational path to social change. Routine involvement in a compelling and enjoyable daily round of activities, the most important of which are a job and a family, is a more important factor in explaining acquiescence to power-elite policies than attempts to shape public opinion. What happens in the economy and in government has more impact on how people act than what is said in the opinion-shaping process and the mass media.[60]

However, public opinion can have an impact when people are forced out of their routines by depressions, wars, and other forms of social disruption. In those cases, public opinion can lead to a strong social movement that threatens one or another aspect of the established order, which in turn leads members of the power elite to seek solutions that will restore social stability. Public opinion that congeals into a social movement also can set limits on corporate actions when there is a major accident, such as an oil spill, mining explosion, or nuclear plant breakdown.[61]

Although research on public opinion suggests there is a large amount of latitude for the power elite to operate as they wish to, this chapter is incomplete in one important respect. It has not considered the potential effect of public opinion through the electoral process.

6

Parties and Elections

Elections hold out the potential that citizens can shape public policy through support for candidates who share their policy preferences. Overwhelming defeats for candidates favored by the power elite would be difficult to overturn because elections are so legitimate. But have elections delivered on their promise in the United States? To provide perspective on this question, it is useful to begin with the gradual development of elections in Western history.

WHEN AND HOW DO ELECTIONS MATTER?

Historically, the first function of elections is to provide a mechanism for rival power groups, not everyday people, to resolve disputes in a peaceful way. It was not until elections were well established that they came to be seen as a way to engage more of the population in governance. This does not mean elections were willingly accepted by the combatants. In fact, elections were not adopted in any European country until the power rivals had compromised their major differences in a pact or settlement, usually after years of violence or in the face of extreme economic crisis.[1]

In the United States, the Constitution was the equivalent of these peace agreements. It dealt with several issues that rival colonial leaders said were not negotiable. Most importantly, Northern wealth holders had to make several concessions to the Southern slave owners to win their agreement to the new constitution. Even in this example, the limited nature of elections is revealed by the Civil War. The slave holders decided to secede from the union and risk war rather than see their way of life gradually eroded by an inability to expand slavery westward.

Within the context of stable power-sharing pacts, elections gradually come to have a second function. They allow average citizens to help determine which of the rival power groups will play the lead role in government. In the case of the United States, this means different occupational and ethnic groups become part of corporate-led coalitions that contend for office on a wide range of appeals, some issue-based, some not. Voters are thus often able to eliminate those candidates they perceive as extremists.

Thirdly, citizens in many countries can have an influence on economic and social issues due to their participation in electoral coalitions. This is best seen in those European countries where social democrats have won a majority and created social insurance systems for unemployment, disability, health, and old age that are far larger than American programs. Finally, elections matter as a way to introduce new policies in times of social disruption caused by extreme domestic problems. In the nineteenth and early twentieth centuries, this role was often fulfilled by third parties that appeared suddenly on the scene, such as the new parties of the 1840s and 1850s that first advocated the abolition of slavery. By the second decade of the twentieth century, the main electoral arena for new ideas became the primary elections of the two major parties.

So, elections can and do matter. They allow for at least some input by citizens who are not wealthy, and they provide an opening for critics of the social system to present their ideas. In the United States, however, elections have yielded far fewer successes for the liberal-labor coalition than might be expected on the basis of social-democratic victories in most Western democracies. The reasons for this difference are explained in the remainder of this chapter.

WHY ONLY TWO MAJOR PARTIES?

In some democratic countries, there are three or more substantial political parties with clearly defined programs understood by voters, who therefore are able to vote on the basis of policy preferences if they so desire. In sharp contrast, there have been only two major parties for most of American history. The only exceptions were a brief one-party era from about 1812 to 1824, after the Federalist Party collapsed, and a few years in the 1850s, when the conflict over extending slavery into Kansas and Missouri led to the break-up of the Whig Party (the party that, roughly speaking, replaced the Federalist Party). Even the Republican Party that developed in the 1850s does not really qualify as a third party, because it replaced the Whigs in the space of just one or two elections.

Why are there only two major parties despite the country's tumultuous history of regional, religious, and class rivalries? Two fundamental features of American government lead to a two-party system. The first is the selection of senators and representatives from states and districts in elections that require only a plurality, not a majority. Such an arrangement is called a *single-member-district plurality system,* and it has led to two-party systems in 90 percent of the 109 countries included in an exhaustive comparative study. The exceptions tend to be in countries where a third party has some strength in a single region for ethnic or religious reasons. The second reason for the American two-party system is relatively unique in the world: the election of a president. The election of a president is, in effect, a strong version of the single-member district plurality system, with the nation serving as the only district. Due to the enormous power of the presidency, the pull toward two parties that exists in any single-member district system is even greater in the United States. The result is that third parties are even more unlikely and smaller than in other countries with district/plurality elections.*[2]

The fact that only one person can win the presidency, or be elected to Congress from a given state or district, which seems trivial, and is taken for granted by most Americans, leads to a two-party system by creating a series of winner-take-all elections. A vote for a third-party candidate of the right or left is in effect a vote for the voter's least-favored candidate on the other side of the political spectrum. Because a vote for a third candidate of the left or right is a vote for "your worst enemy," the usual strategy for those who want to avoid this fate is to form the largest possible preelection coalition, even if numerous policy preferences must be abandoned or compromised. The result is two coalitional parties.

By way of contrast, a parliamentary system provides some room for third parties even in district/plurality electoral systems. This is because a prime minister is selected by the parliament after the elections. There is therefore less pressure toward two preelectoral coalitions, thus making it possible for three issue-oriented parties to

* As shown dramatically in the 2000 elections, the president is selected by the Electoral College, where each state has a number of electors equal to the size of its congressional delegation. The minimum number of electors a small state can have is three—two senators plus one House member. Electors cast their ballots for the candidate who wins in their state. The focus on electoral votes forces candidates to concentrate on winning a plurality in as many states as possible, not simply on winning the most votes in the nation overall. This system creates a further disadvantage for third parties.

exist or for a new third party to grow over the period of several elections. Even more parties are likely to exist if the parliament is elected through a system of proportional representation, which eliminates districts and allots seats in proportion to a party's nationwide vote once a certain minimum is reached (usually about 5 percent). Thus, comparative studies of the relationship between electoral rules and the number of political parties suggest how candidate selection in the United States came to be conducted through a two-party system, despite the existence of the same kinds of class, regional, and ethnic conflicts that have led to three or more parties in other countries.

Although the American system of single-member congressional districts and presidential elections generates an inexorable tendency toward a two-party system, it was not designed with this fact in mind. The Founding Fathers purposely created a system of checks and balances that would keep power within bounds, especially the potential power of an aroused and organized majority of farmers and artisans. However, a party system was not among their plans. Indeed, the Founding Fathers disliked the idea of parties, which they condemned as factions that are highly divisive. Parties are a major unintended consequence of their deliberations, and it was not until the 1830s and 1840s that a new generation of political leaders finally accommodated themselves to the idea that the two-party system was not disruptive of rule by the wealthy few.[3]

A two-party system does not foster parties that articulate clear images and policies, in good part because rival candidates attempt to blur their differences in order to win the voters in the middle. It causes candidates to emphasize personal qualities rather than policy preferences. It may even lead to collusion between the two parties to avoid some issues or to avoid competition in some districts. Moreover, there is reason to believe that a two-party system actually discourages voting because those in a minority of even 49 percent receive no representation for their efforts. Voting increases considerably in countries where districts have been replaced by proportional representation.[4]

For all these reasons, then, a two-party system leads to the possibility that there may be very little relationship between politics and policy. Candidates can say one thing to be elected and then do another once in office, which of course gives people with money and information the opportunity to shape legislation. In short, a two-party system creates a set of circumstances in which the parties may or may not reflect citizen preferences. However, none of this explains why the liberal-labor coalition does not have a party of its own. The historic difference between the Northern and Southern economies, one based in free labor, the other in slavery, provides the explanation for this unusual situation.

REPUBLICANS AND DEMOCRATS

Two contrasting claims predominate in most everyday discussions of the Republican and Democratic parties. One suggests there is not a "dime's worth of difference between them," which reflects the need to appeal to the centrist voters in a two-party system. The other says that the Republicans represent big business and the Democrats the liberal-labor coalition, a belief that comes equally from the scare tactics of ultraconservatives and the mythmaking by liberals about a progressive past. In fact, both parties have been controlled for most of their history by different factions within the power elite.

Although the Constitutional Convention of 1787 settled the major issues between the Northern and Southern rich, at least until the 1850s, it did not take long for political parties to develop. From the day in 1791 when wealthy Virginia plantation owners made contact with landowners in upstate New York to create what was to become the first incarnation of the Democratic Party, the two parties represented different economic interests within the upper class. For the most part, the Democrats were originally the party of agrarian wealth, especially in the South, the Republicans the party of bankers, merchants, and industrialists.*[5]

As with all generalizations, this one needs some qualification. The Democratic-Republican party, as it was first known, also found many of its adherents in the North among merchants and bankers of Irish origins, who disliked the English-origin leaders in the Federalist Party for historical reasons. Then, too, religious dissenters and Protestants of low-status denominations often favored the Democratic-Republicans over the "high church" Federalist Party. These kinds of differences persist down to the present: In terms of social status, the Federalist-Whig-Republican party has been the party of the secure and established, the Democrats the party of those who were in the out-group on some dimension. Today, it is most strongly supported by African-Americans, Hispanics, Jews, and women who work outside the home, although it still has moderate-conservative business leaders at its core.[6]

The characterization of the Democratic Party as a coalition of out-groups even fits the slave holders who controlled the party in its first sixty-nine years, for they were agrarians in an industrializing society, slave holders in a land of free labor. Although they controlled the

---

* The South is defined for purposes of this book as the following fourteen states: Alabama, Arkansas, Florida, Georgia, Louisiana, Kentucky, Mississippi, North Carolina, Oklahoma, South Carolina, Tennessee, Texas, Virginia, and West Virginia. Although there is no standard definition of *the South*, and Missouri might well have been included because it was a slave state, the fourteen listed here are used by many social scientists.

presidency in thirty-two of the first thirty-six years of the country's existence by electing slave owners like Thomas Jefferson, James Madison, and Andrew Jackson, the plantation capitalists were on the defensive, and they knew it. Following the Civil War, the Democratic Party became even more completely the instrument of the southern half of the upper class when all wealthy white Southerners moved into that party. They correctly saw this move as the best strategy to maximize their impact in Washington and at the same time force the Southern populists to accept marginalization within the Democratic Party, or start a third party that could go nowhere.[7]

After the Civil War, the white Southerners gained new allies in the North with the arrival of millions of ethnic Catholic and Jewish immigrants, who were often treated badly and scorned by the Protestant Republican majority. When some of these new immigrants grew wealthy in the first half of the twentieth century, they became major financial backers of urban Democratic organizations (called *machines* in their day). Contrary to ultraconservatives and liberals, the liberal-labor coalition that developed within the Democratic Party in the 1930s was no match for the well-established Southern rich and their wealthy, urban ethnic allies.[8]

Still, the liberal-labor coalition did begin to elect about 100 Democrats to the House starting in the 1930s, where they joined with roughly 100 Southern Democrats and 50 machine Democrats from Northern urban areas to form a strong Democratic majority in all but a few sessions of Congress before 1994. By 1938, however, the Southern Democrats and Northern Republicans had formed a conservative voting bloc that stopped the liberal Democrats from passing legislation concerning union rights, civil rights, and the regulation of business. These are precisely the issues that defined class conflict at the time. This generalization includes civil rights because that was a code phrase for issues concerning the coercive control of the low-wage African-American workforce in the South.[9]

For the most part, the liberal-labor coalition had to settle for small victories on economic issues where it could attract the support of some Southern Democrats, such as housing subsidies. More generally, the Democratic Party became a pro-spending alliance in which Northern Democrats supported agricultural subsidies and price supports that greatly benefited Southern plantation owners. The Southerners in turn were willing to support government spending programs for roads, public housing, hospital construction, school lunches, and even public assistance, but with three provisos. The spending programs would contain no attack on segregation, they would be locally controlled, and they would differentially benefit Southern states. This arrangement hinged on a tacit agreement that the liberal-labor coalition would not vigorously oppose the continuing segregation in the South.[10]

The fact that Democrats formally controlled Congress for most of the years between 1932 and 1994 is therefore irrelevant in terms of understanding the domination of government policy by the power elite. The important point is that a strong conservative majority was elected to Congress throughout the twentieth century and always voted together on the issues that related to class conflict.[11] There are two crucial exceptions to this generalization, the mid-1930s and the mid-1960s, times of great social turmoil. The activism of workers in the 1930s led to the passage of pro-union legislation in 1935 and the Civil Rights Movement of the 1960s led to the Civil Rights Act of 1964 and the Voting Rights Act of 1965. The pro-union legislation is discussed at the end of Chapter 7 and the civil rights legislation at the end of Chapter 8.

There is, of course, far more to the story of the Democratic Party, including the details of how a voting majority is assembled for each particular piece of legislation through complex horse trading. But enough has been said to explain why the liberal-labor coalition does not have a party of its own, as it does in most democratic countries. The electoral rules leading to a two-party system, in conjunction with control of the Democrats by wealthy Southern whites until the last few decades, left the liberal-labor coalition with no good options. It cannot form a third party without assuring the election of even more Republicans, who are its sworn enemies, but it has been unable to win control of the Democratic Party. The result is a sordid bargain from the point of view of leftists and young activists.

The control of both political parties by members of the power elite reinforces the worst tendencies of a two-party system: avoidance of issues, collusion, and an emphasis on the character and personality of the candidates. There is an important political science literature on how elected officials from both parties employ a variety of strategies within this context to vote their policy preferences, even when they are opposed by a majority of voters, and at the same time win reelection.[12] This literature shows the complexity of politics and electioneering at the intersection between the power elite and ordinary citizens. For purposes of this book, the important point is that many people in the United States can be persuaded to vote on the basis of their race, religion, or ethnicity, rather than their social class, because there is no political party to develop and popularize a program reflecting their economic interests and preferences. This is the main reason why the electoral system is best understood from a power perspective as a *candidate-selection process*. Its primary function is one of filling offices, with the minimum possible attention to the policy aspects of politics.

RALPH NADER AND THE GREEN PARTY

The Green Party, and especially the presidential candidacy of Ralph Nader in 2000, repeats a long history of high expectations and great disappointment for left-wing third parties in the United States due to the nature of the electoral system. Although Green Party members have been active in state and local campaigns since the early 1990s, they have had very little success except in New Mexico and parts of Colorado, California, and Oregon. As of 2000, they have elected seventy-nine people in twenty-one states, all at the local level, including five mayors in towns in California.[13] The Nader campaign seemed to many leftists to be an ideal opportunity to give the party greater visibility, along with the 5 percent of the presidential vote needed to qualify for federal campaign funds.

Nader ran an all-out anticorporate campaign that included most of the economic reforms desired by leftwing advocates. He fueled the enthusiasm of a great many activists eager for change. Early polls showed Nader's potential share of the vote at 8 to 10 percent in some states, but it fell to 4 to 5 percent in the weeks before the election, and then to 2.7 percent nationally in the final tally. This downward trajectory parallels the decline in support for previous left-wing presidential candidates when their supporters decided they did not want to risk a Republican victory.*

As so often in the past, the Democrats began by ignoring the leftist candidate almost entirely, hoping that few people would notice him. When polls showed that Nader might make the difference in several key states, they came to regard him as a deadly enemy, and in the end he probably did contribute to their loss of the presidency by winning enough votes in Florida and New Hampshire to give the electoral votes for those states to President George W. Bush. Fearing this outcome, the Gore campaign enlisted the most liberal of Democrats to attack Nader unmercifully as a once-great figure who had lost his way and was serving as a spoiler. Pro-choice women's groups and African-American leaders, who believed their causes would suffer in a Republican administration, urged Nader to stay out of closely contested states, but he rejected their requests. Even a group of former Nader

---

* The fact that H. Ross Perot received 19 percent of the vote in 1992 and nearly 9 percent in 1996, running as the candidate of his Reform Party, does not contradict this analysis because his party was positioned between the two major parties. As a centrist party, it was more likely to draw votes from partisans of both parties, and hence was not more threatening to one than the other. Careful analysis of the 1992 campaign, and exit polls in both 1992 and 1996, show that he did take voters from both parties. Perot's vote is also unusual because he spent $72 million of his own money to promote his candidacy in 1992.

co-workers, who greatly admired him for his work on consumer and environmental issues, urged a vote for Albert Gore, Jr.

At the same time, Republicans ran television ads in closely contested states that showed Nader making very negative comments about Gore, even though his views are closer to those of Gore and he regarded Bush as a lightweight who would do the bidding of his corporate advisers. The Republicans launched this stealth ad campaign with the idea that Nader's attacks on Gore could help Nader pull enough votes to give several states to Bush. Such support of left-wing third parties by Republicans is an old story.

During the 1990s, the Greens had their highest vote counts in gubernatorial and House races in New Mexico, ranging from 5 to 17 percent. Green candidates in one of the House districts there made it possible for a Republican to win the last three elections with about 47% of the vote. Green candidates also took away enough votes in House races in 2000 to elect Republicans in Michigan and New Jersey. The enmity between Greens and liberal Democrats is now very great. This division in the forces seeking egalitarian social change is not likely to go away. For the structural reasons outlined earlier in this chapter, Democrats probably will do everything they can to undermine the Green Party.

But it was not just the Democrats who were hurt in 2000 by a third party. The Republicans suffered at the hands of two extreme right-wing parties, Patrick Buchanan's transformed Reform Party and the Libertarian Party. In Iowa, New Mexico, Oregon, and Wisconsin, where Gore won by anywhere from 500 to 6,500 votes, Buchanan's votes would have been enough to give President Bush 30 more electoral votes. In the state of Washington, where the Democratic challenger for a Senate seat defeated the Republican incumbent by only 2,229 votes, the Libertarian candidate received 49,345 votes.

PARTY PRIMARIES AS GOVERNMENT STRUCTURES

The inexorable two-party logic of the American electoral system led to another unique feature of American politics: the use of primary elections regulated by state governments to determine the parties' candidates. The system was first legislated in 1903 by reformers in Wisconsin, who became convinced there was no hope for third parties. About the same time, a system of white primaries was adopted in the segregationist Southern states as a way for rival white candidates to challenge each other without allowing African-Americans to vote.[14]

As primaries grew in frequency, they gradually became an accepted part of the overall electoral system. It has now reached the point where the use of state-regulated primaries, when combined with long-standing governmental control of party registration, has transformed the two major parties into the official office-filling agencies of the state. From a legislative and legal point of view, the party primaries labeled *Republican* and *Democratic* can be seen as two different pathways legitimated by the government for obtaining its elected officials. Thus, state-sponsored primaries reinforce the point that American politics is a candidate-selection process.

Put another way, parties are no longer fully independent organizations that control membership and choose their own leaders. Since anyone can register with the government to be a member of a party, party leaders cannot exclude people from membership based on political beliefs. By the same token, people registered in the party can run in its primaries for any office, so party leaders and party conventions have very little influence on the policies advocated by its candidates. In effect, a party stands for what the successful candidates in primaries say it stands for. Party leaders can protest and donors can withhold crucial campaign funds, but the winners in the primaries, along with their many political consultants, are the party for all intents and purposes. This is a major difference from political parties in other countries. It is also very different from the situation a few decades ago in the United States, when "urban bosses" selected Northern Democratic candidates.

The use of primaries by insurgents led to some surprising victories early in the twentieth century. In North Dakota, for example, a one-time Socialist Party organizer developed the Nonpartisan League to run candidates in party primaries on a radical platform. The platform called for state-owned grain elevators, a state-owned bank, public housing for farm workers, and other policies that would make farmers less dependent on railroads and grain companies, which were viewed as highly exploitative. Despite vehement opposition from business leaders and mainstream politicians, the Nonpartisan League swept to power in North Dakota in 1916 and instituted much of its program. The Bank of North Dakota, which focuses on credit for farmers and low-income rural people, is still the only one of its kind in the United States. Even though the Nonpartisan League has been gone for many decades and is almost completely forgotten, it had a large impact. As the historian who studied it most closely concludes: "Not only was it to control for some years the government in one state, elect state officials and legislators in a number of midwestern and western states, and send several of its representatives to the Congress—its impact was to help shape the destinies of a dozen states and the political philosophies of an important segment of the nation's voters."[15]

The first major insurgency in Democratic presidential primaries came in 1952 from a Tennessee senator, who shocked party leaders by advocating integration in the South and opposing the influence of organized crime in Democratic machines in the North. Although he won several primaries and fared well in polls, too many convention votes were still controlled by party leaders for him to receive the nomination.[16] By the 1960s, ultraconservatives were using Republican primaries to spread their ideas and recruit activists, and antiwar liberals were using Democratic Party primaries to allow Democrats to register their dissatisfaction with the Vietnam War. Both groups had a strong impact on their parties.[17] Most recently, an African-American leader, Jesse Jackson, ran solid presidential campaigns in the 1984 and 1988 primaries, establishing his credibility with white Democratic politicians who had previously ignored him.[18]

Perhaps even more dramatically, socialists entered Democratic primaries and demonstrated to mainstream party leaders and government officials that there was more support for left-wing economic programs than was generally realized. In 1934, for example, in the midst of the Great Depression, the most famous socialist of his day, the prolific author Upton Sinclair, switched his party registration from Socialist to Democrat and won the California primary for governor with 51 percent of the vote in a field of seven candidates. He lost the general election with 37 percent of the vote, but the party was liberalized for years thereafter because many young liberal and socialist activists ran for other offices as part of his campaign. The wealthy backers of the state's Democratic and Republican parties therefore worked together to contain liberals until conservative Republicans were able to win general elections in the post–World War II era.[19]

The institutionalization of primaries, in conjunction with the changes in the Democratic Party in the South as a result of the Civil Rights Movement, have created new possibilities for the liberal-labor coalition. These possibilities are discussed in the final chapter.

WHY ARE LOCAL ELECTIONS DIFFERENT?

Perhaps some readers at this point are recalling from their own experience that elections in many cities do not conform to the two-party pattern, but are instead nonpartisan in nature (i.e., without parties). The reasons for this and other differences from the county, state, and national levels are well worth considering. They show that electoral rules, and even the structure of American government itself, are subject to change by outside forces. In this case, the rules were changed as part of electoral battles between local growth coalitions and ordinary citizens in the years between 1870 and 1920. The end result was a defeat for average voters in a majority of cities, which made American politics even more atypical among Western democracies and rendered the Democratic Party even less useful as an organizational base for labor unions and their liberal allies.

When American cities were small and relatively homogeneous, and not everyone could vote, they were easily dominated by the local well-to-do. In the second half of the nineteenth century, as the country urbanized and new immigrants poured into the cities, the situation changed dramatically. Ethnic-based political machines, usually affiliated with the Democratic Party, came to control many city governments. In the early twentieth century, these machine Democrats were sometimes joined by members of the Socialist Party, founded in 1900. In 1912, the high point of socialist electoral success, the party elected 1,200 members in 340 cities across the country, including 79 mayors in 24 different states. There were also 20 socialists in nine different state legislatures, with Wisconsin (7), Kansas (3), and Illinois (3) heading the list.[20]

The local growth coalitions were deeply upset by these defeats. They claimed that ethnic machines were raising taxes, appointing their supporters to government jobs, and giving lucrative government contracts to their friends. Even when the established growth coalitions could reach an accommodation with the machines by joining them as financial supporters, as they very frequently did, they also worked to undercut them through a series of so-called reforms and good-government strategies that gradually took shape over a thirty-year period.[21] Although the reforms were presented as efforts to eliminate corruption, reduce costs, and improve efficiency, they in fact made it more difficult for Democrats and Socialists to win elected positions. These reforms and their effects are as follows:

1. *Off-year elections.* It was argued that local elections should not be held in the same year as national elections because city issues are different. This reform broke the policy connections between local and national levels while at the same time reducing voter turnout for local elections, thereby favoring conservative candidates.

2. *Nonpartisan elections.* It was claimed that parties should not play a role at the local level because the citizens of a community have common interests that should not be overshadowed by partisan politics. This reform makes it necessary for candidates to increase their name recognition because voters can no longer rely on labels like *Democrat* or *Socialist* to identify those candidates with whom they sympathize.

3. *Citywide elections.* It was argued that districts do not have the same usefulness they do at the Congressional level because the problems facing members of a city council involve the city as a whole, not

separate neighborhoods. The net effect of this reform is to make it more difficult for neighborhood leaders, whether Democrats, Socialists, or ethnic and racial minorities, to earn seats on city councils, because they do not have the money and name recognition to win citywide elections.

4. *Elimination of salaries for city council members*. It was argued that serving on a city council should be a civic service done in a volunteer fashion in order to eliminate corruption and self-serving motives for seeking office. The effect of this reform is to make it more difficult for average-income people to serve on city councils because they cannot afford to do so.

5. *Creation of a city-manager form of government*. It was claimed that a city is like a corporation, and the city council like a corporate board of directors, so the city council should set general policy and then turn the management of the city over to a trained professional called a *city manager*. The proposed model charters for city-manager governments made it difficult to replace city managers by requiring the votes of five of the seven council members. The effect of this reform is to increase the power of upper-middle-class professionals, who are natural allies of the growth coalitions through training in special university programs (financed by several large foundations).[22]

Most of these reforms were packaged and publicized by the National Municipal League, a national-level policy-planning organization. Formed in 1894 by 150 developers, lawyers, political scientists, and urban planners from twenty-one different cities, the organization embodied many years of experimenting with reform efforts in various cities. Riding a call for unity between the two major parties in the face of large gains by Socialists in 1908 and 1912, the reformers then capitalized on the fear and patriotism created by World War I. They branded the Socialists as antiwar traitors, disrupted their meetings, and removed their newspapers from the U.S. mail. By 1919, the reformers had been able to implement their model charter in 130 cities and could claim partial successes in many more.[23]

The reform movement continued to make gains in the next several decades. A large-scale survey conducted in 1991 revealed that 75 percent of American cities have nonpartisan elections, making that reform the most successful in the entire array. In addition, 59 percent of cities use citywide ("at-large") elections, compared to only 12 percent that rely exclusively on the old district system ("wards"). The other 29 percent use a combination of citywide and ward representation. Finally, 52 percent of cities adopted either the council-manager or commission form of government recommended by the reformers, abandoning the election of a strong mayor who presided over the city council and had responsibility for city employees. Most of the resistance to council-manager government came from large cities with strong Democratic organizations.[24]

At a point before World War I, thousands of blue-collar and lower white-collar workers were serving on city councils, but by the 1940s there were very few such people being elected. Businesspeople and their lawyers, often legitimated for office by service on well-publicized committees of the local chamber of commerce, are now the overwhelming presence on most city councils. They are also the most frequent appointees to the nonelected boards and commissions that matter the most to the local growth coalitions: planning and zoning commissions, off-street parking authorities, water boards, and other local entities concerned with municipal infrastructure or retail sales.[25]

The net result is that there are very few cities where the growth coalition does not shape city government on economic issues. The findings from studies of local power structures from the 1950s to the 1970s are so strikingly similar that most social scientists lost interest in doing them. The exceptions are in a few university towns, where the composition of the electorate changed due to the adoption of the 26th amendment in 1971, giving the vote to eighteen year olds. Wealthy suburbs and retirement cities for the well-to-do provide other exceptions to the rule.[26]

THE CRITICAL IMPORTANCE OF CAMPAIGN FINANCE

In an electoral system where party differences become blurred for structural and historical reasons, the emphasis on the character and image of each candidate becomes very great, along with a concern about her or his stance on symbolic social issues. In fact, personalities and social issues often become more important than policies related to jobs, health, and other substantive issues, even though careful voting studies suggest that many voters are more concerned about policies that affect their everyday well-being than they are about personalities.[27] This tendency to focus on personality and social issues has been increased somewhat with the rise of the mass media, in particular television, but it is a reality of American politics that has existed far longer than is understood by the many newspaper columnists and television pundits who lament what they call the "recent decline of political parties."

Because the candidate-selection process is relatively individualistic, and therefore dependent upon name recognition and personal image, it can be in good part controlled by members of the power elite through large campaign contributions. Serving as both big donors and fundraisers, the same people who direct corporations and take part in policy groups play a central role in the careers of most politicians who advance beyond the local level in states of any size and consequence. The role of wealthy donors and fundraisers seems to be especially crucial in determining which candidates enter primaries and do well in them, because name recognition and image seem to be even more important at this point than in regular elections.

This does not mean that the candidate with the most money usually wins. Far from it, as seen in case studies of big-spending losers, who are usually new to politics and think that money is everything. Instead, the important point is that it takes a very large minimum, now as much as $500,000 in a campaign for the House of Representatives, to be a viable candidate even with the requisite political experience and skills. It is like a high-stakes poker game: Anyone is welcome as long as they have a million dollars to wager.

Several reforms in campaign finance laws during the 1970s restricted the size of donations by large contributors at the national level, but those reforms did not diminish the influence of the corporate community. If anything, they increased it quite inadvertently. Before the reforms, a handful of owners and executives would give hundreds of thousands of dollars to candidates of interest to them. Since the reforms, they have organized luncheons and dinners to which all of their colleagues and friends give a few thousand dollars for specific candidates and party finance committees. The 2000 Bush campaign, for example, organized a group of corporate leaders, the Pioneers, who pledged to raise $100,000 each by contacting 100 friends to give $1,000 apiece.[28] Corporate leaders also form Political Action Committees (PACs) so their stockholders and executives can give another $5,000 each year. In addition, trade associations and professional societies organize PACs, as do trade unions. PACs, in turn, can contribute to individual candidates and other PACs.

The restrictions on the size of individual donations, and on any donations whatsoever by corporations, were in effect lifted in 1979. The Federal Election Commission ruled that unrestricted donations to state parties for party-building were permissible as long as the money was not used to support a particular candidate. In practice, this distinction boils down to the fact that the party's candidate cannot be named even though his or her opponent can be named (and pilloried). This "soft money," as it came to be called, climbed to $46 million for both parties combined in 1992, then jumped to $150 million in 1996, and to over $250 million in 2000. Still, the "hard money" of regular donations has remained much larger and was over $400 million in 2000.[29]

Whether the donations are hard money or soft money, less than half of 1 percent of adults give $1,000 or more. Business groups contribute twelve to fourteen times as much as organized labor, and they

Table 6.1 Donations to Democrats and Republicans by Business, Labor, and Ideological Groups in the 2000 Elections (in millions of dollars)

	Republicans	Democrats
Business	$466.0	$340.3
Labor Unions	$3.8	$52.4
Ideological	$18.4	$17.5
Totals	$488.2	$410.2

Source: Adapted from "Business, Labor, and Ideological Donors" (Center for Responsive Politics, www.opensecrets.org, 30 December 2000).

are the major donors to both Republicans and Democrats. Fifty-nine percent of the business-related donations go to the Republicans, which is 96 percent of the money they collect, and the 40 percent that goes to the Democrats is six times as much as labor gives to the Democrats. Table 6.1 shows the breakdown of donations to Republicans and Democrats in 2000 by corporate and labor groups. Ideological groups, such as pro-choice and anti-handgun groups on the liberal side and pro-life and pro-gun groups on the ultraconservative side, are also listed in that table. They gave over $17 million to each party in 2000.

Although sectors of the corporate community are the largest donors to candidates in both parties, detailed analyses of PAC giving patterns at the congressional level provide strong evidence that the differences between the corporate-conservative and liberal-labor coalitions manifest themselves in the electoral process. They show that corporate and conservative PACs usually support one set of candidates, liberal and labor PACs a different set, and that corporate PACs almost never oppose each other. They may not all give to the same candidate, but they seldom give to two different candidates in the same race.[30] These conclusions, based on statistical techniques, have been bolstered by interviews with PAC executives, which reveal there is indeed a large amount of coordination among corporate PACs. Furthermore, these studies report that when corporate PACs support a Democrat it is usually (1) because the Democrat is a moderate or conservative, and most often from the South or a rural area; (2) to maintain access to a Democrat who sits on a Congressional committee important to the corporation; or (3) as a favor to another corporation that wants to maintain access to the Democrat.[31]

Most corporate leaders in most business sectors favor Republicans, but there are some variations from sector to sector.[32] In 2000, 60 percent of the donations from those in movies and music went to Democrats, whereas 82 percent of automotive and 79 percent of oil and gas donations went to Republicans.[33] There are also religious differences between the wealthy donors to the two parties. Large Republican contributions come overwhelmingly from Christians. Motivated by continuing concerns about anti-Semitism, as well as the Jewish emphasis on sharing with the community, wealthy owners and managers from Jewish backgrounds are more strongly Democratic than Republican, and according to some estimates, may provide the Democrats with as much as half of their individual contributions.[34]

The large amount of money spent on campaigns is a source of great concern to liberal reformers, who try to use the issue to win more voters to their causes. As part of their reform package, some of them call for the abolition of PACs, but that makes their allies in organized labor very uneasy. Although labor is greatly outspent by business in most elections, the union leaders believe that the little influence they have would be dissipated if they were not allowed to accumulate a war chest and then make donations to a few favored candidates. Similarly, several successful campaigns by women have been at least in part due to the collection of funds by feminist PACs, so women activists are also wary of new restrictions on how money is raised.

Given the problems of creating effective campaign finance reforms that are constitutional, acceptable to all elements of the liberal-labor coalition, and acceptable to a congressional majority, it seems likely that large donations will remain an essential part of the electoral system. Thus, campaign donations from members of the corporate community and upper class will continue to be a central element in determining who enters politics with any hope of winning a nomination at the federal level. In particular, it is the need for a large amount of start-up money—to travel around a district or the country, to send out large mailings, to schedule radio and television time in advance—that gives representatives of the power elite a very direct role in the process right from the start, and thereby provides them with personal access to politicians of both parties. Even though they do not try to tie specific strings to their gifts, which would be futile and counterproductive in any event, they are able to ensure a hearing for their views and to work against candidates they do not consider sensible and approachable.[35]

It is important to stress once again, however, that this critical role for campaign finance is made possible by the electoral rules creating the two-party system, combined with the unusual economic history of the southern United States, first as a slaveocracy and then as a segregationist, low-wage society in which few African-Americans could vote until 1965. The net effect is that the Democrat Party, due to its history and warring factions, still cannot project a clear economic image of what it represents. If the Democrats were to develop a distinct programmatic identity in the future, which might make party loyalty more important than personality in voting decisions, then campaign finance would become less important than it has been.

OTHER FINANCIAL SUPPORT FOR CANDIDATES

As important as large campaign donations are in the electoral process, there are numerous other methods by which members of the corporate community can give financial support to the politicians they favor. One of the most direct is to give them corporate stock or to purchase property from them at a price well above the market value. In 1966, for example, just this kind of favor was done for a future president, Ronald Reagan, shortly after he became governor of California. Twentieth Century-Fox purchased several hundred acres of his land adjacent to its large outdoor set in Malibu for nearly $2 million, triple its assessed market value and 30 times what he had paid for it in 1952. The land was never utilized and was later sold to the state. It was this transaction that gave Reagan the financial security that made it possible for him to devote himself full time to his political career.[36]

A very direct way of supporting the many politicians who are lawyers has been to hire them or their law firms as legal consultants or to provide them with routine legal business. Corporations can be especially helpful to lawyer-politicians when they are between offices. For example, the chairman of Pepsico retained former vice president and future president Richard M. Nixon as the company's lawyer in 1963, while Nixon was out of office. He thereafter paid for every trip Nixon made overseas in the next two years. This made it possible for Nixon to remain in the political limelight as a foreign-policy expert while he quietly began his campaign to become president in 1968.[37]

Members of the power elite also can benefit politicians personally by hiring them to give speeches at corporate and trade association events. The Republican presidential candidate in 1996, former Senator Robert Dole of Kansas, earned $800,000 speaking to business groups while he was a senator, a road to wealth now barred for Senate members.[38] But corporations and organizations in the policy-planning network still can support candidates and potential candidates by this method, paying them $30,000 and over per speech. They also hire them as consultants or make them permanent fellows or honorary advisers. One Republican politician of the 1980s and 1990s, Jack Kemp, the party's vice-presidential candidate in 1996, was paid $136,000 a year as an adviser by the Heritage Foundation, while also earning

$1 million between 1992 and 1995 lecturing to business groups and receiving $100,000 a year as a director of six corporations.[39]

Politicians also know from past experience that they can be richly rewarded after their careers in office if they are seen as reasonable and supportive. For example, in early 2000, 144 former senators and House members, evenly split between Democrats and Republicans, were working as registered lobbyists, mostly for corporations and trade associations, usually at salaries many times what they had made while they were in government.[40] Others have become corporate executives or joined corporate advisory boards. Thus, a Democrat from California, the chair of the House committee on public works and transportation, resigned in 1995 to become a vice president at Lockheed Martin. Former House speaker Newt Gingrich, a Republican, joined the advisory board of Forstmann Little and Company, an investment banking firm run by one of the party's largest contributors, when he resigned from Congress in November 1999.[41]

THE RESULTS OF THE CANDIDATE-SELECTION PROCESS

What kinds of elected officials emerge from a candidate-selection process that demands great emphasis on campaign finance and media recognition? The answer is available from numerous studies. First, politicians are from the top 10 to 15 percent of the occupational and income ladders, especially those who hold the highest elective offices. Only a minority are from the upper class or corporate community, but in a majority of cases they share in common a business or legal background with members of the upper class.[42] Nonetheless, politicians feel a need to stress the humble nature of their social backgrounds whenever it is possible.

As shown by a study comparing the rhetoric and reality of the early lives of American presidents, most of the presidents were wealthy or connected to wealth by the time they became president. George Washington was one of the richest men of his day, partly through inheritance, partly through marriage. Andrew Jackson, allegedly of humble circumstances, was raised in a well-to-do, slave-holding family because his father died before he was born, and he became even more wealthy as an adult. He "dealt in slaves, made hundreds of thousands of dollars and accumulated hundreds of thousands of valuable acres in land speculation, owned racehorses and racetracks, bought cotton gins, distilleries, and plantations, was a successful merchant, and married extremely well."[43] Abraham Lincoln became a corporate lawyer for railroads and married into a wealthy Kentucky family.

Few twentieth-century presidents have been from outside the very wealthiest circles. Theodore Roosevelt, William H. Taft, Franklin D. Roosevelt, John F. Kennedy, George H. W. Bush, and George W. Bush are from upper-class backgrounds. Herbert Hoover, Jimmy Carter, and Ronald Reagan were millionaires before they became deeply involved in national politics. Lyndon B. Johnson was a millionaire several times over through his wife's land dealings and his use of political leverage to gain a lucrative television license in Austin, Texas. Even Richard M. Nixon, whose father ran a small store, was a rich man when he finally attained the presidency in 1968, after earning high salaries as a corporate lawyer between 1963 and 1968 due to his ability to open political doors for corporate clients.

Bill Clinton, elected president in 1992 and 1996, tries to give the impression he is from an impoverished background, claiming he is just a poor boy from little Hope, Arkansas, born of a widowed mother. But Clinton was gone from Hope, where he lived in comfortable circumstances with his grandparents, who owned a small store, by the age of six. At that time, his mother married Roger Clinton, whose family owned a car dealership in the nearby tourist town of Hot Springs. He grew up playing golf at the local country club and drove a Buick convertible. His mother sent him money throughout his years in college. Clinton is not wealthy or from the upper class, but he has a very solid middle-class upbringing and education that he artfully obscures.

The second general finding about elected officials is that a great many of them are lawyers. In the past, between 50 and 60 percent of Congressional members were lawyers, and 27 of the American presidents had law degrees.[44] The large percentage of lawyers in the American political system is highly atypical when compared with other countries, where only 10 to 30 percent of legislators have a legal background. Insight into this high representation of lawyers among American officials is provided by comparing the United States with a deviant case at the other extreme, Denmark, where only 2 percent of legislators are lawyers. The class-based nature of Danish politics since the late nineteenth century, and the fact that political careers are not pathways to judicial appointments, are thought to discourage lawyer participation in politics in that country. In contrast, the marginalization of class issues by the two main American political parties, combined with the intimate involvement of the parties in the judicial system, creates a climate for strong lawyer involvement in the U.S. political system.[45]

Whatever the reason for their involvement, lawyers are the occupational group that by training and career needs are ideal go-betweens and compromisers. They have the skills to balance the relationship between the corporate community that finances them on the one hand

and the citizens who vote for them on the other. They are the supreme pragmatists in a nation that prides itself on a pragmatic and can-do ideology. They have an ability to be dispassionate about the issues, and they are generally respectful of the process by which things are done.

Taken together, business executives, bankers, realtors, and lawyers account for 79 percent of Congress. A study of the occupational backgrounds of members of the Congress for 2001 shows that the number of business executives, bankers, and realtors in the House has risen to 183, surpassing the number of lawyers, who fell to 155. Fifty-eight of the businesspeople are Democrats, 125 are Republicans; 84 lawyers are Democrats, 71 are Republicans. In the Senate, there are 28 members in the business/banker/realtor category and 53 lawyers. Ten of the 28 businesspeople are Democrats and 18 are Republicans; the lawyers are evenly balanced between the two parties. There is one former union official in the House, none in the Senate.[46]

Whether elected officials are from business or law, the third general result of the candidate-selection process is a large number of very ambitious people who are eager to "go along to get along." To understand the behavior of a politician, concludes one political scientist who studies political careers in detail, "it is more important to know what he wants to be than how he got to where he is now."[47] This great ambition, whether it be for wealth or higher office, makes politicians especially available to those people who can help them realize their goals. Such people are often members of the corporate community or upper class, who have money to contribute and connections to other districts, states, or regions where striving candidates need new friends. Thus, even the most liberal or ultraconservative of politicians may develop a new circle of moderate supporters as they move from the local to the congressional to the presidential level, gradually becoming more and more involved with leading figures within the power elite.

The fourth generalization about most successful political candidates is that they are either conservative or silent on the highly emotional social issues. Basically, very few candidates can win if their views fall outside the limits that have been set by the actions and television advertising of the ultraconservatives. As long as 75 percent of the people say they believe in the death penalty, for example, and a significant minority of fervent single-issue voters oppose strict gun-control laws, it is unlikely that anyone who openly challenges these beliefs can be elected to any office except in a few liberal districts and cities. Here, then, is an instance in which public opinion has a direct effect on the behavior of candidates and elected officials, even though it is also true that most voters make their voting decisions based on their party identification and degree of satisfaction with the state of the economy.[48]

The fifth general finding, alluded to earlier in the chapter, is that the majority of elected officials at the national level are pro-business conservatives. For most of the twentieth century, this conservative majority consisted of Northern Republicans and Southern Democrats. In the 1980s and early 1990s, Republicans replaced Southern Democrats in both the House and the Senate, which contributed heavily to the Republican takeover of Congress in 1994. As late as 1996, however, with conservative white Southern Democrats accounting for less than thirty votes in the House, the conservative voting coalition still formed on 11.7 percent of the congressional votes and was successful 98.9 percent of the time. The Southern Democratic votes were essential to thirty-three of fifty-one victories in the House and nineteen of thirty-seven victories in the Senate, offsetting defections by the handful of moderate Republicans from the Northeast who are still in office despite ultraconservative challenges in primaries and a drift to the Democrats by Northeastern voters.[49]

Even in the Congress elected in 2000, closely divided between Republicans and Democrats, there is a majority of conservatives because there are thirteen "New Democrats" in the Senate and sixty-four in the House who are conservatives on the issues of concern to the power elite. They differ from Republicans primarily on social issues. They are also somewhat more sympathetic to the liberal-labor coalition on issues relating to health and social security.[50]

THE LIBERAL-LABOR
COALITION IN ELECTORAL POLITICS

The liberal-labor coalition has very little independent influence at the presidential level. Fearing the antiunion and antiliberal stance of the Republican Party, it ends up trying desperately to turn out voters for the centrist or moderate conservative who wins the Democratic presidential nomination. However, despite the importance of campaign contributions and corporate-conservative involvement at the Congressional level, the liberal-labor coalition is nonetheless able to elect some sympathizers and supporters to both the House and the Senate. Using 75 percent favorable ratings over a four-year period by the liberal Americans for Democratic Action as an indicator of liberalism, a study done for this book shows that about 30 percent of Senators and 35 percent of House members are liberals. While a liberal group of this size is not large enough to win on its own, it can pose a potential threat to the power elite.

Moreover, politicians who are supported by and feel sympathetic toward the power elite may vote with the liberals and labor under some conditions, which means that a majority of elected officials could disagree with the power elite on specific issues. Such alliances do occur, although they usually do not involve issues relevant to the corporate community. For example, a liberal-led arms-control coalition defeated the Reagan Administration's proposal in 1984 to build an additional 100 MX missiles. The coalition included members of the defense community, such as former secretaries of defense, directors of the CIA, and retired army generals who once held leadership roles in nuclear defense. These defense leaders were essential in reassuring lawmakers that the MX missiles were not necessary. Then, too, the liberal lobby initiated the battle to extend the lifetime of the Voting Rights Act in 1982, but there was no lobbying opposition, and moderate Republicans agreed that legislative oversight in Southern states was needed in the face of evidence of continuing discrimination there.[51]

The liberal-labor coalition also was successful in blocking the nomination of Robert J. Bork to the Supreme Court in 1987. The AFL-CIO, civil rights groups, and women's groups formed a large and vigorous coalition to claim that Bork was an ideological extremist, as evidenced by assertions in his many speeches, articles, and court briefs. He argued, for example, that courts had no right to rule on civil rights and abortions. Ultraconservative groups were unable to counter this liberal-labor pressure, and Bork was rejected in the Senate by a 58–42 vote. But the corporate community was silent on the issue, as it often is on court appointments. Moreover, even some moderate civic groups opposed Bork. The centrist Federation of Business and Professional Women's Clubs was open in its opposition. Most important of all, Bork also was opposed by some of the most distinguished conservative law professors in the country as well as by a great many centrist law professors. Simply put, the liberal-labor coalition could not have won in the Senate without the support of centrists, moderate Republicans, and conservative law professors.[52]

Still, the liberal-labor coalition has won some victories in the face of opposition from many sectors of the corporate community. These victories show, as emphasized at the end of Chapters 2 and 4, that there is too much uncertainty and volatility in the workings of government for the power elite to leave anything to chance. The power elite therefore have a need to influence government directly in order to augment their structural economic power and their large reservoir of respectable policy options. The explanations for the handful of liberal-labor successes on some issues of concern to the corporate community, which at first glance may seem to contradict much of what has been said in this and the preceding chapter, is presented as part of the next chapter.

7

How the Power Elite Dominate Government

The power elite build on their structural economic power, their storehouse of policy expertise, and their success in the electoral arena to dominate the federal government on the issues about which they care. Lobbyists from corporations, law firms, and trade associations play a key role in shaping government on narrow issues of concern to specific corporations or business sectors, and the policy-planning network supplies new policy directions on major issues, along with top-level governmental appointees to implement those policies.

However, victories within government are far from automatic. As is the case in the competition for public opinion and electoral success, the power elite face opposition from a minority of elected officials and their supporters in labor unions and liberal advocacy groups. These liberal opponents are sometimes successful in blocking the initiatives of ultraconservatives or the New Christian Right, but the corporate-conservative coalition itself seldom loses when it is united. In fact, most of the victories for the liberal-labor coalition come because of support from moderate conservatives, usually in situations of extreme social disruption, such as economic depressions or wars.

There is only one major issue that does not fit these generalizations, the National Labor Relations Act of 1935. This legislation gave employees, with the exception of agricultural, seasonal, and domestic workers, the right to join unions and enter into collective bargaining with their employers. It was vigorously opposed by virtually every major corporation in the country, but the liberal-labor coalition nonetheless prevailed in the context of strong labor militancy. This defeat for the corporate community is due in large part to an unusual defection from the conservative voting bloc that is explained at the end of the chapter.

THE ROLE OF GOVERNMENTS

Governments are potentially autonomous because they have a unique function: territorial regulation. They set up and guard boundaries and then regulate the flow of people, money, and goods in and out of the area for which they have responsibility. They also have regulatory functions within a territory, such as settling disputes through the judicial system and setting the rules that shape the economic marketplace.[1]

Neither business, the military, nor churches are organized in such a way that they could provide these necessary functions. The military sometimes steps in—or forces its way in—when a government is weak or collapsing, but it has a difficult time carrying out routine regulatory functions for very long. Nor can competing businesses regulate themselves. There is always some business that will try to improve its market share or profits by adulterating products, reducing wages, colluding with other companies, or telling half-truths. As most economists and all other social scientists agree, a business system could not survive without some degree of market regulation. Contrary to claims about markets being free, they are historically constructed institutions dependent upon governmentally sanctioned enforcement of property and contract rights.[2] Table 7.1 presents a list of illegal corporate actions that were stopped or penalized by the federal government in the first ten months of 2000.

Sometimes the federal government has to act to protect markets from being completely destroyed by the anticompetitive practices of a company that thereby grows very large. That is what happened in 1911, when the Supreme Court ordered the break-up of the Rockefellers' huge Standard Oil of New Jersey because of the illegal strategies used by John D. Rockefeller, Sr., to destroy rivals. It is also what happened in the case of Microsoft, when Netscape sent the Department of Justice a 222-page paper in 1996, which was later backed up by testimony from representatives of Sun Microsystems, AOL, and others. What seemed at first to be innovation turned out to be manipulation and intimidation in the tradition of Rockefeller, Sr.[3]

Governments are also essential in creating money, setting interest rates, and shaping the credit system. Although the United States tried to function without a central bank for much of the nineteenth century, the problems caused by a privately controlled money system were so great that the most powerful bankers of the day worked together to create the Federal Reserve System in 1912.[4] The system was

Table 7.1 Selected Reports from the *New York Times*, Jan.–Oct., 2000, Concerning Illegal Actions by Corporations

---

Koch Industries, one of the nation's largest oil and gas pipeline operators, was fined $30 million for contaminating water in six states. January 14, p. A21.

Chevron, a large oil company, agreed to pay $95 million to resolve claims that it underpaid royalties for eleven years for oil production on federal and Indian lands. January 14, p. C2.

Nine West Group, which makes women's shoes, agreed to pay $34 million to settle charges that it had illegally fixed shoe prices since 1988. March 7, p. C1.

The **five largest music companies** settled an antitrust case for using illegal marketing agreements to overcharge customers by an estimated $500 million for CDs. June 11, p, A1.

AOL paid a fine of $3.5 million on charges brought by the Securities and Exchange Commission that it had improperly inflated profit reports by hundreds of millions of dollars. May 16, p. C6.

Columbia/HCA Healthcare, the nation's largest healthcare company, agree to pay $745 million to resolve an inquiry into whether it had defrauded federal health programs. June 19, p. C1.

WorldCom agreed to pay a $3.5 million fine for switching customers telephone carriers without permission. June 7, p. C10.

Lockheed Martin was fined a record $13 million for illegally giving China information on satellites. June 14, p. A1.

Three former executives of **CUC International** pleaded guilty to charges of accounting fraud that cost investors $19 billion. June 15, p. C1.

Provident Financial, the seventh largest issuer of credit cards, agreed to reimburse customers at least $300 million for misleading and improperly billing them. June 29, p. C1.

BP Amoco agreed to pay several million in fines and spend $500 million for pollution control technologies due to environmental violations in nine states. July 26, p. A19.

Mylan Laboratories agreed to pay $147 million to settle a charge that it improperly cornered the market on two widely used drugs and raised prices by as much as 3,000 percent. July 13, p. A1.

Publishers Clearing House, which mails out notices that look like gift checks for large amounts, agreed to pay $18 million to settle accusations of deceptive advertising. August 23, p. A14.

American Home Products agreed to pay the government $30 million for repeated violations of manufacturing regulations at two of its drug factories. October 4, p. C18.

---

improved during the 1930s and is now an essential tool of the corporate community in keeping a highly volatile business system from careening off in one direction or another. When the stock market crashed in 1987, for example, the Federal Reserve made sure there would be no repeat of the Great Depression by instructing large New York banks to keep making loans to temporarily insolvent debtors. Similar bailouts were performed in the 1990s for problems in Mexico, Korea, and a Wall Street investment firm, Long Term Capital Management, that could have caused large-scale bankruptcies.[5]

The federal government also is essential in providing subsidy payments to groups in trouble, such as farmers and low-income workers, in ways that bolster the market system and benefit large corporations. Farmers received a record $28 billion in direct payments in 2000, which is half of all farm income. This program allows large corporations to buy commodities at low prices, while at the same time providing purchasing power in rural communities throughout the South, Midwest, and Great Plains.[6] Low-income employees who work full time and have children received $30 billion in 2000 through a program called *Earned Income Tax Credits*. Both corporate leaders and Republicans prefer these year-end government bonus payments to the old system of welfare payments because they increase the labor pool and reinforce the work ethic.[7]

Nor is the state any less important in the context of a globalizing economy. If anything, it is even more important because it has to enforce rules concerning patents, intellectual property, quality of merchandise, and much else in an unregulated international arena. The international economy simply could not function without the agreements on monetary policy and trade that the governments of the United States, Japan, Canada, and Western Europe uphold through the International Monetary Fund, World Trade Organization, and other international agencies. For the American corporate community, domination of the state on economic issues also remains essential because the laws favoring American corporations that move production overseas could be easily changed. Tax breaks to offset taxes paid overseas could be eliminated, for example, or laws could be passed stipulating that goods could not enter the United States from countries that ban unions and use government force to suppress wages.

APPOINTEES TO GOVERNMENT

The first way to see how the power elite shapes the federal government is to look at the social and occupational backgrounds of the people who are appointed to manage the major departments of the executive branch, such as state, treasury, defense, and justice. If the power elite is as important as this book claims, they should come disproportionately from the upper class, the corporate community, and the policy-planning network.

There have been numerous studies of major governmental appointees under both Republican and Democratic administrations, usually focusing on the top appointees in the departments that are represented in the president's cabinet. These studies are unanimous in their conclusion that most top appointees in both Republican and Democratic administrations are corporate executives and corporate lawyers, and hence members of the power elite. Moreover, they are often part of the policy-planning network as well, supporting the claim in Chapter 4 that the network plays a central role in preparing members of the power elite for government service.[8]

Two major historical studies of cabinet appointees provide relevant background information on major government appointees from the founding of the country through the Carter Administration. A comparison of the top appointees in the Clinton and George W. Bush administrations brings the information forward to 2000. The most ambitious of these studies—a three-volume work that covers cabinet officers, diplomats, and Supreme Court justices from 1978 to 1980—defines the economic elite as those who were among the top wealth holders or sat on the boards of the largest companies of their era. It shows that (1) 96 percent of the cabinet and diplomatic appointees from 1780 to 1861 were members of the economic elite, with a predominance of landowners, merchants, and lawyers; (2) from 1862 to 1933, the figure was 84 percent, with an increasing number of financiers and corporate lawyers; and (3) from 1934 to 1980, the overall percentage was 64, but with only 47 percent during the New Deal.[9] The second large-scale study, which focuses on the 205 individuals who served in presidential cabinets between 1897 and 1972, reports that 60 percent were members of the upper class and 78 percent members of the corporate community. There are no differences in the overall percentages for Democrats and Republicans or for the years before and after 1933.[10]

The most systematic study of the factors leading to appointments shows that corporate executives who have two or more outside directorships are four times more likely to serve in a federal government advisory position than executives from smaller companies. In addition, participation of corporate directors in at least one policy group increases their chances of an appointment by a factor of 1.7. An accompanying interview study supported the quantitative findings by showing that chief executive officers often mention participation in a policy group as a qualification for an appointment to government.[11]

Reflecting the different coalitions that make up the two parties, there are some differences between the second-level and third-level appointees in Republican and Democratic administrations. Republicans frequently appoint ultraconservatives to agencies that are thoroughly disliked by the appointee, such as the Environmental Protection Agency, the Occupational Safety and Health Administration, The National Highway Traffic Safety Administration, and the Office of Civil Rights. Democrats, on the other hand, often place liberals in the same agencies, creating a dramatic contrast when a Democratic administration replaces a Republican one. The Clinton Administration's appointments to the Office of the Attorney General, for example, were far more vigorous in using the antitrust laws to challenge monopolistic corporate practices than those of the Reagan and Bush administrations.[12] As an even more dramatic example, the Food and Drug Administration took on the tobacco companies during the Clinton years and won, to the amazement of everyone.[13]

The way in which presidents rely on corporate leaders and experts from the policy groups in making appointments can be seen in both the Clinton and Bush administrations. President Clinton's first secretary of state was a director of Lockheed Martin, Southern California Edison, and First Interstate Bancorp, a trustee of the Carnegie Corporation, a recent vice-chair of the Council on Foreign Relations, and officially a corporate lawyer. The second secretary of state, the daughter of a Czechoslovakian diplomat who immigrated to the United States and became a dean at the University of Denver, married into great wealth, earned a Ph.D. in international relations, raised money for the Democratic Party, and became active in several foreign policy groups. The first secretary of defense, a former professor and longtime member of Congress, came from a business family in Wisconsin. The first secretary of treasury inherited millions from his rancher father and founded his own insurance company in Texas. He was succeeded by a codirector of the Wall Street investment banking firm of Goldman, Sachs who was also a trustee of the Carnegie Corporation and had a net worth between $50 and $100 million in 1992. The first director of the CIA was a corporate lawyer and a director of Martin Marietta, a large defense contractor; the second CIA director, a professor and administrator at MIT, was a director of Citicorp, Perkins-Elmer, and CMS Energy.

The secretary of agriculture was an African-American from the Mississippi Delta whose grandfather and father were major landowners and business owners. The secretary of commerce, also an African-American, came from a family that owned a hotel in Harlem; at the time of his appointment he was a lawyer with one of the leading corporate firms in Washington, which paid him $580,000 in 1992 even though he spent most of his time as chairman of the Democratic Party. The secretary of energy was both African-American and female; she is also the former executive vice president of Northern States Power, a utility company in Minnesota, and the daughter of two physicians. The secretary of housing and urban development, a Mexican-American who had been mayor of San Antonio, was the chair of an investment firm, the head of an air charter company, and a trustee of the Rockefeller Foundation at the time of his appointment. The least-connected major figure who was in the Clinton cabinet, the attorney general, is the daughter of journalists in Florida and was once a state attorney in Miami.

The administration drew many of its key members from a small group of current or recent directors on the board of the Council on Foreign Relations. In addition to the secretary of state, who was a Council director from 1982 to 1991, three other Council directors held top positions in the State Department at one point or another. The secretary of health and human services was a Council director at the time of her appointment, as well as the chancellor of the University of Wisconsin, a trustee of the Committee for Economic Development, and a trustee of the Brookings Institution. Other Council directors who served in the Clinton Administration at one point or another were the White House special counsel, the director of the Office of Management and Budget, and the head of the Federal Reserve Board.

The top levels of the Bush Administration are as directly connected to the corporate community as any set of high government officials could be, but President Bush's cabinet also contains a significant number of ultraconservatives with strong views on a wide range of social issues. President Bush and his father are both graduates of Andover and Yale, and the younger Bush is also a graduate of Harvard Business School. Both owned oil companies before they went into politics, and the new president is a former owner of the Texas Rangers baseball team as well, thanks to the generosity of some of Bush, Sr.'s, main campaign donors.[14] Vice President Richard Cheney spent the eight years prior to his appointment as president of Halliburton, an oil drilling company, where he made several million dollars a year and exercised over $20 million in stock options when he left. He was also on the board of directors of Electronic Data Systems, Procter & Gamble, and Union Pacific. He served as a director of the Council on Foreign Relations from 1987 to 1989, and was vice-chair of the board of the American Enterprise Institute when he became vice president.

The president's chief of staff, Andrew Card, came to his position after seven years as the chief lobbyist for General Motors, where his title was vice president for governmental affairs. The national security advisor, Condoleezza Rice, an African-American woman from the middle class in Birmingham, with a Ph.D. in international relations from the University of Denver, was the provost of Stanford University and a director of Chevron and Transamerica. The head of the Office of Management and Budget, Mitchell E. Daniels, Jr., was a senior executive at Eli Lilly & Co., the former president of a conservative think tank, and a former aide in the Reagan White House.

The secretary of state, retired army general Colin Powell, the chair of the Joint Chiefs of Staff during the Persian Gulf War, and an African-American, made millions after his retirement as a speaker to corporate employees at $60,000 to $75,000 an appearance. He served as a director of Gulfstream Aerospace until its merger with General Dynamics in 1999, where he earned $1.49 million from stock options in exchange for helping the company sell its corporate jets in Kuwait and Saudi Arabia.[15] He was a director of America Online at the time of his appointment to the state department, walking away with $8.27 million in stock options, and his overall worth since retiring from the army came to over $28 million in 2001. Powell is also a member of the Council on Foreign Relations.

The secretary of defense, Donald Rumsfeld, who held numerous positions in the Nixon and Ford administrations, including secretary of defense for eighteen months between 1975 and 1977, spent eight years as the chief executive officer of G.D. Searle & Co., and three years in the same position for General Instruments. He sat on 4 corporate boards in 1998: Kellogg, Sears Roebuck, The Tribune Publishing Co., and Gulfstream Aerospace (where, like his fellow director, General Powell, he made over $1 million from stock options for his help in selling corporate jets). He was a trustee of 2 think tanks, the American Enterprise Institute and the Rand Corporation. In 1998, he headed a bipartisan congressional commission to assess the ballistic missile threat from North Korea and Iran, which concluded that the United States was in great danger.

The secretary of treasury, Paul H. O'Neill, was the recently retired chair of Alcoa and a director of Lucent Technologies. He holds over $50 million in Alcoa stock. He was a member of the Business Council and the Business Roundtable, the chair of the board of trustees at the Rand Corporation, where he rubbed elbows with Rumsfeld, and a trustee of the American Enterprise Institute, where he served with Rumsfeld and Cheney. The secretary of commerce, Donald L. Evans, a longtime friend of President Bush and his chief fundraiser for the 2000 campaign, bringing in $100 million, is the son of a Shell Oil manager and the chief executive officer of Tom Brown, Inc., a mid-sized oil company in Midland, Texas.

The secretary of transportation, Norman Mineta, an Asian-American and former Democratic congressman, inherited his father's insurance agency in San Jose, where he was elected to the city council and the office of mayor before going to Congress in 1975. He resigned from Congress and then worked as a vice president at Lockheed Martin from 1995 until July 2000, when President Clinton appointed him secretary of commerce. The secretary of labor, Elaine Chao, a Chinese-American, is a daughter of wealthy immigrants from Taiwan. She graduated from Mount Holyoke and the Harvard Business School, worked in management for the Bank of America and Citicorp, and served as deputy secretary of transportation and then head of the Peace Corps in the George H. W. Bush Administration. She has served on the boards of Clorox, Dole Foods, and Northwest Airlines and is affiliated with the Heritage Foundation.

The secretary of agriculture, Ann Veneman, is the daughter of a well-to-do California farmer who worked as the undersecretary of health, education, and welfare in the Nixon Administration. She is a lawyer and served as a deputy to the undersecretary of agriculture in the Reagan Administration. After her service in the Reagan Administration, she joined a corporate law lobbying firm in Washington for two years before going to Sacramento to practice corporate law. The director of the Environmental Protection Agency, Christine Todd Whitman, the governor of New Jersey at the time of her appointment, is from a very wealthy family. She is a member of the Council on Foreign Relations.

The secretary of education, Rod Paige, an African-American born and raised in Mississippi, has a doctorate in physical education from the University of Indiana, and was the dean of the School of Education at Texas Southern University before becoming the superintendent of schools in Houston, where his firm approach caught the eye of George W. Bush while he was governor of Texas. The secretary of housing and urban development, Melquiades Martinez, was the highest elected official in the Florida county that encompasses the city of Orlando. He is the first Cuban-American to be appointed to the cabinet. He has a net worth of $3 million from his personal-injury law practice.

The secretary of veterans affairs, Anthony J. Principi, a decorated Vietnam War veteran with an undergraduate degree from the U.S. Naval Academy and a law degree from Seton Hall, is a longtime advocate for veterans, He was deputy secretary of veterans affairs from 1989 to 1992 and acting secretary of veterans affairs in 1992 and 1993. After leaving government, he joined a corporate law firm in San Diego for two years, then moved into the corporate world as a vice president at a subsidiary of Lockheed Martin and the head of a telecommunications company. He was president of QTC Medical Services, Inc., in San Diego at the time of his appointment.

The remainder of the Bush cabinet is from the ultraconservative wing of the party. The attorney general, John Ashcroft, the son and grandson of ministers, is a former governor and senator from Missouri, but he did spend 6 years in private law practice before going into politics. He is a strong opponent of abortion, except when a woman's own life is endangered, and is very close to leaders in the New Christian Right. The secretary of health and human services, Tommy G. Thompson, the longtime governor of Wisconsin at the time of his appointment, also is strongly opposed to abortion and has been a leader in cutting back on welfare. He has close ties with tobacco and brewing companies, which made his appointment to the department that looks after health of great concern to liberals.

The secretary of energy, Spencer Abraham, strongly in the ultra-conservative camp on all issues, is the grandson of a Christian Lebanese immigrant and the first Arab-American to serve in the cabinet. Ironically, during his term as the Republican senator from Michigan, he advocated the abolishment of the department he now heads. The secretary of the interior, Gale Norton, served as the attorney general of Colorado from 1992 to 1998 when she joined a corporate law firm in Denver and became a registered lobbyist for NL Industries, a major manufacturer of lead-based paint. She spent much of her earlier career fighting court battles against environmental regulations in the West. Her husband is a commercial real estate developer.

As these thumbnail sketches show, the ethnic, racial, and gender diversity of Bush's appointments is at least as wide as Clinton's, but the political orientations are even more corporate and conservative, and dramatically so on social issues. The nature of the Bush Cabinet suggests that the diversity fought for by liberal women, minorities, and gays and lesbians since the 1960s does not necessarily transfer into a liberal social outlook. It may even be that the power elite has been strengthened by calls for diversity that did not include an emphasis on the liberal social philosophy that energized the activists. Leaders in the power elite have been able to defuse criticism based on gender, ethnicity, and race while at the same time appointing people with the class backgrounds and values that are important in reinforcing the structure and distribution of power.[16]

The general picture that emerges from this information on the overrepresentation of members of the corporate community and policy network in appointed governmental positions is that the highest levels of the executive branch, especially in the State, Defense, and Treasury departments, are interlocked constantly with the corporate community through the movement of executives and corporate lawyers in and out of government. Although the same person is not in governmental and corporate positions at the same time, there is enough continuity for the relationship to be described as one of revolving interlocks. Corporate leaders resign from their numerous directorships to serve in government for two or three years, then return to the corporate community.

This practice gives corporate officials temporary independence from the narrow concerns of their own companies and allows them to perform the more general roles they have learned in the policy-discussion groups. However, it does not give them the time or inclination to become fully independent from the corporate community or to develop a perspective that includes the interests of other classes and groups. In terms of the *Who governs?* indicator of power, then, it is clear that the power elite are the predominant voice in top-level appointive positions in the executive branch.

SUPREME COURT APPOINTMENTS

The Supreme Court has a special and unique role in the American system of governance. As the final arbiter in major disputes, it has been imbued with a mystique of reverence and respect that makes it the backstop for the American power elite.[17] While its members are to some extent constrained by legal precedent, there is in fact a fair degree of discretion in what they decide, as seen in the numerous great reversals of opinion down through the years.[18] Such reversals have occurred most dramatically on the issue of rights for African-Americans. Then, too, a switch in precedents in 1937 by two members of the court legitimated the crucial legislation having to do with union organizing that is discussed toward the end of this chapter.[19] Coming closer to home, the independent power of the Supreme Court was on display for all Americans in the 2000 elections: A highly conservative court that preached against judicial activism and emphasized states rights nonetheless overrode the Florida Supreme Court and found a way to put a stop to the counting of uncounted votes that might have tipped the presidential election to the Democrats. As constitutional scholars argued vociferously about the legal reasoning behind the court's majority, the Democratic Party and most ordinary Americans accepted the decision.

As the court's prevention of the Florida recount shows, Supreme Court appointments, and deference to their decisions, do matter, which is yet another reason why the power elite work so hard to win elections. As standard sources conclude from an examination of Supreme Court appointments, virtually all appointees have shared the ideological and political views of the presidents who appointed them.[20] In effect, this means that the Supreme Court reflects the range of acceptable opinion within the corporate-conservative coalition. The appointees are also primarily from the upper and upper-middle classes, and an "inordinate number had served as corporate attorneys before their appointments."[21] However, they also tend to be from elite law schools, to have experience as lawyers for lower-level judicial appointments or as professors at prestigious law schools, and to have been active in a political party. They are subject to strong scrutiny by leaders of the American Bar Association and confirmation by the Senate.[22]

The current court reflects most of these generalities. Four are graduates of Harvard Law School, including three Reagan-Bush appointments and one Clinton appointment. Two are from Stanford Law School, one from Yale Law School, and one from Columbia Law School. The justice most clearly from the upper class, a corporate lawyer appointed by President Gerald Ford, received his law degree at Northwestern. Most had corporate law experience, except for the two women justices, who found it difficult to find positions in a law firm despite their high rankings upon graduation from Stanford and Columbia. Six of the nine are millionaires, including the two Clinton appointees. Some inherited their wealth, some married into wealth, and others acquired wealth from their corporate law practices.

Two of the nonmillionaires, Antonin Scalia and Clarence Thomas, are also the most conservative justices. Scalia worked for a corporate law firm for six years after graduation from Harvard, then became a law professor. Thomas's work experience after graduation from Yale included two years as a corporate attorney for Monsanto Chemical Company, followed by two years as a legislative assistant to the millionaire Republican senator from Missouri, John C. Danforth, who later urged his appointment to the Supreme Court as the African-American replacement for the first African-American ever appointed to the Supreme Court, civil rights lawyer Thurgood Marshall. The third nonmillionaire, Anthony M. Kennedy, is the son of a corporate lawyer and a graduate of Harvard, and was a corporate lawyer before he became a judge.

As might be expected by this point in the book, the biggest differences among the justices concern volatile social issues. Women's rights, affirmative action, civil liberties, and the separation between church and state are the main targets of the ultraconservatives on the court. There is much less disagreement on issues of concern to the corporate community. On these issues, court opinions can be seen as the best rationales that can be constructed for the defense of the corporate economic system.

THE SPECIAL-INTEREST PROCESS

The special-interest process consists of the many and varied means by which specific corporations and business sectors gain the favors, tax breaks, regulatory rulings, and other governmental assistance they need to realize their narrow and short-run interests. The process is carried out by people with a wide range of experiences: former elected officials, experts who once served on congressional staffs or in regulatory agencies, employees of trade associations, corporate executives whose explicit function is government liaison, and an assortment of lawyers and public-relations specialists. The process is based on a great amount of personal contact, but its most important ingredients are the information and financial support that the lobbyists have to offer. Much of the time this information comes from grassroots pressure generated by the lobbyists to show that voting for a given measure will or will not hurt a particular politician.[23]

The most powerful lobbyists are gathered into a few large firms that are large businesses in themselves. The 10 biggest firms reported fees of $67 million for the first six months of 2000. These firms, in turn, are often owned by the public relations firms that have a major role in the opinion-shaping network discussed in Chapter 5. Two former Senate majority leaders, one Democratic and one Republican, are the leading figures in the second-largest lobbying firm, whose many clients include Citigroup, Merrill Lynch, and Brown & Williamson Tobacco. The issues these firms handle are typical of the special-interest process. For example, Pfister, a pharmaceutical manufacturer, paid one firm $400,000 to try to work against a National Transportation Safety Board proposal to ban the use of antihistamines by truck drivers. The Magazine Publishers of America paid another firm $520,000 to oppose a possible 15 percent increase in magazine postal rates.[24]

Intricate and arcane tax breaks are one of the most important aspects of the special interest process. Thanks to successful efforts in 1993 to relax rules concerning minimum corporate taxes, and changes in 1997 making it possible for corporations to spread tax breaks over several years, 12 of 250 profitable large firms studied for the years 1996 to 1998 paid no federal income taxes. Seventy-one of the 250 paid taxes at less than half the official rate during those three years. General Electric alone saved $6.9 billion.[25] Examples such as this could be multiplied endlessly.

Special interests also work through Congress to try to hamstring regulatory agencies or reverse military purchasing decisions they do not like. When the Federal Communications Commission tried to issue licenses for over 1,000 low-power FM stations for schools and community groups, Congress blocked the initiative at the behest of big broadcasting companies, setting standards that will restrict new licenses to a small number of stations in the least populated parts of the country. When the Food and Drug Administration tried to regulate tobacco, Congress refused authorization in 2000 in deference to the tobacco industry. In 1989, the Pentagon tried to cancel a new helicopter that was considered too costly and dangerous, but Congress deferred to the defense industry, allocating funds to keep it in production, and there have been three deadly crashes since.[26]

Some special-interest conflicts pit one sector of business against another, such as when broadcasters jockey for advantage against movie or cable companies. Sometimes the arguments are within a specific industry, as occurred when smaller insurance companies moved their headquarters to Bermuda in 1999 and 2000 to take advantage of a tax loophole worth as much as $4 billion annually. Since the bigger insurance companies cannot take advantage of this opportunity, they support bipartisan legislation to end the tax benefits of setting up in Bermuda. They have hired a lobbying firm, several law firms, and a public relations firm to press their cause. The small companies countered by hiring a different set of law firms and public relations companies.[27]

The special-interest process often is used to create loopholes in legislation that is accepted by the corporate community in principle. "I spent the last 7 years fighting the Clean Air Act," said a corporate lobbyist in charge of PAC donations, who then went on to explain why he gave money to elected officials who voted for the strengthening of the Clean Air Act in 1990:

> "How a person votes on the final piece of legislation is not representative of what they have done. Somebody will do a lot of things during the process. How many guys voted against the Clean Air Act? But during the process some of them were very sympathetic to some of our concerns."[28]

Translated, this means there are forty pages of exceptions, extensions, and other loopholes in the 1990 version of the act after a thirteen-year standoff between the Business Roundtable's Clean Air Working Group and the liberal-labor coalition's National Clean Air Coalition. For example, the steel industry has thirty years to bring twenty-six large coke ovens into compliance with the new standards. Once the bill passed, lobbyists went to work on the Environmental Protection Agency to win the most lax regulations possible for implementing the legislation. As of 1998, after twenty-eight years of argument and delay, the agency had been able to issue standards for less than ten of the many hazardous chemicals emitted into the air.[29]

Although most studies of the special-interest process recount the success of one or another corporation or trade association in gaining the tax or regulatory breaks it seeks, or discuss battles between rival sectors of the corporate community, there are occasional defeats for corporate interests at the hands of liberals and labor within this process. In 1971, for example, environmentalists convinced Congress to end taxpayer subsidies for construction of a supersonic transport.

In 1977, a relatively strong antistrip mine bill was adopted over the objections of the coal industry. Laws that improved auto safety standards were passed over automobile industry objections in the 1970s, as were standards of water cleanliness opposed by the paper and chemical industries.[30]

The liberal-labor coalition also can claim some victories for its own initiatives in Congress. For example, the Family and Medical Leave Act of 1993 allows both male and female employees of companies with fifty or more employees to take up to twelve weeks of unpaid leave a year for child care or family illness. The bill was opposed by corporate groups when it was first introduced in 1986, and vetoed twice by President George H. W. Bush before President Clinton came into office. The act covers 55 percent of American workers if government agencies are included. The fact that the leaves are unpaid limits the number of workers who can take advantage of them, and conservatives were able to exempt small companies and reduce the amount of leave from eighteen weeks to twelve, but health benefits are still in place during the leave. Seventeen percent of the workforce took advantage of this opportunity over an eighteen-month period during 1994 and 1995.[31]

The special-interest process is the most visible and frequently studied aspect of governmental activity in Washington. It also consumes the lion's share of the attention devoted to legislation by elected officials. There is general agreement among a wide range of theorists about the operation of this dimension of American politics. The special-interest process is very important to the corporate community, but it is not the heart of the matter when it comes to a full understanding of corporate power in the United States.

THE POLICY-MAKING PROCESS

General policy-making on issues of concern to the corporate community as a whole is the culmination of work done in the policy network described in Chapter 4. However, the differences between moderate conservatives and ultraconservatives sometimes lead to major conflicts over new policies within the executive branch and the legislative process. This was especially the case before the mid-1970s, although the moderate conservatives stopped ultraconservatives from going too far on some issues during the Reagan Administration. In addition, the power elite have to fend off alternative legislative proposals put forward by the liberal-labor coalition at this point in the policy process.

The recommendations developed in the policy-planning network reach government in a variety of ways. On the most general level, their reports, news releases, and interviews are read by elected officials and their staffs, if not in their original form, then as they are summarized by commentators and columnists in the *Washington Post, New York Times,* and *Wall Street Journal.* Members of the policy organizations also appear before congressional committees and subcommittees that are writing legislation or preparing budget proposals. During one calendar year, for example, 134 of the 206 trustees of the Committee for Economic Development testified at least once before Congress on issues ranging from oil prices to tax reductions to cutting regulatory red tape. Not all of this testimony related directly to CED projects, but all of it related to issues of concern to the corporate community. In several instances, the testimony was written for the trustees by CED staff members; three of these staff members also presented their own testimony on behalf of CED.

Impressive as these numerous appearances before legislative committees are, the most important contacts with government are more direct and formal in nature. First, people from the policy-planning network are often members of the many unpaid committees that advise specific departments of the executive branch on general policies. Second, they are prominent on the presidential and congressional commissions that have been appointed from time to time since World War II to make recommendations on a wide range of issues from highway construction to Social Security to a new missile defense system. Third, corporate leaders have personal contact with both appointed and elected officials as members of the two policy organizations with the most access to government, the Business Council and the Business Roundtable. Fourth, they serve as informal advisers to the President in times of foreign policy crisis. Finally, as shown in an earlier section of this chapter, they are appointed to government positions with a frequency far beyond what would be expected if all groups had an equal chance, putting them in a position to endorse the policy suggestions brought to them by their colleagues and former employees in the policy-planning network.

For the most part, the positions taken by moderate conservatives determine the outcome of policy battles. If they do not wish to see any change, they side with their ultraconservative counterparts in the power elite to defeat any programs suggested by liberals or labor. There were only a few instances in the twentieth century when the conservative voting bloc did not unite to block class-oriented liberal-labor legislation through an outright majority, maneuvering within key congressional committees, or a filibuster in the Senate.*

---

* It was not until 1917 that a filibuster could be ended with a two-thirds vote. Since 1974, it takes three-fifths of the votes to end a filibuster. Because both Republicans and Democrats now resort to filibusters more frequently than they did in the past, in effect it is now necessary to have 60 votes in the Senate to pass highly liberal or highly conservative legislation.

If the moderate conservatives favor policy changes opposed by the ultraconservatives, they seek the backing of liberal-labor elected officials for a program developed in moderate think tanks or policy-discussion groups, or else they modify a plan advocated by liberals. They are especially likely to take this course in times of extreme social disruption like the late 1960s, when they were dealing simultaneously with an antiwar movement, major upheaval in inner cities, and an overheated economy. In this context, for example, many corporate leaders welcomed the idea for the first Earth Day in 1970, and openly sponsored it, although many came to regret the "excesses" of the environmental movement just a few years later.[32]

Sometimes general policy battles pit one or two industries against the rest of the corporate community, with the aggrieved industries eventually losing out. This is what happened to a large extent in the 1950s and 1960s when the textile and chemical sectors blocked attempts to reduce tariff barriers and increase world trade. When leaders from the Committee for Economic Development were able to forge a compromise with textile and chemical spokespersons, the opposition in Congress disappeared immediately.[33] The same thing happened in 1987 when the U.S. Chamber of Commerce and the National Federation of Independent Business objected on general principle to a call by the American Electronics Association, the Chemical Manufacturers Association, and organized labor for a federal program to monitor and notify workers exposed to toxic substances in the workplace. The legislation was defeated by a Republican filibuster in the Senate because the corporate community as a whole feared that such a program might provide a thin entering wedge for further demands for regulation.[34]

None of this means that congressional voting coalitions develop any more quickly and easily on large-scale issues than they do on special-interest ones. Instead, each coalition has to be carefully constructed by elected officials, with the help of corporate lobbyists and grassroots publicity. It is here that the political leaders do their most important work. They are specialists in arranging trades with other politicians for votes, and in being sensitive to the electoral risks for each colleague in voting for or against any highly visible piece of legislation. They are also experts at sensing when the moment is right to hold a vote, often keeping the final outcome hanging in the balance for weeks or months at a time. Sometimes they wait until a lame-duck session shortly after elections have been held, or slip controversial legislation into omnibus bills that are hard for voters to fathom. Finally, their constant interaction with constituents and the media gives them the experience and sensitivity to create the rhetoric and symbols needed to make the new legislation palatable to as many people as possible.

THE POLICY PROCESS
AND THE ORIGINS OF SOCIAL SECURITY

Several detailed studies could be used to demonstrate how the policy process operates. They are of necessity historical in nature so that all of the essential information can be assembled, including the behind-the-scenes story of how the last few votes were secured. These studies encompass the most important twentieth-century initiatives of the power elite, everything from the creation of agricultural subsidies to the origins of several key regulatory agencies. They also include the success of the conservative voting coalition in defeating strong economic proposals from the liberal-labor coalition in 1946 and 1976.[35]

For purposes of this book, however, the one best historical study concerns the origins of the Social Security Act passed in 1935. Although Social Security is perhaps the most popular program ever developed by the federal government, and it has reduced the previous high incidence of poverty among the elderly, it is nonetheless heavily criticized by Wall Street financiers and ultraconservative think tanks, and its future solvency is a topic of constant concern. The tenor of the ongoing debate gives the impression that Social Security is the work of the liberal-labor coalition, or the invention of academic experts, who must have been opposed by the corporate community at the time the legislation passed. In fact, the situation is just about the exact opposite. The liberal-labor coalition did not even exist when the program was being formulated in the early 1930s, and independent academic experts had very little to do with it. Nor did elected officials craft the legislation, although some of them made significant alterations in the way the program operated before they passed it.

Instead, the program is the product of the executives and experts who worked for the fabled Rockefeller family in the 1920s and 1930s. The Rockefeller fortune, based in the ownership and control of three of the largest corporations of the era, including the companies now called Exxon/Mobil and Chevron, along with one of the largest banks and several smaller companies, was 2.5 times larger than its nearest rivals. Three Rockefeller foundations accounted for 58 percent of the money given out by the 20 largest foundations in 1934. This complex of corporations and foundations in turn financed several think tanks concerned with labor relations and social welfare.[36]

The main ideas for Social Security came from the employees of Industrial Relations Counselors, Inc., founded in 1921 by John D. Rockefeller, Jr., to search for ways to deal with labor unrest and avoid unionization. The organization often worked directly for the family's oil companies (today no longer controlled by the family). It was funded by family foundations for some purposes, although most of its money came straight from the Rockefellers' personal bank accounts. These employees were aided by experts from several university labor relations institutes, created with Rockefeller money about the same time. The ideas then were discussed in committees of business leaders and academic experts, which were organized by the Social Science Research Council, a policy-discussion group funded almost entirely by Rockefeller foundations.* The ideas received wider attention through two conferences attended by government officials and leaders in the field of social welfare.

In terms of describing the policy-process, there are two critical aspects to the program, old-age insurance and unemployment insurance. Corporate leaders understood both of these programs as ways to control labor markets and make them more efficient. Old-age insurance is a way to remove older people and make way for younger, more efficient employees. Unemployment insurance is a way to keep the unemployed from becoming destitute or desperate, and thereby potentially disruptive. In the case of old-age insurance, the philosophy behind the program is best explained by a Rockefeller-funded professor in the Labor Relations Section of the Department of Economics at Princeton, who worked closely with Industrial Relations Counselors, Inc. He also was a key member of the team that created Social Security:

> The acceptance by the larger American corporation of the obligation to pay contributions to a social insurance program, although influenced by the traditional concept of employer responsibility, was probably more directly the result of the need for a perpetual corporation to assure a flow of effective and well-motivated personnel for the year-by-year operation of the company. Retirement programs with adequate pensions became necessary to prevent an excessive aging of staff or the loss of morale which the discard of the old without compensation would involve. Such programs became a charge on current production to be passed on to the consumer.[37]

The Rockefeller group insisted that government old-age insurance had to be based on three principles it developed during several years of experience with private pension plans. First, the level of benefits would be tied to salary level, thus preserving and reinforcing the values established in the labor market. Second, unlike the case in many countries, there were to be no government contributions from

---

* The Social Science Research Council lost its discussion-group role by World War II. Drawing on funds from the major foundations, it is now an organization that sponsors academic conferences and gives grants to social scientists.

general tax revenues. Instead, there had to be a separate tax for old-age insurance, which would help to limit the size of benefits. Third, there were to be both employer and employee contributions to the system, which would limit the tax payments by the corporations.

These general principles were well known to President Franklin D. Roosevelt, who was familiar with the Rockefeller philanthropies and think tanks as a native of New York state, and its governor from 1929 to 1932. He discussed them at length with the president of General Electric, who worked closely with the Rockefeller group, in March 1934.[38] Then, in June 1934, the president announced he was appointing a Committee on Economic Security to propose legislation for a social security system. The committee consisted of several of his key cabinet members, who were authorized to hire a staff to make the necessary studies and draft the legislation. The Committee on Economic Security also had an Advisory Council to assist it, made up of the most prominent business, labor, and social welfare leaders of the time.

The executive director of the staff, a labor economist from the University of Wisconsin, in effect hired the Rockefeller experts to write the plans for old-age and unemployment insurance. Although they were now government appointees, they remained in New York and were paid by Industrial Relations Counselors, Inc., which means, in essence, that the Rockefeller group was subsidizing the government.

The old-age plan the Cabinet members endorsed was almost exactly like the one originally proposed by the Rockefeller employees. However, it did not cover agricultural employees even though the staff recommended their inclusion. This exclusion was made in anticipation of likely opposition from Southern plantation capitalists.[39] Although the plan was conservative and uncontroversial, some cabinet members and Roosevelt began to think about waiting to introduce it until unemployment legislation was passed. The Rockefeller experts leaked this possibility to the press, and the corporate leaders on the Advisory Council insisted that the president keep old-age insurance in the package.[40]

Unemployment insurance proved to be a far more controversial topic for the committee and its staff. At one level, this was because experts from the University of Wisconsin believed, contrary to the Rockefeller group, that each state should administer its own program on unemployment, with financial help from the federal government. This approach was consistent with their longstanding tendency to avoid federal programs. In this instance, there are also indications that these experts were anticipating the opposition of Southern Democrats to any federal initiative that might undercut their low-wage agrarian economy. This is best seen in the fact that the state-administered plan approved by the Committee on Economic Security did not even include any federal minimum standards, which were strongly advocated by the Wisconsin experts. Tax and benefit levels were entirely at the discretion of the states. As one of the two most important Rockefeller experts explained in a letter to a professor at the University of Virginia early in 1935:

> Almost without exception, congressmen and senators from the South indicated extreme skepticism of the wisdom of any legislation of a social character which would concentrate further power in Washington. Behind this feeling was obviously a fear that unsympathetic administrations in Washington would require southern states to pay Negroes a benefit which would be regarded locally as excessive.[41]

Just as the plan was being discussed in Congress, a Supreme Court ruling in May 1935, almost undermined the rationale for the new legislation and endangered its constitutionality. In a case concerning a new government retirement program for railroad employees, the court ruled that pensions and unemployment relief are not "proper objects" of legislation under the constitution. Nor are the alleged positive effects of pensions on the efficiency and morale of the workforce. The preamble justifying the social security proposal therefore had to be rewritten. It now emphasized that such legislation would contribute to the general welfare of the country, which it is permissible to support under the constitution. In other words, an ideology based in social welfare had to be constructed that stressed needs, not efficiency. This change in justification caused the labor-market basis of the plan to be lost from sight and led to the false notion that social workers, liberals, and unions had created the Social Security Act.[42]

Once the plan finally arrived in Congress, Southern Democrats objected to a number of features concerning old-age assistance. They modified it so that states could hire their own personnel for local administration, set their own pension levels, and determine eligibility.[43] However, they accepted the unemployment plan much as it had been written because it gave so much discretion to individual states and already allowed them to set their own benefit levels. Labor leaders also had their say at this point, objecting to the fact that workers had to pay into the unemployment fund. The plan was amended at their behest, but it was a shortsighted victory that makes unemployment insurance less generous and harder to legitimate than old-age insurance, where both workers and employers are taxed.

The U.S. Chamber of Commerce and the National Association of Manufacturers testified against the plan, suggesting disagreements between the moderate conservatives in the Rockefeller group and hardline conservatives. At one level, their objections were a surprise, because leaders of both groups had indicated their begrudging approval of the plan in late 1934 and early 1935. However, in May 1935, these two groups had come out in full opposition to Roosevelt and the New Deal because of other proposed legislation, especially the labor legislation discussed in the next section of this chapter. Thus, their opposition to this proposal was primarily political, not substantive. The real battle was between Northern corporate interests and Southern plantation capitalists, and the legislation passed with ease once their differences were compromised.

The Rockefeller group also played a very large role in the implementation of the new legislation after it passed. With the aid of large grants from the Rockefeller Foundation, the Social Science Research Council created a Committee on Social Security and augmented its Committee on Public Administration, both of which helped solve administrative problems and supplied staff personnel for departments of the Social Security Administration.[44] In addition, the Rockefeller professor at Princeton became head of the advisory committee that made many changes in 1939.[45] The system later expanded to include agricultural workers, became slightly more generous to low-income retirees, and added a regular cost-of-living adjustment.

Despite its conservative origins and great success, the system has been under constant attack since the 1990s by ultraconservative experts from the Cato Institute and the Heritage Foundation who want to privatize it. Using projections based on very low and unlikely estimates concerning the rate of economic growth, they claim that the system may not be solvent in thirty or forty years. Their scare campaign through the media has convinced many young people that the system may not be around when it comes time for them to retire. The ultraconservatives claim Social Security is a bad investment for people, because it does not earn a high enough rate of return. They therefore suggest that people be allowed to withdraw from Social Security and invest their money for retirement purposes through Wall Street.

The defense of the system has fallen to the liberal-labor coalition, which is joined on this issue by a large and potent lobbying force, the American Association of Retired Persons. The defenders note that social insurance is a communal concept that insures a decent life for those who happen to live to an old age, not an individual investment strategy. They argue that any future deficits can be averted with a combination of very small changes. They point to the long downturn in the stock market in the 1970s to suggest that the stock market is not always as rosy as it was in the 1990s, which means that many people might not have what they thought they would a few years from now.

Since nearly everyone agrees that Social Security is sound until at least 2030, this argument is likely to go on for a long time. It is very useful symbolic politics for the power elite, even if few changes are actually made. It allows them to broadcast their antigovernment ideology, creates potential wedges between the younger and older generations, and keeps the liberal-labor coalition on the defensive.

The way in which the Social Security Act was formulated in a policy-planning network created with Rockefeller money, and then amended in Congress by Southern Democrats, reinforces several general points made throughout this book. First, it demonstrates that the federal government employs very little expertise of its own and has to rely on the policy-planning network for new initiatives. Second, it illustrates the great power of the Southern plantation capitalists in Congress until well after World War II, which provides perspective for younger people on why American social programs are so meager. Third, the large role of the Southern rich in the Democratic Party highlights the limits that the two-party system placed on the liberal-labor coalition as long as African-Americans could not vote in the South.

THE GREAT EXCEPTION: LABOR POLICY

The corporate community suffered its two biggest setbacks of the twentieth century on the issue that matters most to it, labor policy. The first came in the turmoil of the Great Depression and in the face of determined union-organizing drives. The second happened in the midst of the social upheaval and new environmental movement in the late 1960s. In both cases, the aftermath of the defeats is very instructive for understanding the full scope of corporate domination in the United States.

Labor Relations and Union Organizing

The National Labor Relations Act of 1935 affirmed the right of workers to organize unions and placed government sanctions behind any illegal attempts (called "unfair labor practices") to interfere with this right. The unusual twist to this anticorporate legislation is that all of the precedents for it were created by corporate leaders, dating back to the early years of the twentieth century. In 1900, they founded a policy-discussion group to meet with the leaders of the few unions that existed in order to see if the violence and volatility of American labor relations could be reduced. The new group, with the help of hired experts, evolved the idea of *collective bargaining,* meaning voluntary meetings between representatives of business and labor to try to come to agreement on matters concerning wages, hours, and working conditions. Although the idea sounds simple, it is actually a complex power relationship that embodies the strengths and weaknesses of both sides. Its narrowness shows the power of corporate leaders to deflect the larger changes that many workers had demanded earlier, including a voice in the production process. Its existence reveals the power of workers through strikes and work stoppages to force corporate leaders to talk with them as a group, which corporate leaders previously had refused to do. [46]

Still, the unionism the corporate leaders were willing to support was a limited one, focused almost exclusively on skilled or craft workers, with no provision for unskilled workers in mass-production industries. Furthermore, they wanted to deal with each craft union separately, and they insisted that collective bargaining be voluntary. Government appointees or special committees sometimes could be called in to mediate, but they could not mandate. This kind of arrangement was given its first serious trial during World War I, when the necessity of regimenting the economy also allowed for temporary government sanctions, and it worked well enough.

The 1920s were a time of corporate ascendancy and union failure in the midst of a growing economy, and it looked like even the small union movement that had survived in the building trades, coal mining, and garment making was on its way to extinction. But the Great Depression that began suddenly in 1929, and grew worse for the next three years, changed everything. Desperate corporate leaders finally decided in early 1933 that they had to create a government regulatory agency, the National Recovery Administration. They believed this agency could help to restart the economy by bringing business leaders together to set minimum wages, minimum prices, and maximum levels of productive output. The hope was that the elimination of wage cutting and overproduction, which produced cutthroat competition and a vicious downward spiral in profits, would allow for the reemployment of workers and an increase in purchasing power.[47]

As one small part of this plan, there was a clause stating that workers had the right to be organized into unions. Although the National Association of Manufacturers fought this clause, which came to be known simply as *Section 7a,* most corporate leaders saw it as a goodwill gesture toward weak union leaders, several of whom were fellow Republicans besides. They thought Section 7a would solidify union support for the unprecedented powers the new plan gave to corporations to change the nature of market relations. Besides, there was no enforcement power behind it, and they could fall back on employee representation plans if necessary. These in-plant consultation sessions, known as "company unions" by their critics, were designed in the early 1920s for the Rockefellers by Industrial Relations Counselors, Inc., and put into practice in several of their oil companies. Shortly after the legislation passed, however, Section 7a turned out to provide a wedge that led to totally unexpected results.

The National Recovery Administration was a complete failure that did not contribute to the recovery and was abandoned in less than two years, but Section 7a had an electrifying effect on workers and union organizers. They interpreted it to mean that the president of the United States wanted them to join a union, and within months there were strikes and protests in hundreds of locations across the country, with workers demanding the right to join unions of their own choosing. In the midst of this upheaval, surprised corporate leaders from General Electric and Exxon suggested a reincarnation of the wartime mediating board, and then their real troubles began. They hoped the new National Labor Board would be able to put an end to the disruption, but the simple fact of its existence, as a seeming fulfillment of Section 7a, generated even more labor militancy and a new political crisis that the corporate community could not control.[48]

The new labor board consisted of three corporate leaders, three union leaders, and New York Senator Robert F. Wagner, who ultimately wrote the legislation that the corporate leaders vigorously opposed. Ironically, corporate leaders had suggested Senator Wagner as the ideal leader for the board because he was supportive of policy suggestions from moderate-conservative think tanks and enjoyed the trust of labor leaders.[49] The board developed a set of rules for bringing business and labor into collective bargaining, including the idea that a union should be recognized if a majority of workers in a factory voted in favor of having it represent them. Members of the board then met with both sides of the dispute to see if they could mediate, but they still had no enforcement power.

The labor board had some success in its first few months, in part because it was dealing primarily with small companies that did not have the collective strength to resist. Coal miners and garment workers especially benefited. However, large companies, notably in mass-production industries, began to defy the board's authority as the economy improved. Moreover, union leaders on the board insisted that there should not be more than one union representing workers in each company, which they had not demanded in the past. The corporate moderates resisted this step. They did not want to risk the possibility that most American workers would be organized into inclusive unions that might eventually provide a challenge to corporate power inside and outside the workplace.

The idea of collective bargaining was acceptable to the sophisticated conservatives in the corporate community if it was voluntary and primarily involved a number of separate craft unions, and left room for their employee representation plans to hold on to some workers, which meant in practice that the corporations could divide and conquer. But even in the midst of an economic crisis, they continued to bitterly oppose collective bargaining if it was mandated by law and had the potential to unite craft and industrial workers.[50] When Senator Wagner and several liberal Democrats suggested that majority rule should be made into law and that fines should be levied against those who refused to follow governmentally sanctioned rules that spelled out good-faith collective bargaining, the corporate leaders serving on the board turned against it. In addition, many corporations began to fire union organizers, hire detectives to break up strikes, stockpile weapons and dynamite, and in a few cases make contact with right-wing vigilante groups.[51]

Meanwhile, Senator Wagner's staff and the lawyers working for the board, a few of them experienced corporate lawyers who had become liberals, introduced new legislation that would embody and strengthen the practices that they had worked out through experience. The new board would not have representatives from business and labor, but would instead consist of three experts appointed by the president, who in practice turned out to be primarily lawyers and labor relations specialists. Instead of trying to mediate, it would serve as a mini Supreme Court for labor disputes. It would have the power to determine if corporations had used illegal means to impede unionization, such as firing or attacking striking workers. The board would have the power to administer fines and to enforce its rulings through the courts.

Deeply disturbed by this unanticipated turn of events, the corporate community mounted a very large lobbying campaign against the proposed National Labor Relations Board. This campaign was coordinated by the same Rockefeller group that created the Social Security Act, this time working hand-in-hand with the U.S. Chamber of Commerce and the National Association of Manufacturers. The employees who wrote the Social Security Act were not involved in the lobbying, but the former assistant to the president at Exxon, then employed by Industrial Relations Counselors, Inc., coordinated both efforts. The lobbying initiative included a legal brief signed by the famous corporate lawyers of the day, claiming that the act was unconstitutional. To the great embarrassment of the corporate community, the details of this lobbying battle, and the plans some of them had for violence against union organizers, became known shortly after the legislation passed. The Senate's Committee on Civil Liberties subpoenaed the papers of the corporate coordinating committee as part of its investigation into antiunion activities.[52]

Although there was a large Democratic majority in Congress at this juncture due to Roosevelt's great popularity, and labor unions were gearing up for another big organizing drive after the 1936 elections, these facts do not fully explain why the act passed by a large majority in both the House and Senate in the summer of 1935. They are not sufficient because Southern Democrats controlled the congressional levers of power. Moreover, President Roosevelt was reluctant to oppose the Southerners because they were longtime allies and personal friends who had been among his major supporters when he won the presidential nomination in 1932. In addition, their cooperation was necessary to pass any future legislation he might find essential to nurture the economic recovery. Southern Democrats and their moderate Democratic allies therefore could have sided with the handful of Republicans remaining in the Congress to weaken or block the legislation.

Instead, the Southern Democrats sided with the liberal Democrats. This unusual agreement on a labor issue was possible due to a simple expedient, the exclusion of agricultural, seasonal, and domestic workers from the protection of the act, the same bargain made in the case of the social security act. The exclusion of agricultural workers also made it easier for the Progressive Republicans from the predominantly agrarian states of the Midwest and Great Plains to support the legislation, leaving the employers of Northern industrial labor almost completely isolated. As a perceptive observer from the 1930s wrote:

> Most of our social legislation, in fact, has been enacted as a result
> of a political "deal" between organized labor and the farm groups.
> The basis of this deal has always been: we, the farm representatives,
> will not object to this legislation, if you, the representatives of
> organized labor, will agree to exempt agricultural employees.[53]

This compromise was fully understood at the time. When the leader of the Socialist Party wrote Senator Wagner to ask why agricultural workers had been excluded from the bill, he replied that he was "very regretful of this," but that they had not been included because he thought it "better to pass the bill for the benefit of industrial workers than not to pass it at all, and the inclusion of agricultural workers would lessen the likelihood of passage so much as not to be desirable."[54]

Further support for this analysis can be found in events that unfolded after the legislation passed. Due to disruptive sit-down strikes throughout the North in 1937, along with attempts to create racially integrated industrial unions in some parts of the South, the Southern Democrats turned against the act, doing everything they could to undermine it throughout the years leading up to World War II. When Republicans gained control of Congress for a two-year period after the war, the Southerners joined with them in passing conservative amendments that had severe consequences for the union movement. When the liberal-labor coalition worked very hard to elect a Democratic Congress and president in 1948, it argued that the Democrats should remove the conservative amendments because of the large liberal-labor contribution to their victory. But the Southern Democrats would not agree to do so.[55]

Unions lost more ground to the conservative voting bloc on union issues in 1959, 1961, and 1967. Then, they were defeated in 1978 by a filibuster in the Senate in their attempt to make improvements in the laws concerning union organizing. In effect, then, the history of union-related legislation since 1935 is as follows: During the New Deal, the union leaders conceded to government the right to regulate methods of union organizing in exchange for governmentally protected rights, then had those rights taken away gradually by a series of legislative amendments, negative rulings by the National Labor Relations Board, and court decisions.[56]

Although the fact remains that the corporate community lost on the National Labor Relations Act, it is the aftermath of this defeat that gives us insight into the power of the corporate-conservative coalition and the power elite when they are united.

The Occupational Safety and Health Administration

The corporate community suffered its other unambiguous legislative loss in 1970 on another labor issue, health and safety in the workplace. Although the legislation is not nearly as consequential as the National Labor Relations Act, the corporate leaders and their trade organizations nonetheless strongly opposed it. Until that time, occupational safety and health issues had been under their control through a network of corporate-funded private organizations, the most prominent of which are the National Safety Council and the American National Standards Institute. Although this organizational network set some minimal standards for the workplace, they were voluntary and often ignored. The greatest emphasis was on weeding out allegedly accident-prone employees and preaching that safe practices were the responsibility of the workers themselves.

Occupational safety and health arrived on the legislative agenda due to the general social upheaval, environmentalism, and tight labor markets of the late 1960s, along with the increasing scientific evidence that asbestos and some industrial chemicals are dangerous to workers. President Lyndon Johnson had his staff prepare new legislation on the issue as part of his anticipated reelection campaign of 1968, and then President Nixon decided to back a weaker version of the program as part of his strategy to win blue-collar workers as Republican voters. The standards created by the corporate community's own American National Standards Institute were written into the legislation as a starting point.[57]

Despite reassurances from the Nixon Administration, and the fact that the standards were ones they had legitimated, the corporate community opposed this legislation as an unwarranted extension of government regulatory power and a possible advantage for union organizers. The U.S. Chamber of Commerce went so far as to argue that the new agency called for by the legislation probably would hire unemployed workers, who would then take their revenge on corporations by applying the standards unfairly. Although the union movement as a whole had paid very little attention to the development of this legislation, at this point several unions lobbied vigorously for passage.

As the new Occupational Safety and Health Administration slowly tried to develop its own standards, the corporate community fought back with a strategy of withholding information, delay, and litigation. The corporate leaders also launched a strong ideological campaign, blaming government regulation for a recent decline in economic productivity, but public opinion remained supportive of safety and health regulations nonetheless. In the 1980s, however, the enforcement powers of the agency were scaled back through legislative amendments, budget cuts, and court rulings.[58] Once again, the passage of legislation does not tell the full story.

Predictably, the corporate community registered a massive protest in November 2000, when the Occupational Safety and Health Administration issued its first new standards in twenty years. The rulings, intended to reduce repetitive stress injuries such as back strain and carpal tunnel syndrome, covered 102 million workers at 6 million workplaces. The U.S. Chamber of Commerce, the National Association of Manufacturers, and numerous trade associations claimed the standards were a parting gift to organized labor by President Clinton, even though the intent to create such standards was first announced in 1990 by a Republican appointee, and then delayed by Congress in 1995, 1996, and 1998 through legislative amendments. They were overturned by Congress in March 2001 after a vigorous lobbying effort by the corporate-conservative coalition.[59]

WHY BUSINESS LEADERS FEEL POWERLESS

Despite the strong *Who governs?* and *Who wins?* evidence that the power elite have great power over the federal government on the issues of concern to them, many corporate leaders feel they are relatively powerless in the face of government. To hear them tell it, the Congress is more responsive to organized labor, environmentalists, and consumers than it is to them. They also claim to be harassed by willful and arrogant bureaucrats who encroach upon the rightful preserves of the private sector, sapping them of their confidence and making them hesitant to invest their capital.

These feelings have been documented by a journalist and political scientist who observed a series of meetings at a policy discussion group in which the social responsibilities of business were being discussed. The men at these meetings were convinced that everybody but them was listened to by government. Government was seen as responsive to the immediate preferences of the majority of citizens. "The have-nots are gaining steadily more political power to distribute the wealth downward," complained one executive. "The masses have turned to a larger government." Some even wondered whether democracy and capitalism are compatible. "Can we still afford one man, one vote? We are tumbling on the brink," said one. "One man, one vote has undermined the power of business in all capitalist countries since World War II," announced another. "The loss of the rural vote weakens conservatives."[60]

The fear business leaders express of the democratic majority leads them to view recessions as a saving grace, because recessions help to keep the expectations of workers in check. Workers who fear for their jobs are less likely to demand higher wages or government social programs. For example, different corporate executives made the following comments:

> This recession will bring about the healthy respect for economic values that the Great Depression did.
>
> People need to recognize that a job is the most important thing they can have. We should use this recession to get the public to better understand how our economic system works. Social goals are OK, provided the public is aware of their costs.
>
> It would be better if the recession were allowed to weaken more than it will, so that we would have a sense of sobriety.[61]

The negative feelings these corporate leaders have toward government are not a new development in the corporate community. A study of business leaders' views in the nineteenth century found that they believed political leaders to be "stupid" and "empty" people who go into politics only to earn a living. As for the ordinary voters, they are "brutal, selfish and ignorant." A comment written by a businessman in 1886 could have been made at the meetings just discussed: "In this good, democratic country where every man is allowed to vote, the intelligence and the property of the country is at the mercy of the ignorant, idle and vicious."[62] Even in the 1920s, when everyone agrees that business was at the zenith of its powers, corporate leaders sang the same tune.[63] These findings undercut any claim that business hostility toward government stems largely from the growth of government programs during the New Deal.

The emotional expressions of businesspeople about their lack of power cannot be taken seriously as power indicators, although they give pause to thoughts on how corporate leaders might react in the face of a large-scale democratic social and political movement that seriously challenges their prerogatives and privileges. The investigation of power concerns actions and their consequences, which are in the realm of sociology, economics, and politics, not in the realm of subjective feelings. Still, it is worthwhile to try to understand why corporate leaders complain about a government they dominate. There are three intertwined aspects to the answer.

First of all, complaining about government is a useful power strategy, a form of action in itself. It puts government officials on the defensive and forces them to keep proving that they are friendly to business, out of concern that corporate leaders will lose confidence in economic conditions and stop investing. A political scientist makes this point as follows:

> Whether the issue is understood explicitly, intuitively, or not at all, denunciations serve to establish and maintain the subservience of government units to the business constituencies to which they are actually held responsible. Attacks upon government in general place continuing pressure on governmental officers to accommodate their activities to the groups from which support is most reliable.[64]

There also seems to be an ideological level to the corporate stance toward government, which is based in a fear of the populist, democratic ideology that underlies American government. Since power is in theory in the hands of all the people, there is always the possibility that some day the people, in the sense of the majority, will make the government into the pluralist democracy it is supposed to be. In the American historical context, the great power of the dominant class is illegitimate, and the existence of such power is therefore vigorously denied.[65]

The most powerful reason for this fear of popular control is revealed by the corporate community's unending battle with unions, as described throughout this book. It is an issue-area like no other in evoking angry rhetoric and near-perfect unity among corporate leaders. It also has generated more violence than any other issue except civil rights for African-Americans. The uniqueness of the corporate community's reaction to any government help for unions supports the hypothesis that the corporate community, small businesses, and the growth coalitions are antigovernment because they fear government as the only institution that could challenge corporate control of labor markets, thereby changing the functioning of the system to some extent and reducing the power of employers. The federal government can influence labor markets in five basic ways:

1. The government can hire unemployed workers to do necessary work relating to parks, schools, roadways, and the environment. Such government programs were a great success during the New Deal, when unemployment reached 25 percent and social disruption seemed imminent, but they were quickly shut down at the insistence of business leaders when order was restored and the economy began to improve.[66]

2. It can support the right to organize unions and bargain collectively, as described in the previous section. This kind of government initiative is opposed even more strongly than government jobs for the unemployed because it would give workers a sustained organizational base for moving into the political arena.

3. Although the power elite appreciate the value of old-age, disability, and unemployment insurance, they worry that politicians might allow these programs to become too generous. In fact, these programs expanded in response to the turmoil of the 1960s and 1970s to the point where the Reagan Administration felt it necessary to cut them back in order to reduce inflation and make corporations more profitable.[67]

4. The government can tighten labor markets by limiting immigration. The immigration of low-wage labor has been essential to the corporate community throughout American history. When conservative Republicans began to think about passing anti-immigration legislation in the mid-1990s, as called for in their campaign rhetoric, they were met with a barrage of employer opposition, particularly from leaders in agribusiness, and quickly retreated.

5. Government can reduce unemployment and tighten labor markets by lowering interest rates through the operations of the Federal Reserve System. This fact has been made obvious to a large per-

centage of the public by the way in which the Federal Reserve increases unemployment by increasing the interest rates whenever the unemployment rate dips too low. Although the issue is cast in terms of inflation, the economics of inflation are often the politics of labor markets.

Given the many ways that the government could tighten labor markets and thereby reduce profits and increase the economic power of American workers, it is understandable that the corporate community would be fearful of the government it dominates.

THE LIMITS OF CORPORATE DOMINATION

Involvement in government is the final and most visible aspect of corporate domination, which has its roots in the class structure, control of the investment function, and the operation of the policy-planning network. If government officials did not have to wait on corporate leaders to decide where and when they will invest, and if government officials were not further limited by the general public's acceptance of policy recommendations from the policy-planning network, then power elite involvement in elections and government would count for a lot less than it does under present conditions.

Domination by the power elite does not negate the reality of continuing conflict over government policies, but few conflicts, it has been shown, involve challenges to the rules that create privileges for the upper class and the corporate community. Most of the numerous battles within the interest-group process, for example, are only over specific spoils and favors; they often involve disagreements between competing business interests.

Similarly, conflicts within the policy-making process sometimes concern differences between the moderate conservatives and ultraconservatives in the power elite. Many issues that at first appear to be legislative defeats for the corporate community turn out to be situations where the moderate conservatives decided for their own reasons to side with the liberal-labor coalition. At other times, the policy disagreements involve issues where the needs of the corporate community as a whole come into conflict with the needs of specific industries, which is what happened in the past on trade policies and also on some environmental legislation.

The single most consequential loss for the corporate community, the National Labor Relations Act of 1935, played a role in creating a strong labor movement in the North in the mid-1900s. As mentioned, this loss occurred in a context of great labor militancy and a willingness on the part of Southern plantation capitalists to side with liberal

Democrats in exchange for the exclusion of their own labor force. The defeat, although tempered by later legislation, had a major effect on the nature of the American power structure. It suggests that limits can be placed on corporate power under some conditions.

The legislation establishing the Occupational Safety and Health Administration in 1970 is the only instance of any significance that reflects a liberal-labor victory over a united corporate community. The fact that it occurred in a time of social upheaval again suggests that the corporate community can lose in some contexts. On this issue, however, the success of the power elite and the conservative voting bloc in the aftermath of this legislative defeat shows why the full picture of corporate domination is best demonstrated through sociological analyses with a historical dimension.

8

The Big Picture

This book began with two seeming paradoxes. How can the owners and managers of highly competitive corporations develop the policy unity to shape government policies? How can large corporations have such great power in a democratic country? The step-by-step argument and evidence presented in previous chapters provide the foundation for a theory that can explain these paradoxes—a *class-domination theory of power* in the United States.

Domination means that the commands of a group or class are carried out with relatively little resistance, which is possible because that group or class has been able to establish the rules and customs through which everyday life is conducted. Domination, in other words, is the institutionalized outcome of great distributive power. The upper class of owners and high-level executives, based in the corporate community, is a dominant class in terms of this definition because the cumulative effect of its various distributive powers leads to a situation where its policies are generally accepted by most Americans. The routinized ways of acting in the United States follow from the rules and regulations needed by the corporate community to continue to grow and make profits.

The overall distributive power of the dominant class is first of all based in its structural economic power, which falls to it by virtue of its members being owners and high-level executives in corporations that sell goods and services for a profit in a market economy. The power to invest or not invest, and to hire and fire employees, leads to a political context where elected officials try to do as much as they can to create a favorable investment climate to avoid being voted out of office in the event of an economic downturn. This structural power is augmented by the ability to create new policies through a complex policy-planning network, which the upper class has been able to institutionalize because common economic interests and social cohesion have given the corporate community enough unity to sustain such an endeavor over many decades.

But even these powers might not have been enough to generate a system of extreme class domination if the bargains and compromises embodied in the Constitution had not led unexpectedly to a two-party system in which one party was controlled by the Northern rich and the other by the Southern rich. This in turn created a personality-oriented candidate-selection process that is heavily dependent on large campaign donations—now and in the past as well. The system of party primaries is the one adaptation to this constrictive two-party system that has provided some openings for insurgent liberals and trade unionists.

Structural economic power and control of the two parties, along with the elaboration of an opinion-shaping network, results in a polity where there is little or no organized public opinion independent of the limits set by debates within the power elite itself. There is no organizational base from which to construct an alternative public opinion, and there have been until recently no openings within the political system that could carry an alternative message to government.

Finally, the fragmented and constrained system of government carefully crafted by the Founding Fathers led to a relatively small federal government that is easily entered and influenced by wealthy and well-organized private citizens, whether through Congress, the separate departments of the executive branch, or a myriad of regulatory agencies. The net result is that the owners and managers of large income-producing properties score very high on all three power indicators: who benefits, who governs, and who wins. They have a greater proportion of wealth and income than their counterparts in any other capitalist democracy, and through the power elite they are vastly over-represented in key government positions and decision-making groups. They win far more often than they lose on those issues that make it to the government for legislative consideration, although their lack of unity in the face of worker militancy in the 1930s made it possible for organized workers to have far more independence, income, and power than they ever had in the past.

Americans feel a sense of empowerment because they have religious freedom, free speech, and a belief that they can strike it rich or rise in the system if they try hard enough. They experience a degree of dignity and respect because there is no tradition of public degradation for those of average or low incomes. Liberals and leftists can retain hope because in recent decades they have had success in expanding individual rights and freedom—for women, for people of color, and most recently for gays and lesbians. But individual rights and freedoms do not necessarily add up to distributive power. In the same time period, when individual rights and freedoms expanded, corporate power also became greater because unions were decimated and the liberal-labor coalition splintered. This analysis suggests there is class domination in spite of individual freedoms and the right to vote.

THE MAIN ALTERNATIVE VIEWS

The Pluralism Theory

It is now possible to look at three other theories of power in America to see how they compare with the one suggested in this book. The main alternative, pluralism, is that power is more widely dispersed among groups and classes than a class-dominance view allows. According to this theory, the general public has power on many issues through forming voluntary associations that shape public opinion and lobby elected officials. Citizens also have the power to influence the general direction of public policy by supporting candidates who are sympathetic with their preferences.

But the little evidence there is for any influence of public opinion on policy is almost entirely correlational, which means that it can tell us nothing about causality. Pluralist claims based on correlations overlook the role of the opinion-shaping network (outlined in Chapter 5) in bringing public opinion into conformity on many issues with the policy preferences of the power elite. The claim that voting has a major influence on legislation is based in good part on theoretical arguments and the experience of other countries, not evidence about elections in the United States. It does not take into account the several factors shown in Chapter 6 to dilute this potential influence. In particular, it ignores the way in which a two-party system leads candidates to blur policy differences as they try to win the centrist voters, leaving elected officials relatively free to say one thing in the campaign and do another once in office. It also misses the major role of the Southern rich in the Democratic Party until very recently, and the veto power of the conservative voting bloc in Congress.

Other pluralists claim that experts have an independent role in developing new public policies. These theorists are right that experts provide many of the new policy ideas, but they seem unaware of the policy-planning network discussed in Chapter 4. They do not appreciate that the most visible experts are selected and sponsored by one or more organizations within the policy network, and that their ideas are discussed and criticized by corporate leaders before appearing in reports and proposals. Pluralists do not realize the degree to which the careers of experts who hope to have an impact within government, or receive an appointment to a government position, are shaped by the corporate leaders who direct policy organizations, fund political candidates, and serve as appointed officials within the government.

Some pluralists hold to the notion that corporate leaders are too divided among themselves to dominate government. They believe there are divisions between owners and managers of large corporations, or that corporations are only organized into narrow interest groups that sometimes argue among themselves. These theorists are right that corporations are organized into interest groups that lobby Congress and the regulatory agencies, but they ignore the evidence presented in Chapter 3 for the assimilation of corporate managers into the upper class through a wide range of social occasions and economic incentives. By focusing on the occasional squabbles among corporations on narrow, short-range issues, pluralists miss the degree of unity that is generated through common ownership, interlocking directorships, and participation in the policy-planning network.

The most recent version of pluralism suggests a new liberalism has arisen in which citizen's lobbies proliferate.[1] This view puts great emphasis on the battles between liberals and the New Christian Right over cultural values, noting that the liberals often win, but this is irrelevant in analyzing corporate power, except when social issues are used as an election ploy. It grants that major foundations, especially the Ford Foundation, funded many citizen groups at their outset, but claims they are now independent due to money raised through direct mailings and other outreach efforts. In fact, many of the advocacy groups for low-income minority groups are still very dependent on foundation money. More generally, minimizing the role of foundation grants overlooks the importance of discretionary money in the functioning of any organization.

All environmental groups are counted as part of this new liberalism, but as Chapter 4 shows, the key groups as far as policy formulation are still funded by large foundations and are part of the policy-planning network. Strong environmentalists have had great success in sensitizing public opinion on environmental issues. They have been able to create watchdog groups whose reports receive major attention in the mass media when they are released. They have developed new ideas and technologies for controlling pollution that have been grudgingly accepted by the corporate community. Their activism has been crucial in stopping many specific development projects and in saving old forests. But since 1975 they have not been able to pass any legislation that is opposed by the Business Roundtable, and they often become very annoyed with the moderate environmentalists. The environmental movement as a whole, and the liberal wing in particular, is more marginal in a power sense than its public reputation would suggest.[2]

The consumer movement that developed out of the activism of the civil rights and antiwar movements of the 1960s is also held out as evidence for the success of the new liberalism. Inspired in good part by the efforts of Ralph Nader, the movement led to the passage of many new consumer protection laws between 1967 and 1974. When Jimmy Carter became president in 1976, he appointed the leader of the Consumer Federation of America as an undersecretary of agriculture and the head of Nader's congressional watchdog group as the chair of the National Highway Traffic Safety Administration. In addition, a respected academic researcher was put in charge of the Occupational Safety and Health Administration, and a Senate staff member who helped to draft many of the new consumer safety laws became chair of the Federal Trade Commission.

However, there is less evidence of liberal power in this story than meets the eye, because the relevant business groups either agreed with the legislation or forced modifications to make it acceptable. Although the U.S. Chamber of Commerce registered its usual protestations, there was little or no business opposition to any of the consumer protection legislation of the 1960s. The important exception is the automobile industry's objections to the National Traffic and Motor Vehicle Safety Act, an effort to force them to make safer cars.[3]

The profound weakness of the consumer movement was exposed as long ago as 1978, when it could not win enactment for its mild proposal for an Agency for Consumer Advocacy. The envisioned agency would not have had any power to enforce laws or issue regulations, but only to gather information and help consumer groups when they approached federal agencies or asked for judicial reviews of agency actions. Nevertheless, the Business Roundtable and other corporate organizations strongly opposed the idea through the Roundtable's Consumers Issues Working Group. Although the act passed both houses of Congress in 1975, a final version was not sent to the White House because President Ford said he would veto it. Two years later, despite support from the newly elected Democratic president, the conservative voting bloc in the House rejected the bill.

The movement also failed in all its efforts to legislate greater corporate responsibility. Congress refused to consider the idea of federal charters for corporations, leaving them free to continue to incorporate in states like Delaware with very weak laws governing corporations. Nor did whistle-blowers within corporations receive any protections, leaving them at great risk for being disloyal to their employers. Plans to increase shareholder rights and strengthen the laws on corporate crime were rejected. A flurry of new initiatives at the Federal Trade Commission led to a strong reaction by Congress when it was inundated by complaints from the car dealers, funeral directors, and other business groups that felt put upon and harassed. Every reform was lost. In the early 1980s the ultraconservatives tried to abolish the Federal Trade Commission entirely, but it was saved with the help of corporate moderates who believe it has some uses.[4]

Surveying the successes and failures of consumer activists from the vantage point of the 1990s, the most detailed study of this movement concludes pluralists are wrong to claim that the new regulation starting in the 1970s is different from earlier forms of business regulation, even though it usually covers a wider array of industries. More generally, its authors conclude that business is the dominant force in the interest-group community despite the increase in nonbusiness interest groups in the 1970s.[5]

When all is said and done, the only significant defeat for a united corporate community since the 1960s is the establishment of the Occupational Safety and Health Administration, which was strongly opposed by corporate leaders as both a possible precedent for enlarging government regulation and a potential stronghold for unions. However, as stressed in Chapter 7, the ensuing history of this new agency is instructive in terms of corporate power, making it possible to go beyond the matter of success and failure on a specific piece of legislation to demonstrate the overall domination of government by the power elite. By the 1980s, as detailed studies show, the corporations had turned the agency into a political prisoner through delays in providing information, legislative amendments limiting its power, legal victories that further reduce its power, and budget cuts that make inspections fewer and more superficial.[6] As if to make this case even more difficult for pluralists, these changes occurred despite strong public sentiment in favor of enforcing workplace safety laws.

The Elite Theory

Another perspective, elite theory, intersects with class-dominance theory, agreeing with it on some crucial points, but disagreeing on others. The starting point for elite theorists is that all modern societies are dominated by elites, who are leaders based in bureaucratically structured organizations. Power is lodged at the top of these organizations, whether they are aimed at making a profit or not. The persons who hold this power have the money, time, contacts with other organizations, and authority over lower-level employees to shape political and many other outcomes outside their organizations. Still, the theory does not claim that everyday people are completely powerless; they sometimes have the ability to set limits on the actions of elites.[7]

Elite theorists are primarily interested in explaining historical and cross-national variations in the stability and representativeness of political regimes, so they pay relatively little attention to how and why specific constellations of elites dominate American society. They are more interested in how and why elites in all of today's rich democracies have developed political rules and behavioral patterns that enable them to resolve their conflicts peacefully, whereas in most other countries today, as well as in most of the rich democracies historically, elites have been deeply divided and prone to resolve their competitions violently.[8]

Elite theorists contribute important insights. Organizations are indeed the basis of power, because their leaders command great resources, have more information than those below them in the hierarchy, and can reward followers and punish critics. They can shape lower-level jobs so that the flexibility and information available to employees is limited. They can make alliances with the leaders of other organizations to strengthen their own positions.[9] Elite theorists also stress that American democracy provides one of history's most peaceful working and living environments, where ordinary people have achieved an unprecedented degree of prosperity, even though it disproportionately favors the corporate-based upper class They emphasize that the upper class remains open to challenge by other elite and nonelite interests, and that the task for these challengers is to achieve a more balanced distribution of power and privilege while preserving the overarching norms of elite restraint and conciliation that constitute the foundation of America's stable democracy.

However, elite theorists do not fully appreciate the class bias that is built into the policy-planning network and other nonprofit organizations in the United States. Historically, they are as antithetical to the concept of class as most class-oriented theorists are to organizational theory. Their lack of attention to class also leads them to underestimate the differences between business-dominated organizations and organizations based in the working class, especially unions and political parties. The leaders of unions and working-class parties work with the leaders of business-oriented organizations as elite theorists would emphasize, but many of their objectives remain class based.

Thus, as this book shows, it is the combination of insights from the class and elite traditions that explains the strength of the American power elite. Capitalism creates an ownership class that has great economic resources and the potential for political power. It also generates ongoing class conflict over wages, profits, works rules, taxes, and government regulation. Organizations give owners institutional resources that incorporate and legitimate their class resources. It is the interaction of class and organizational imperatives at the top of all American organizations, including government institutions, that leads to class domination in the United States. This viewpoint is in keeping with the basic starting point of the power structure research tradition that first developed in American sociology in the 1950s.[10]

The State Autonomy Theory

A final alternative perspective, state autonomy theory, suggests that predominant power is located in government, not in any class or coalition of groups. Following European usage, advocates of this theory talk of the state rather than of government, in part to emphasize the government's independence from the rest of society. This state independence, usually called *autonomy*, is said to be due to several intertwined factors: (1) its monopoly on the legitimate use of force within the country; (2) its unique role in defending the country from foreign rivals; and (3) its regulatory and taxing powers. Due to these powers, government officials have the capacity to impose their views on business groups no matter how united the corporate leaders might be. State autonomy theorists believe a growing budget and an increasing number of employees are indicators of the power of an agency or department within government. More generally, the alleged continued expansion of the federal government is sometimes said to be good evidence for the power of state officials.[11]

State autonomy theorists also stress that the institutional structure of the state—e.g., whether it is parliamentary or presidential, centralized or decentralized—has an important role in shaping party systems and political strategies. They also note that some institutions within the state can have a greater capacity for autonomy than others, and that state institutions sometimes strive for independence from one another.[12]

"The state" indeed has the potential for autonomy, but this book shows that this potential does not manifest itself in the United States. State autonomy is only possible when a state is unified and relatively impermeable to the employees and representatives of private organizations, but the American government is neither. For historical reasons explained in the next section, it is a fragmented government completely open to outside agents and therefore vulnerable to domination through the electoral process explained in Chapter 6 and through the appointments from the corporate community and policy-planning network documented in Chapter 7. The movement by members of the power elite between the private sector and government blurs the line between the corporate community and the state, which does not fit with the idea of state autonomy.

However, the state-oriented theorists are right to stress that the institutional structure of the state shapes the way in which political power is organized and exercised in the United States. As shown in Chapter 6, the election of a president by the country as a whole and the election of Congress on a state-by-state and district-by-district basis accounts for the strength of the two-party system. Moreover, the historic lack of large planning staffs in most executive departments made it possible for a private policy-planning network to flourish. Then, too, the division of American government into national, state, and local levels helps to explain why growth coalitions can be so powerful in most cities.

The state autonomy theorists are wrong for three reasons when they use increases in federal budgets and number of agency employees as power indicators. First, the size of a government does not necessarily say anything about how it is controlled. The government could grow and still be controlled by the power elite, as the establishment of the Social Security Administration discussed in Chapter 7 shows. There are no substitutes for the three power indicators. Second, the growth of government since at least the 1960s has been at the state and local levels, which does not fit with the image of an independently powerful federal government that aggrandizes more resources to itself. Third, as the most detailed and sophisticated study of federal government budgets reveals, budgets actually declined in size from 1950 to 1977 by 8.8 percent as a percentage of Gross Domestic Product when various biasing factors such as inflation are taken into account.[13] That decline continued from 1980, when federal spending was 21.6 percent of Gross Domestic product, to 2000, when the figure was 18.7 percent.

The findings on the number of government employees also contradict the expectations of state autonomy theory because the number of federal civilian and military employees declined in the 1990s, both in absolute numbers and as a percentage of the nation's total population. The main finding that emerges from a comparison of departments is that the Department of Defense dwarfs all others, employing over half of all federal employees when military personnel are included. When only civilian employees are counted, that department is still three to seven times bigger than its nearest rivals.

To conclude this brief discussion of three alternative views, it can be added that none of them can account for the strong findings in this book on all three power indicators. They do not explain why the wealth and income distributions would be so highly skewed if the corporate owners are not disproportionately powerful, or why women and men from the power elite would be overrepresented in key government positions and decision-making groups. They also do not comprehend the power alignments in legislative battles, as outlined in

Chapter 7. Finally, the pluralist and state autonomy views do not have the historical and comparative scope to explain why the corporate community is so powerful in the United States.

WHY IS THE CORPORATE COMMUNITY SO POWERFUL?

How is such a high concentration of corporate power possible? This question can be answered with the insights gained by comparing America's history to the histories of democratic countries in Europe. There are two separate but intertwined historical reasons for class domination in the United States. First, the corporate community in America is stronger because it didn't have to contend with feudal aristocrats, strong states, and the hierarchy of an established church. Second, those who work for wages and salaries are weaker as a class than in other democratic countries because they never have been able to establish an organizational base in either the economy or the political system.

The historical factors leading to a decentralized and relatively powerless federal government are especially important in understanding modern corporate dominance. The pre-Revolutionary history of the United States as a set of separate colonial territories, only lightly overseen by the appointed governors representing the British crown, left plenty of room for the development of wealthy merchants and slaveholders, primarily because the colonial governments were so small. The Founding Fathers, as the representatives of the separate colonial capitalist classes, were therefore able to create a government with divided and limited powers that was designed to accommodate the concerns of both Southern slave owners and Northern merchants and manufacturers. They took special care to deal with the fears of the Southern rich, who rightly worried that a strong federal government might lead to the abolishment of slavery in an industrializing society. Although the plan failed in that differences over the expansion of slavery into western territories led to a murderous Civil War, afterwards the Southern and Northern rich could once again agree in opposing any federal program or agency that might aid those who work with their hands in factories or fields, an agreement that came to be known as the conservative voting bloc during the 1930s.

The federal government also remained small because of the absence of any dangerous rival nations along the country's borders. In addition, the British navy provided a deterrent against invasion by any other European states throughout most of the nineteenth century, and U.S. involvement in World War I was relatively brief, with no postwar European military obligations. Thus, the United States did not have a permanent military establishment until World War II. By contrast, the nation-states that survived the severe competition among rival groups in Europe were the ones with strong central governments and large military organizations. These countries came into the modern era with strong states that intertwined with the old aristocracy, so capitalists had to compete for power. The result is a more complex power equation.

Within this context, it is very important that there were big corporations by the second half of the nineteenth century, well before there was any semblance of a so-called big government at the national level. These corporations and their associated policy-planning organizations were able to play the major role in shaping the regulatory agencies and White House offices that became important in the twentieth century. The power elite also dominated the creation of the large military machine during World War II.[14]

For all the early divisions between property owners in the North and South, ordinary Americans were even more divided from the beginning—free white farmers and artisans in the North and black slaves in the South. These divisions were exacerbated by the arrival of immigrants from eastern and southern Europe in the late nineteenth century, who were viewed by entrenched skilled workers of northern European origins as a threat to the tight labor markets they enjoyed.[15] To make matters worse, there was no good way to overcome these divisions because bold activists could not develop strong trade unions in the North, where governments were dominated by capitalists.

Despite these problems, the working-class movement in the Northern United States was very similar to the ones in Britain and France between the 1830s and the 1880s. Then, its attempts at class-wide organization were defeated by highly organized and violence-prone employers, who had the support of the local and state governments controlled by the political parties they dominated. In that atmosphere, only skilled workers were able to unionize, usually in business sectors where there were a large number of highly competitive small owners. such as construction, coal mining, and garment making. By contrast, capitalists in Britain and France were forced by government, still dominated by landed aristocrats and administrative elites, to compromise with unions.[16]

More generally, most large-scale attempts at union organizing between the 1880s and 1936 were broken up by government troops or the armed private police forces controlled by corporations. More violence was directed against the American labor movement than any other labor movement in a Western democracy. It was not until early 1937, shortly after the landslide reelection of Franklin D. Roosevelt to the presidency, along with the election of liberal governors in Pennsylvania and Michigan, that industrial unions were able to organize in some Northern states. Braced by their electoral victories, and facing highly organized union activists, these elected officials refused to send federal troops or state police to arrest workers when they took over factories.[17]

This refusal to honor repeated requests from corporate leaders for armed intervention—on the grounds that sit-down strikes were a form of trespassing on private property—marked the first time in American history that government force was not used to break a major strike.* The result was a victory for union organizers in the automobile, rubber, and other heavy industries. Just a year later, however, state police in Ohio, Indiana, and Illinois helped owners defeat strikers who were trying to organize the steel industry.[18] This sequence of success and failure supports an important claim by a historian specializing in American radicalism, who concludes that "the central importance of government mediation, and of the alliance with the Democrats, has been glossed over" in many accounts of this surge in union organizing.[19] Pro-labor authors instead focus solely on the leadership provided at the grassroots by leftists and the courage of the workers.

Nor could workers gain a toehold in the political system because the government structure and electoral rules led inexorably to a two-party system, as explained in Chapter 6. Thus, there was no way for people to come together to create programs that might help to transcend the white-black and old immigrant–new immigrant divisions. Once again, the situation was different in European countries, mainly because their parliamentary systems made the development of a labor or socialist party more feasible.[20]

Workers in America also suffered from the fact that they were unable to form a solid alliance with middle-class and well-off liberals. This difficulty had its roots in two atypical factors not present in European countries. First, the small trade union movement that developed in the late nineteenth century was strongly antigovernment because it saw government as controlled by capitalists. It was therefore suspicious of the liberals' desire to use government to tame and reform the big corporations. Second, due to the absence of a liberal or labor party, there was no meeting ground where the potential allies could work out their differences and develop a common program.[21] Only after 1935 did the Democratic Party fill part of this need, when the leadership of the new industrial union movement and liberals formed

---

*In 1939, the Supreme Court ruled sit-down strikes unconstitutional on the grounds that they violated the rights of private property.

the liberal-labor coalition within the context of the larger New Deal coalition.[22]

Lacking an organizational base in unions and a party that could formulate and popularize a communal, pro-government ethos, there was little possibility for the American working class to overcome the strong individualism and racial prejudice that has pervaded the United States. Thus, these divisive orientations persist among nonunionized white workers and matter in terms of union organizing and voting patterns.

In closing this discussion of why the corporate community is so powerful in the United States, it needs to be emphasized that the strong case for class domination in the United States does not demonstrate that there is class domination everywhere. In fact, the ubiquity of class domination is in great dispute in the social sciences. The Marxist theoretical school argues that the dominant power group is usually the economic class that owns the means of production, but it does allow for government autonomy or mixed power structures in times of large-scale societal transitions. It also claims that class struggle between owners and nonowners is the major determinant of historical change.[23]

Non-Marxist class theorists doubt that class domination and class conflict are always at the center of the power equation. They believe that governmental, military, and religious power have an independent status, and that they have been important in some times and places in Western history. For example, they argue that the empires at the dawn of civilization were dominated by state rulers, not property owners, and that the military had greater power than owners in the Roman Empire. Even after the development of capitalism, the non-Marxists continue, feudal lords and state leaders remained powerful longer than Marxists believe.[24]

This book does not try to adjudicate these long-standing theoretical disputes. They are tangential to its purpose, which is simply to demonstrate and explain class domination in the United States. Because the present study is narrowly focused as to time and place, its conclusion of class domination is compatible with Marxian and non-Marxian theories of history and power.

Nor does this book imply that the extreme degree of class domination found in the United States is inevitable in the future. It recognizes that power structures do change, as demonstrated most dramatically by the nonviolent collapse of the Soviet Union and the relatively peaceful replacement of white rule and a repressive system of apartheid in South Africa. Rather obviously, nothing so large-scale seems likely in the United States, but the potential for changes in the

American power structure created by the Civil Rights Movement are explored in the final section.

THE TRANSFORMATION OF AMERICAN POLITICS

With the Northern rich dominating the Republicans and the Southern rich dominating the Democrats, and a conservative voting bloc of Northern Republicans and Southern Democrats controlling Congress on class issues, there was little chance of egalitarian social change through the electoral system for much of American history. Those who had social grievances therefore resorted to social movements outside of the electoral system to try to win new rights, including in some cases the right to vote. In terms of challenges to the corporate community, the successes of the antinuclear movement are a good recent example of the power of social movements.[25]

The largest, most sustained, and best known of these social movements, the Civil Rights Movement of the 1950s and 1960s, not only transformed the lives of African-Americans in the South and made possible the growth of a black middle class throughout the nation, it altered the underlying nature of the American power structure as well. It created political openings that may or may not be utilized in the future. Specifically, the Voting Rights Act of 1965 made it possible for African-Americans to help defeat open segregationists and other ultraconservatives in Democratic primaries in the South, thereby pushing them into the Republican Party. This in turn provides the opportunity to remake the national Democratic Party as an expression of the liberal-labor coalition. The pressure on conservative Democrats from black voters was complemented by the fact that the gradual industrialization of the South since World War II made the situation of the Southern segment of the corporate community even more similar to that of its Northern counterpart.[26] When the Democratic Party could no longer fulfill its main historical function, namely, keeping African-Americans powerless, it was relatively easy for wealthy white conservatives to become Republicans.

Although the changing political economy of the South made the complete oppression of African-Americans less crucial for the white rich, civil rights did not come easily, or simply through changes in public opinion, although most Americans favored civil rights for African-Americans by 1964. In fact, the civil rights acts of 1964 and 1965 would not have passed without the social disruption created by the movement, because the conservative voting bloc was not prepared to budge despite moral appeals to decency and the clear ring of public opinion at that point. The Northern Republicans did not abandon the Southern Democrats on this issue until the power elite, confronted with the potential for ongoing social turmoil in inner cities across the nation, decided to move in an accommodating direction to bring the South more in line with practices in the rest of the country. It was only at this juncture that enough Republicans finally broke with the Southern Democrats to end a thirteen-week filibuster, the longest in Senate history.[27]

Once civil rights and voting rights legislation was enacted, the white Southern rich used racial resentments and religious conservatism to carry middle- and low-income white Southerners into the Republican Party with them. At the presidential level, this exodus led to the collapse of the New Deal coalition that had governed for most of the years after 1932. As a result, Republicans held the presidency for all but four years between 1968 and 1992, and gradually consolidated a nationwide conservative Republican majority that gained control of both the Senate and the House in 1994. The abandonment of the Democrats at the congressional level did not happen even faster primarily because the seniority enjoyed by many Southern Democrats gave them considerable power in national politics as long as that party maintained a majority in Congress. Wherever possible, then, Southern whites continued to control the Democratic Party at the local level, even while usually voting Republican at the national level. The result was a split party system in the South from 1968 to 1994.

In the long run, however, the Civil Rights Movement created the possibility for developing a stronger liberal-labor coalition that could use the nationwide Democratic Party as an organizing base for the first time in American history. This could allow the Democrats to develop a distinct program and image, which would make name recognition, personality, and campaign finance less important as its voters came to identify more strongly with the party. Whether its image has changed very fast or not, the opening of the Democratic Party normalized American politics at the national level. The result is that the two parties have never been more different along a liberal-conservative dimension than they are now. Unlike the situation just ten to fifteen years ago, there are few Democrats who are as conservative as the most moderate Republicans.[28]

For a nationwide liberal-labor coalition to be successful, however, it would need to have sixty votes in the Senate, which is the number now necessary to break a filibuster, a majority in the House, and a moderate to liberal Democrat as president. Winning that number of seats in Congress would be a daunting task because of the conservatism of the Southern and Great Plains states. The greatest opportunity lies in trying to create liberal black-white voting coalitions in the fourteen Southern states, which have roughly 30 percent of congressional seats and hence 30 percent of the Electoral College votes needed to win the presidency. Since African-Americans are now so important to the Democratic Party in the South, this would have to be a coalition of equals, but racial resentments and feelings of superiority would make it difficult for whites to accept such a coalition. There is also the problem that neither white nor black Southerners are as supportive of social liberalism as Democrats outside the South.

The difficulties of winning liberal Democratic victories in very many parts of the South is best demonstrated in a study of six special congressional elections between 1981 and 1993, all made necessary by deaths or resignations. Surprisingly, all six were won by white conservative Democrats, who took several steps to defeat even more conservative Republicans: (1) They first established their conservatism on key social issues like school prayer, the death penalty, and gun control; (2) then they pointed out that the extraordinarily antigovernment stance of the Republicans could be bad for the South if it led to a reduction in federal subsidies of various kinds; (3) they emphasized their long-standing local ties; and (4) they quietly cultivated the African-American vote by advertising on black radio stations, visiting black churches in the company of black campaign workers, and saying they would uphold civil rights legislation.[29]

As these cases show, there has been very little trend toward a more liberal politics in the South. All of the Southern Republicans in the Senate and House are conservatives, as are all but one or two of the Democratic senators and ten to fifteen of the remaining white Southern Democrats in the House. Overall, three-fourths of the congressional representatives from the South are conservatives. The major change has been the election of sixteen liberal African-Americans to the House, all from majority black districts when they were originally elected.

ENVOI

Even if a nationwide liberal-labor coalition were able to transform the Democratic Party through coordinated challenges in its primaries from precinct to president, there would be no guarantee of success in winning control of the federal government and altering or softening its pro-corporate policies. The corporate community described in this book commands great wealth, the best advice money can buy, and direct access to government officials. Its employees in the policy-planning and opinion-shaping networks have polished antigovernment rhetoric and rags-to-riches success stories to a small science. Its success in the policy arena put unions on the defensive and created a low-wage economy that allows for both high levels of employment and corporate control of the labor market.

In addition, the men and women of the power elite enjoy the admiration of a great many voters, and their political operatives are adept at subordinating economic issues by making subtle symbolic appeals based on race and religion. Most of all, the structural power conferred upon the corporate community by the system of private property and markets would be difficult to overcome without very creative new programs that build on the flexibility that markets provide.[30]

Still, as stressed earlier in this chapter, social change does occur in unexpected ways and times, and that holds true for the United States. No one imagined there would be a New Deal in the face of the Great Depression, or that a massive, nonviolent Civil Rights Movement would come roaring out of the Silent Fifties, generating antiwar, feminist, and environmental movements in its train. Social scientists and historians can outline the structure of power and analyze trends, but they cannot predict the future. All anyone knows for sure, thanks in good part to historical hindsight, is that societies do change. The analysis presented in this book is based on that open-ended spirit.

APPENDIX A

How to Do Research on Power

NETWORK ANALYSIS

The empirical study of power begins with a search for connections among the people and organizations that are thought to constitute the powerful group or class. As noted in Chapter 1, this procedure is called *membership network analysis*. The results of a membership network analysis are usually presented in the form of a matrix, as shown in Table A.1. The people are listed from the top to bottom and the organizations are arrayed from left to right. The *cells* or boxes created by the intersection of a person and organization are filled with *relational information* such as member, director, owner, or financial donor. The attitudes the person has toward any given organization in the matrix also can be included, such as supporter or opponent. The information used in filling the cells of the matrix is obtained in a variety of ways described later in this appendix.

The information contained in the matrix is used to create the *organizational* and *interpersonal* networks explained in Chapter 1. Fig-

Table A.1 Hypothetical Membership Network

	Organizations			
Individuals	A	B	C	D
1	X	X		
2	X		X	
3	X			X
4			X	X
5*				

* Person 5 is an *isolate* with no connections.

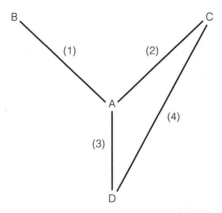

Figure A.1 Hypothetical Organization Network Created by Overlapping Members

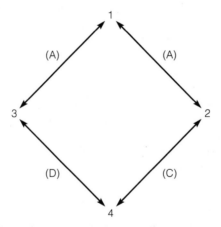

Figure A.2 Hypothetical Interpersonal Network Created by Common Organizational Affiliations

ure A.1 displays an organizational network based on the overlapping members in Table A.1. It shows that organization A is at the center of the network. Figure A.2 shows the interpersonal network that emerges from Table A.1. Note that no one person is at the center of the network even though the organizational network had a center. Note also in Table A.1 that one person is an *isolate*, with no connections, a not uncommon situation for most Americans in terms of power networks.

Large and complicated membership networks can be analyzed using computer software based on sophisticated mathematical techniques, such as graph theory, matrix algebra, and boolean algebra (an algebra that detects *hierarchies* or *levels* in a large complex network). Most of this software, except the boolean program, is available in UCINET 4, a DOS program that is menu driven and can be set up to run under the Windows operating system. It can be downloaded for free on the Internet. For advanced applications, UCINET 5 for Windows can be obtained by students for $40 from Analytic Technologies, Inc. For information, see the Analytic Technologies Web page at www.analytictech.com; information is also available through sales @analytictech.com, and at 978-456-7372.

Once the membership networks have been established, there are many other types of links that might be analyzed, such as kinship ties or flows of information between organizations. One of the most important of these other types of links concerns the size and direction of money flows in the network. In theory, money flows are another kind of relationship between people or institutions, but in practice it is a good idea to consider them separately because they are socially distinct in most people's minds. There are four kinds of money flows:

1. people to people (e.g., gifts, loans, campaign donations);
2. people to institutions (e.g., taxes to government, individual or family gifts to foundations);
3. institutions to people (e.g., corporate dividends to stockholders, foundation grants to research experts);
4. institutions to institutions (e.g., foundation grants to policy-discussion groups, corporate donations to foundations).

The first finding from network analyses using relational data or money flows is whether or not the group or class under consideration actually exists as a social reality. If no connections among corporations are found, for example, then it makes no sense to speak of a *corporate community*. If there are few or no overlapping memberships among exclusive social clubs in different cities, then it is less likely that there is a nationwide *upper class*. If there are no money flows from wealthy people to foundations or from foundations to policy discussion groups, then there is very little basis for talking about a *policy-planning network*.

The second finding from membership network analysis concerns various characteristics of organizational and interpersonal networks, such as their density and the existence of central points or subgroups. Some parts in a social network may have more interconnections than others, for example, or some types of businesses might be more central in the corporate community, or there might be moderately conservative and extremely conservative subgroups within the overall policy-planning network.

CONTENT ANALYSIS

Once a membership network is constructed, it is possible to take the next necessary step in the study of social power, an analysis of the ideology and policy preferences of the group or class under scrutiny. This is done by studying the verbal and written output of strategically located people or organizations in the network; that is, speeches, policy statements, campaign literature, and proposed legislation. Technically speaking, such studies are called *content analysis* in the social sciences. Content analyses are not always done formally, but content analysis is what investigators are doing when they infer on the basis of a speech or policy statement that a person or organization has specific values or policy preferences. That is, many content analyses are informal and intuitive, based on implicit categories that exist in the culture. To insure against personal biases, however, an objective and systematic content analysis is far more useful.

In the past, a systematic content analysis always began with the creation of carefully defined categories that related to the attitude or issue being studied. Categories could be constructed, for example, to determine a person or organization's stance toward corporations or labor unions. Once the categories were developed, relevant texts were studied to determine the frequency and intensity of elements that fit into one or more of the categories. Then, the various frequencies were analyzed by calculating averages or percentages. Finally, the averages or percentages for two or more groups were compared.

Thanks to the advent of personal computers, computer-assisted content analyses now can be done without a set of predefined categories. Word searches of computerized text give instant frequency comparisons. Texts also can be compared for tell-tale phrases that might reveal a connection between a private policy group and governmental legislation. There is also software to determine what concepts or phrases are interconnected in documents, a technique known as *semantic network analysis.* Moreover, many important texts are available on the Web and can be downloaded for analysis.[1] For two free and easy-to-use software programs for text processing see **WORDS** at http://www.dsu.edu/~johnsone/ and **VBPro** at http://excellent.com.utk.edu/~mmiller/bvppro.html.

SOURCES OF INFORMATION

Many different sources of information are employed to create membership networks or find textual material for content analysis. First, a wide variety of biographical reference volumes, magazines, and newspapers are used to gather relational information. They include the eighteen different *Who's Who*'s published by Marquis, which contain 770,000 names on a CD-ROM; the hundreds of magazines on MAGS in the University of California's computerized library information system (Melvyl); and the five newspapers included in NEWS on the same system (*New York Times, Los Angeles Times, Washington Post, Wall Street Journal,* and *Christian Science Monitor*). Then, too, *Who Knows Who,* Standard and Poor's *Register of Corporations and Directors,* the *Foundation Directory,* the *Grants Index,* Federal Elections Commission reports on campaign donations, and the annual reports of many organizations can be consulted.

Some of these standard sources, and many new ones, are now available on the Internet. For an exceptional Web site that provides an excellent overview of research on power and access to all of these sources, see *Who Rules?: An Internet Guide to Power Structure Research,* created by sociologist Val Burris at the University of Oregon. It is available at http://darkwing.uoregon.edu/~vburris/whorules/. This site provides direct links to Internet sources of data that make it possible to study, among many topics: (1) the backgrounds, economic interests, and social connections of individual members of a powerful group or class; (2) the internal power structures of major corporations and the political activities in which they are engaged; (3) the flow of money from corporations and wealthy business owners to political candidates and parties; (4) the role of special interests in lobbying congress and shaping legislation; and (5) the role of foundations, think tanks, and business associations in creating public policy. It also contains an excellent discussion of network analysis, a guide to library resources, and a list of suggested readings.

HOW TO STUDY LOCAL POWER

Information for the study of power at the city level may not be readily available via the Internet. For city studies, the following steps can be taken to assemble relevant information in a relatively quick fashion. The starting point is at the reference desk at the library:

1. Use the *Dun and Bradstreet Million Dollar Directory,* which has a section organized by city, to locate the major banks and corporations in the city under study.

2. Use the *Martindale-Hubbell Law Directory*, which is organized by state and city, to locate the major law firms for the city. It often will list the major clients for each firm, which makes it possible to see which law firms are related to the corporations located through the *Dun and Bradstreet* volume. *Martindale-Hubbell* also contains background information on the members of the law firms. (It is used by lawyers to make contacts for clients in other cities.)

3. Use the *Foundation Directory* to see if there are any major foundations in the city. Study the directors of these foundations to see if any of them come from the corporations and law firms located through steps 1 and 2.

4. Use the *Foundation Grants Index* to determine the organizations to which the local foundations gave grants. These organizations may be important ones in the city for areas ranging from the arts to public policy to social welfare. Study their boards of directors to see if they include people located through steps 1, 2, and 3.

5. Use the library indexes to find local social histories that might be a useful starting point for the study of social classes in the city. Ask the library archivist if the library contains the papers of prominent local people, which sometimes include social club membership lists and interesting correspondence related to past policy issues.

6. Go to the local chamber of commerce, city hall, United Way, labor unions, and other organizations in the city for copies of all printed material on their personnel and policies that they make available to the public. Integrate this material with information gained through steps 1 through 5.

7. Go to the local newspaper and ask to use its clip files, or "morgue," as its files are sometimes called. Ask if past issues of the newspaper have been put on a CD-ROM or a Web site that can be searched. Local newspapers are invaluable sources on businesses, law firms, people, and policy issues. They often have folders full of stories going back over many years on the organizations and people relevant to a power study.

8. Use the by-lines on stories, or ask newspaper employees, to determine the names of the reporters who are most knowledgeable on the topic being researched. Try to interview these people. If social class is a component of the study, ask to interview the "society" or "people" editor to gather information on high-status social clubs and other social institutions. From a social-science point of view, reporters are excellent informants. Always end interviews with reporters, and anyone else, for that matter, by asking for their suggestions as to other people it would be helpful to interview.

9. It is also possible to study power at the city level through an interview technique called the *reputational method*. With this method, the evidence for the power of a person or group is based on a reputation for being powerful, as determined by a series of interviews. It also can be used as a supplement or cross-check to the series of steps outlined above. The process begins in one of two ways.

First, nominations can be obtained from a cross-section of observers who are thought to be knowledgeable about the powerful on the basis of their occupational roles (e.g., reporter, administrator, fundraiser). Second, the people found through steps 1 through 4 to sit on several corporate or nonprofit boards of directors can be used as a starting point. Either way, the people on the list are then interviewed and asked for their nominations as to the most powerful people in the locale being studied, as well as for their opinions regarding the power of the other people on the original list. Any new nominees are then interviewed and asked for their opinions.

The process ends, usually within three or four rounds, when the same names keep coming up and no new names are added to the list. For brief studies, it can be decided beforehand to do only one or two rounds of interviewing. The method has a further advantage: The people being interviewed can be asked other questions, such as, What are the major issues in the city? How is policy made in this city? What was your role in one or more of the major issues?

The reputational method works best at the community or city level, where it is less expensive and time-consuming to apply than at the state or national level. It is especially valuable for small towns where very little printed information is available. However, the method has been used with good results in two studies of national power in the United States and in studies of Australia and Norway.[2]

ANALYZING POWER STRUCTURES

Now that membership network analysis and content analysis have been explained, and sources of information have been outlined it is also possible to provide a generic definition of a *power structure*. A power structure is the network of people and institutions in the city or nation under study that stands at the top on the power indicators it was possible to utilize in the study (Who Benefits?, Who Governs?, Who Wins?, and a Reputation for Power). See Chapter 1 for a discussion of the first three of these power indicators.

The methodological approach outlined in this appendix makes it possible to discover any concentration or configuration of power. It can be used by researchers of any theoretical persuasion because it is not biased for or against any given theory. It contains only one assumption: There is a power structure of some kind or another, no matter how weak or fragmented, in any large-scale society or social group. The method can discover that power is highly concentrated or more dispersed, depending on the degree of difference between rival networks on the power indicators. It can show that some groups or classes have power in one arena, some in another arena. It can reveal changes in a power structure over time by changes in the power indicators.

Although the methodological approach described in this appendix can be used in a general and exploratory way, in this book it is used with a focus on corporations as a starting point.

APPENDIX B

Indicators of Upper-Class Standing

Registers or Blue Books

The Social Register
Detroit Social Secretary
New Orleans Social Register
Seattle Blue Book

Coed and Boys' Schools

Asheville (Asheville, N.C.)
Buckley (New York, N.Y.)
Cate (Carpinteria, Calif.)
Catlin Gabel (Portland, Oreg.)
Choate (Wallingford, Conn.)
Country Day School (St. Louis, Mo.)
Cranbrook (Bloomfield Hills, Mich.)
Deerfield (Deerfield, Mass.)
Episcopal High (Alexandria, Va.)
Gilman (Baltimore, Md.)
Groton (Groton, Mass.)
Hill (Pottstown, Pa.)
Hotchkiss (Lakeville, Conn.)
Kent (Kent, Conn.)
Lake Forest (Lake Forest, Ill.)
Lakeside (Seattle, Wash.)
Lawrenceville (Lawrenceville, N.J.)
Middlesex (Concord, Mass.)
Milton (Milton, Mass.)
Pomfret (Pomfret, Conn.)
Ponahou (Honolulu, Hawaii)
Portsmouth Priority (Portsmouth, R.I.)
St. Andrew's (Middlebury, Del.)
St. Christopher's (Richmond, Va.)
St. George's (Newport, R.I.)
St. Mark's (Southborough, Mass.)
St. Paul's (Concord, N.H.)
Shattuck (Faribault, Minn.)

Taft (Watertown, Conn.)
Thatcher (Ojai, Calif.)
University School (Cleveland, Ohio)
Webb (Bell Buckle, Tenn.)
Westminster (Atlanta, Ga.)
Woodberry Forest (Woodberry Forest, Va.)

Girls' Schools

Abbot Academy (Andover, Mass.)
Agnes Irwin (Wynnewood, Pa.)
Anna Head (Berkeley, Calif.)
Annie Wright (Tacoma, Wash.)
Ashley Hall (Charleston, S.C.)
Baldwin (Bryn Mawr, Pa.)
Berkeley Institute (Brooklyn, N.Y.)
Bishop's (La Jolla, Calif.)
Brearly (New York, N.Y.)
Brimmer's and May (Chestnut Hill, Mass.)
Brooke Hill (Birmingham, Ala.)
Bryn Mawr (Baltimore, Md.)
Chapin (New York, N.Y.)
Chatham Hall (Chatham, Va.)
Collegiate (Richmond, Va.)
Concord Academy (Concord, Mass.)
Convent of the Sacred Heart (New York, N.Y.)
Dalton (New York, N.Y.)
Dana Hall (Wellesley, Mass.)
Emma Willard (Troy, N.Y.)
Ethel Walker (Simsbury, Conn.)
Foxcroft (Middleburg, Va.)
Garrison Forest (Garrison, Md.)
Hathaway Brown (Cleveland, Ohio)
Hockaday (Dallas, Tex.)
Katherine Branson (Ross, Calif.)
Kingswood (Bloomfield Hills, Mich.)
Kinkaid (Houston, Tex.)
Lake Forest Country Day (Lake Forest, Ill.)
Laurel (Cleveland, Ohio)
Louise S. McGehee (New Orleans, La.)
Madeira (Greenway, Va.)
Marlborough (Los Angeles, Calif.)
Mary Institute (St. Louis, Mo.)
Master's (Dobbs Ferry, N.Y.)
Miss Hall's (Pittsfield, Mass.)
Miss Hewitt's (New York, N.Y.)
Miss Porter's (Farmington, Conn.)
Mt. Vernon Seminary (Washington, D.C.)
Rosemary Hall (Greenwich, Conn.)
Salem Academy (Winston-Salem, N.C.)

Shipley (Bryn Mawr, Pa.)
Spence (New York, N.Y.)
St. Agnes Episcopal (Alexandria, Va.)
St. Catherine's (Richmond, Va.)
St. Mary's Hall (San Antonio, Tex.)
St. Nicholas (Seattle, Wash.)
St. Timothy's (Stevenson, Md.)
Stuart Hall (Staunton, Va.)
Walnut Hill (Natick, Mass.)
Westminster (Atlanta, Ga.)
Westover (Middlebury, Conn.)
Westridge (Pasadena, Calif.)

Country and Men's Clubs

Arlington (Portland, Oreg.)
Bohemian (San Francisco, Calif.)
Boston (New Orleans, La.)
Brook (New York, N.Y.)
Burlingame Country Club (San Francisco, Calif.)
California (Los Angeles, Calif.)
Chagrin Valley Hunt (Cleveland, Ohio)
Charleston (Charleston, S.C.)
Chicago (Chicago, Ill.)
Cuyamuca (San Diego, Calif.)
Denver (Denver, Colo.)
Detroit (Detroit, Mich.)
Eagle Lake (Houston, Tex.)
Everglades (Palm Beach, Calif.)
Hartford (Hartford, Conn.)
Hope (Providence, R.I.)
Idlewild (Dallas, Tex.)
Knickerbocker (New York, N.Y.)
Links (New York, N.Y.)
Maryland (Baltimore, Md.)
Milwaukee (Milwaukee, Wis.)
Minneapolis (Minneapolis, Minn.)
Pacific Union (San Francisco, Calif.)
Philadelphia (Philadelphia, Pa.)
Piedmont Driving (Atlanta, Ga.)
Piping Rock (New York, N.Y.)
Racquet Club (St. Louis, Mo.)
Rainier (Seattle, Wash.)
Richmond German (Richmond, Va.)
Rittenhouse (Philadelphia, Pa.)
River (New York, N.Y.)
Rolling Rock (Pittsburgh, Pa.)
Saturn (Buffalo, N.Y.)
St. Cecelia (Charleston, S.C.)
St. Louis County Club (St. Louis, Mo.)

Somerset (Boston, Mass.)
Union (Cleveland, Ohio)
Woodhill Country Club (Minneapolis, Minn.)

Women's Clubs

Acorn (Philadelphia, Pa.)
Chilton (Boston, Mass.)
Colony (New York, N.Y.)
Fortnightly (Chicago, Ill.)
Friday (Chicago, Ill.)
Mt. Vernon Club (Baltimore, Md.)
Society of Colonial Dames (Washington, D.C.)
Sulgrave (Washington, D.C.)
Sunset (Seattle, Wash.)
Vincent (Boston, Mass.)

Notes

Introduction: Why Bother to Read This Book?

1. Aaron Bernstein, "Too Much Corporate Power?," *Business Week*, 11 September 2000, 145–149.
2. Tim Smart, "Pay Gap Widens between Workers, Top Execs," *Washington Post*, 30 August 1999, 2; Chuck Collins, Betsy Leondar-Wright, and Holly Sklar, *Shifting Fortunes: The Perils of the Growing American Wealth Gap* (Boston United for a Fair Economy, 1999).
3. Don Van Natta and John Broder, "With Finish Line in Sight, An All-Out Race for Money," *New York Times*, 3 November 2000, A24.
4. Harold Meyerson, "Powerlines: Here Comes the Democratic Majority," *LA Weekly*, 22 December 2000, 1; Stanley B. Greenberg, *Middle Class Dreams: The Politics and Power of the New American Majority* (New Haven: Yale University Press, 1996).
5. Steven Greenhouse, "Corruption Tests Labor While It Recruits," *New York Times*, 3 January 1999, 14.
6. Thomas Byrne Edsall, *Chain Reaction: The Impact of Race, Rights, and Taxes on American Politics* (New York: Norton, 1992).
7. Marjorie Connelly, "Who Voted: A Portrait of American Politics, 1976–2000," *New York Times*, 12 November 2000, 4; Michael X. Delli Carpini and Scott Keeter, *What Americans Know about Politics and Why It Matters* (New Haven: Yale University Press, 1996); Richard Flacks, *Making History: The Radical Tradition in American Life* (New York: Columbia University Press, 1988).

Chapter 1: Class and Power in America

1. Robert R. Palmer, *The Age of the Democratic Revolution: A Political History of Europe and America, 1760–1800* (Princeton: Princeton University Press, 1959), p. 203.
2. Jackson T. Main, *The Social Structure of Revolutionary America* (Princeton: Princeton University Press, 1965), pp. 239, 284.
3. Robert R. Palmer, *The Age of the Democratic Revolution: A Political History of Europe and America, 1760–1800* (Princeton: Princeton University Press, 1959), p. 3.

4. Richard P. Coleman, Lee Rainwater, and Kent A. McClelland, *Social Standing in America: New Dimensions of Class* (New York: Basic Books, 1978).

5. Richard P. Coleman, Lee Rainwater, and Kent A. McClelland, *Social Standing in America: New Dimensions of Class* (New York: Basic Books, 1978), p. 25.

6. August de Belmont Hollingshead and Fredrick C. Redlich, *Social Class and Mental Illness: A Community Study* (New York: Wiley, 1958), p. 69.

7. Susan Ostrander, "Upper-class Women: Class Consciousness as Conduct and Meaning," in *Power Structure Research*, ed. G. William Domhoff (Beverly Hills: Sage Publications, 1980), pp. 78–79.

8. John Goldthorpe, "Rent, Class Conflict, and Class Structure: A Commentary on Sorensen," *American Journal of Sociology* 105, no. 6 (2000): 1572–1582; Aage Sorensen, "Toward a Sounder Basis for Class Analysis," *American Journal of Sociology* 105, no. 6 (2000): 1523–1558; Erik O. Wright, "Class, Exploitation, and Economic Rents: Reflections on Sorensen's 'Sounder Basis,'" *American Journal of Sociology* 105, no. 6 (2000): 1559–1571.

9. Michael Mann, "Ruling Class Strategies and Citizenship," *Sociology* 21, no. 3 (1987): 339–354; Michael Mann, *The Sources of Social Power: A History of Power from the Beginning to A.D. 1760*, vol. 1 (New York: Cambridge University Press, 1986).

10. Ronald L. Breiger, "The Duality of Persons and Groups," *Social Forces* 53, no. 2 (1974): 181–190.

11. E. Digby Baltzell, *Philadelphia Gentlemen: The Making of a National Upper Class* (Glencoe, Ill.: Free Press, 1958).

12. G. William Domhoff, *The Higher Circles* (New York: Random House, 1970), chapter 1.

13. Richard P. Coleman, Lee Rainwater, and Kent A. McClelland, *Social Standing in America: New Dimensions of Class* (New York: Basic Books, 1978).

14. G. William Domhoff, *Who Rules America Now?* (New York: Simon & Schuster, 1983).

15. Richard L. Zweigenhaft and G. William Domhoff, *Jews in the Protestant Establishment* (New York: Praeger, 1982).

16. Robert R. Palmer, *The Age of the Democratic Revolution: A Political History of Europe and America, 1760–1800* (Princeton: Princeton University Press, 1959).

17. David Vogel, "Why Businessmen Mistrust Their State: The Political Consciousness of American Corporate Executives," *British Journal of Political Science* 8 (1978): 45–78.

18. Dennis Wrong, *Power: Its Forms, Bases, and Uses* (New Brunswick, N.J.: Transaction Publishers, 1995), p. 2.

19. Paul Lazarsfeld, "Concept Formation and Measurement," in *Concepts, Theory, and Explanation in the Behavioral Sciences*, ed. Gordon DiRenzo (New York: Random House, 1966), 144–202.

20. Christopher Hewitt, "The Effect of Political Democracy and Social Democracy on Equality in Industrial Societies: A Cross-National Comparison," *American Sociological Review* 42, no. 3 (1977): 450–464.

21. John Stephens, *The Transition from Capitalism to Socialism* (London: Macmillan, 1979).
22. W. L. Guttsman, *The English Ruling Class* (London: Weidenfeld & Nicholson, 1969).
23. Richard L. Zweigenhaft and G. William Domhoff, *Diversity in the Power Elite: Have Women and Minorities Reached the Top?* (New Haven: Yale University Press, 1998).

Chapter 2: The Corporate Community

1. Robert F. Dalzell, *Enterprising Elite: The Boston Associates and the World They Made* (Cambridge: Harvard University Press, 1987).
2. David Bunting, "Origins of the American Corporate Network," *Social Science History* 7 (1983): 129–142.
3. William G. Roy, "Interlocking Directorates and the Corporate Revolution," *Social Science History* 7 (1983): 143–164.
4. William G. Roy, *Socializing Capital: The Rise of the Large Industrial Corporation in America* (Princeton: Princeton University Press, 1997).
5. Mark S. Mizruchi, *The American Corporate Network, 1904–1974* (Beverly Hills: Sage Publications, 1982); Mark S. Mizruchi, "Relations among Corporations, 1904–1974," *Social Science History* 7 (1983): 165–182.
6. Myles L. Mace, *Directors, Myth and Reality* (Boston: Harvard Business School Press, 1986); Mayer N. Zald, "The Power and Functions of Boards of Directors: A Theoretical Synthesis," *American Journal of Sociology* 75 (1969): 97–117.
7. Michael Useem, *The Inner Circle: Large Corporations and the Rise of Business Political Activity in the U.S. and U.K.* (New York: Oxford University Press, 1984); Joseph Galaskiewicz et al., "The Influence of Corporate Power, Social Status, and Market Position on Corporate Interlocks in a Regional Network," *Social Forces* 64 (1985): 403–432.
8. Richard L. Zweigenhaft and G. William Domhoff, *Jews in the Protestant Establishment* (New York: Praeger, 1982); Richard L. Zweigenhaft and G. William Domhoff, *Diversity in the Power Elite: Have Women and Minorities Reached the Top?* (New Haven: Yale University Press, 1998).
9. Mayer N. Zald, "The Power and Functions of Boards of Directors: A Theoretical Synthesis," *American Journal of Sociology* 75 (1969): 97–117; Nancy DiTomaso, "Organizational Analysis and Power Structure Research," in *Power Structure Research*, ed. G. William Domhoff (Beverly Hills: Sage Publications, 1980), 255–268; Susan Ostrander, "Elite Domination in Private Social Agencies: How It Happens and How It Is Challenged," in *Power Elites and Organizations*, ed. G. William Domhoff and Thomas Dye (Beverly Hills: Sage Publications, 1987), 85–102.
10. Peter Mariolis, "Interlocking Directorates and Control of Corporations," *Social Sciences Quarterly* 56 (1975): 425–439.
11. Thomas R. Dye, *Who's Running America?: The Clinton Years* (Englewood Cliffs, N.J.: Prentice Hall, 1995).
12. Gerald F. Davis and Mark S. Mizruchi, "The Money Center Cannot Hold: Commercial Banks in the U.S. System of Corporate Governance," *Administrative Science Quarterly* 2 (June 1999): 215.

13. Thomas Koenig and Robert Gogel, "Interlocking Corporate Directorships as a Social Network," *American Journal of Economics and Sociology* 40, no. 1 (1981): 37–50; Donald Palmer, "Broken Ties: Interlocking Directorates and Intercorporate Coordination," *Administrative Science Quarterly* 28, no. 1 (1983): 40–55.

14. Richard L. Zweigenhaft and G. William Domhoff, *Diversity in the Power Elite: Have Women and Minorities Reached the Top?* (New Haven: Yale University Press, 1998).

15. David Bunting, "Origins of the American Corporate Network," *Social Science History* 7 (1983): 129–142; William G. Roy, "Interlocking Directorates and the Corporate Revolution," *Social Science History* 7 (1983): 143–164.

16. Michael Useem, *The Inner Circle: Large Corporations and the Rise of Business Political Activity in the U.S. and U.K.* (New York: Oxford University Press, 1984).

17. Bennett Harrison, *Lean and Mean: The Changing Landscape of Corporate Power in the Age of Flexibility* (New York: Basic Books, 1994).

18. Bennett Harrison, *Lean and Mean: The Changing Landscape of Corporate Power in the Age of Flexibility* (New York: Basic Books, 1994), p. 47.

19. James A. Gross, *Broken Promise: The Subversion of U.S. Labor Relations Policy, 1947–1994* (Philadelphia: Temple University Press, 1995).

20. James Fallows, "Internet Illusions," *New York Review,* 16 November 2000, 28–31.

21. Mark Leibovich, "A Case of Global Ambition," *Washington Post Weekly,* 26 June 2000, 6.

22. Jacob Goldman, "Innovation Isn't the Microsoft Way," *New York Times,* 10 June 2000, A27.

23. Steven Pearlstein, "What Goes Up Must Come Down," *Washington Post Weekly,* 6 November 2000, 16; Paul M. Sherer, "ICG Files for Chapter 11, Lines Up Chase Loan," *Wall Street Journal,* 15 November 2000, C17(W), C17(L).

24. Saul Hansell, "Holiday Traffic at Online-Only Stores Lags Chains' Sites," *New York Times,* 4 December 2000, C8.

25. Janet Abbate, *Inventing the Internet* (Cambridge: MIT Press, 1999).

26. Barnaby Feder, "New Economy," *New York Times,* 18 November 2000, C4.

27. Reed E. Hundt, *You Say You Want a Revolution: A Story of Information Age Politics* (New Haven: Yale University Press, 2000).

28. Kathleen Pender, "Giant Cisco Didn't Pay Any Federal Income Tax," *San Francisco Chronicle,* 8 October 2000, 1; Gretchen Morgenstern, "Options Seen to Be Coming Home to Roost," *New York Times,* 8 October 2000, C1; Floyd Norris, "Levitt to Leave S.E.C. Early; Bush to Pick 4," *New York Times,* December 21 2000, C1.

29. Elizabeth Palmer, "Well-Timed Push on H-1B Bill Gives Businesses All They Asked," *CQ Weekly,* 7 October 2000, 2331–2333.

30. Neil Munro, "For Richer and Poorer," *National Journal,* 18 July 2000, 1676–1680.

31. Rachel Parker-Gwin and William G. Roy, "Corporate Law and the Organization of Property in the United States: The Origin and Institutionalization of New Jersey Corporation Law, 1888–1903," *Politics & Society,* June 1996, 111(25).

32. Robert L. Nelson, "Partners with Power: The Social Transformation of the Large Law Firm," (Berkeley: University of California Press, 1988), p. 232.

33. Robert L. Nelson, "Partners with Power: The Social Transformation of the Large Law Firm," (Berkeley: University of California Press, 1988), pp. 264, 269.

34. Robert Granfield, *Making Elite Lawyers: Visions of Law at Harvard and Beyond* (New York: Routledge, 1992).

35. Dan Carney, "Mr. Class Action Goes to Washington?," *Business Week*, 11 September 2000, 100–104.

36. Michael Useem, *Investor Capitalism: How Money Managers Are Changing the Face of Corporate America*, 1st ed. (New York: Basic Books, 1996).

37. Hilary Rosenberg, *A Traitor to His Class: Robert A.G. Monks and the Battle to Change Corporate America* (New York: Wiley & Sons, 1999).

38. Judith H. Dobrzynski, "Tales from the Boardroom Wars: CALPERS' Hanson on His Long Fight for Shareholders' Rights," *Business Week*, 6 June 1994, 71(2).

39. George Anders, "Restless Natives: While Head of CALPERS Lectures Other Firms, His Own Board Frets," *Wall Street Journal* 1993, A1; Judith Dobrzynski, "Is Pete Wilson Trying to Mute a Shareholder Activist?," *Business Week*, 1 July 1991, 29; Jack Egan, "The Elephant That Roared," *U.S. News & World Report*, 7 October 1991, 95(1); Martha Groves, "CALPERS Plans to Take Softer Line in Tactics," *Los Angeles Times*, 8 October 1991, D2; Margaret M. Blair, *Ownership and Control: Rethinking Corporate Governance for the Twenty-first Century* (Washington, D.C.: Brookings Institution Press, 1995), pp. 184ff.

40. Judith H. Dobrzynski, "Investor Group's Leadership Vote Is a Rebuff to Union Members," *New York Times*, 2 April 1996, C2(N), D23(L); Judith H. Dobrzynski, "Shareholder-Rights Group Faces a Fight over Its Own Leadership," *New York Times*, 1 April 1996, A1(N), D2(L).

41. Kathleen Day, "A Voice for Stockholders," Washington Post Weekly, 4 September 2000, 18–19.

42. Margaret M. Blair, *Ownership and Control: Rethinking Corporate Governance for the Twenty-first Century* (Washington, D.C.: Brookings Institution Press, 1995).

43. G. William Domhoff, *State Autonomy or Class Dominance? Case Studies on Policy Making in America* (Hawthorne, N.Y.: Aldine de Gruyter, 1996), Chapter 3; Grant McConnell, *The Decline of Agrarian Democracy* (Berkeley: University of California Press, 1953).

44. William Browne et al., *Sacred Cows and Hot Potatoes* (Boulder: Westview Press, 1992); Barnaby Feder, "For Amber Waves of Data," *New York Times*, 4 May 1998, C1; David Barboza, "Is the Sun Setting on Farmers?," *New York Times*, 28 November 1999, C1.

45. John L. Shover, *First Majority, Last Minority: The Transforming of Rural Life in America* (DeKalb: Northern Illinois University Press, 1976); *Farms and Land in Farms*, (Washington, D.C.: National Agricultural Statistical Services, 2000).

46. Jennifer Erickson, "The 400 Largest Farms in the U.S.," *Successful Farming*, April 1992, 18–27; Betty Freese, "Pork Powerhouses," *Successful Farming*, October 1996, 27–32.

47. Clark Williams-Derry and Ken Cook, *Bumper Crop: Congress' Latest Attempt to Boost Subsidies for the Largest Farms*, (Washington, D.C.: Environmental Working Group, 2000); Clark Williams-Derry, *Report on Farm Subsidies, 1996–1999*, (Washington, D.C.: Environmental Working Group, 2001).
48. Vicki Monks, *Amber Waves of Gain* (New York: Defenders of Wildlife, 2000).
49. Wesley McCune, *Who's Behind Our Farm Policy?* (New York: Praeger, 1957).
50. Small Business Administration, *The Facts about Small Business* (Washington, D.C.: Small Business Administration, 1996).
51. Scott Hodge, "For Big Franchisers, Money to Go," *Washington Post Weekly*, 8 December 1997, 23; "Franchise Bytes," (Washington, D.C.: International Franchise Association, 1999).
52. William Browne et al., *Sacred Cows and Hot Potatoes* (Boulder: Westview Press, 1992), p. 24.
53. *Handbook of Small Business Data* (Washington, D.C.: Small Business Administration, 1988).
54. John R. Logan and Harvey L. Molotch, *Urban Fortunes: The Political Economy of Place* (Berkeley: University of California Press, 1987), p. 23.
55. Barry Bluestone and Bennett Harrison, *The Deindustrialization of America: Plant Closings, Community Abandonment, and the Dismantling of Basic Industry* (New York: Basic Books, 1982).
56. G. William Domhoff, *Who Really Rules? New Haven and Community Power Re-examined* (New Brunswick, N.J.: Transaction Books, 1978), pp. 49–75; Clarence N. Stone, *Economic Growth and Neighborhood Discontent: System Bias in the Urban Renewal Program of Atlanta* (Chapel Hill: University of North Carolina Press, 1976).
57. Charles Lindblom, *Politics and Markets: The World's Political Economic Systems* (New York: Basic Books, 1977).
58. Robert Kuttner, *Everything for Sale: The Virtues and Limits of Markets* (New York: Alfred A. Knopf, 1997).
59. Stephen K. Bailey, *Congress Makes a Law: The Story behind the Employment Act of 1946* (New York: Columbia University Press, 1950); G. William Domhoff, *The Power Elite and the State: How Policy Is Made in America* (Hawthorne, N.Y.: Aldine de Gruyter, 1990), chapter 7.
60. Irving Bernstein, *Turbulent Years: A History of the American Worker, 1933–1941* (Boston: Houghton Mifflin, 1970).
61. Dan Clawson, Alan Neustadtl, and Denise Scott, *Money Talks: Corporate PACS and Political Influence* (New York: Basic Books, 1992), p. 121.

Chapter 3: The Corporate Community and the Upper Class

1. Michael Hogg, *The Social Psychology of Group Cohesiveness* (New York: New York University Press, 1992).
2. Albert Lott and Bernice Lott, "Group Cohesiveness As Interpersonal Attraction," *Psychological Bulletin* 64 (1965): 259–309.
3. Gabriel Abraham Almond, *Plutocracy and Politics in New York City* (Westview Press, 1998), p. 108.

4. Harold Hodges, "Peninsula People: Social Stratification in a Metropolitan Complex," in *Education and Society,* ed. Warren Kallenach and Harold Hodges (Columbus: Merrill, 1963), p. 414.

5. Peter W. Cookson and Caroline Hodges Persell, *Preparing for Power: America's Elite Boarding Schools* (New York: Basic Books, 1985).

6. Susan A. Ostrander, *Women of the Upper Class* (Philadelphia: Temple University Press, 1984), p. 85.

7. Deborah Samuels, "Interview Study Conducted as Research Assistant for G. William Domhoff" (unpublished interview, 1975).

8. Michael Gordon, "Changing Patterns of Upper-Class Prep School College Placements," *Pacific Sociological Review* 12, no. 1 (1969): 23–26.

9. These figures were obtained from the admissions offices at Cate and St. John's in 1997.

10. Christopher Armstrong, "Privilege and Productivity: The Cases of Two Private Schools and Their Graduates," Ph.D. Dissertation, University of Pennsylvania, 1974.

11. G. William Domhoff, "Social Clubs, Policy-Planning Groups, and Corporations: A Network Study of Ruling-Class Cohesiveness," *Insurgent Sociologist* 5, no. 3 (1975): 173–184.

12. G. William Domhoff, "Social Clubs, Policy-Planning Groups, and Corporations: A Network Study of Ruling-Class Cohesiveness," *Insurgent Sociologist* 5, no. 3 (1975): 173–184; G. William Domhoff, *Who Rules America?,* 1st ed. (Englewood Cliffs, N.J.: Prentice-Hall, 1967).

13. Bohemian Club, "Bohemian Grove 1994: Midsummer Encampment," (San Francisco: Bohemian Club, 1994).

14. G. William Domhoff, *Who Rules America Now?* (New York: Simon & Schuster, 1983), p. 70.

15. Peter Martin Phillips, "A Relative Advantage: Sociology of the San Francisco Bohemian Club," Ph.D. Dissertation, University of California, Davis, 1994.

16. Reed Madsen Powell, *Race, Religion, and the Promotion of the American Executive* (Columbus: College of Administrative Science, Ohio State University, 1969), p. 50.

17. Susan A. Ostrander, *Women of the Upper Class* (Philadelphia: Temple University Press, 1984); Margo MacLeod, "Influential Women Volunteers: Reexamining the Concept of Power" (paper presented at the American Sociological Association, San Antonio, August 6–9 1984); Arlene Kaplan Daniels, *Invisible Careers: Women Civic Leaders from the Volunteer World* (Chicago: University of Chicago Press, 1988).

18. Susan A. Ostrander, *Women of the Upper Class* (Philadelphia: Temple University Press, 1984), pp. 128–129.

19. Susan A. Ostrander, *Women of the Upper Class* (Philadelphia: Temple University Press, 1984), p. 113.

20. Susan A. Ostrander, *Women of the Upper Class* (Philadelphia: Temple University Press, 1984), pp. 132–137.

21. Beth Wesley Ghiloni, "New Women of Power: An Examination of the Ruling Class Model of Domination," Ph.D. Dissertation, University of California, Santa Cruz, 1986, p. 122.

22. Arlene Kaplan Daniels, *Invisible Careers: Women Civic Leaders from the Volunteer World* (Chicago: University of Chicago Press, 1988), p. x.
23. Susan A. Ostrander, *Money for Change: Social Movement Philanthropy at Haymarket People's Fund* (Philadelphia: Temple University Press, 1995).
24. William Miller, "American Historians and the Business Elite," *Journal of Economic History* 9 (1949): 184–208.
25. Ann Marsh, "The Forbes Four Hundred," *Forbes*, 14 October 1996, 100.
26. Chuck Collins, *Born on Third Base: The Sources of Wealth of the 1996 Forbes 400* (Boston: United for a Fair Economy, 1997).
27. Richard L. Zweigenhaft and G. William Domhoff, *Diversity in the Power Elite: Have Women and Minorities Reached the Top?* (New Haven: Yale University Press, 1998).
28. "Wayne Huizenga," in *Current Biography* (New York: H.H. Wilson, 1995), p. 100.
29. Gary Solon, "Intergenerational Income Mobility in the United States," *American Economic Review* 82 (1992): 393–409; Harold R. Kerbo, *Social Stratification and Inequality: Class Conflict in Historical, Comparative, and Global Perspective* (Boston: McGraw-Hill, 2000).
30. T. D. Schuby, "Class, Power, Kinship and Social Cohesion: A Case Study of a Local Elite," *Sociological Focus* 8, no. 3 (1975): 243–255.
31. David Broad, "The Social Register: Directory of America's Upper Class," *Sociological Spectrum* 16 (1996): 173–181.
32. Philip H. Burch, *The Managerial Revolution Reassessed: Family Control in America's Large Corporations* (Lexington, Mass.: Lexington Books, 1972).
33. Stephen Albrecht and Michael Locker, *CDE Stock Ownership Directory: Fortune 500* (New York: Corporate Data Exchange, 1981).
34. Edward S. Herman, *Corporate Control, Corporate Power* (Cambridge, England, and New York: Cambridge University Press, 1981).
35. Marvin Dunn, "The Family Office: Coordinating Mechanism of the Ruling Class," in *Power Structure Research*, ed. G. William Domhoff (Beverly Hills: Sage Publications, 1980), 17–45.
36. Roger Lowenstein, *Buffett: The Making of an American Capitalist* (New York: Random House, 1995).
37. Connie Bruck, *The Predators' Ball: The Junk-Bond Raiders and the Man Who Staked Them* (New York: Simon & Schuster, 1988); James B. Stewart, *Den of Thieves* (New York: Simon & Schuster, 1991).
38. Edward S. Herman, *Corporate Control, Corporate Power* (Cambridge, England, and New York: Cambridge University Press, 1981), chapter 4; Edward Herman, *Conflicts of Interest: Commercial Bank Trust Departments* (New York: Twentieth Century Fund, 1975).
39. Michael Useem, "Corporations and the Corporate Elite," *Annual Review of Sociology* 6 (1980): 41–77; Michael Useem and Jerome Karabel, "Pathways to Top Corporate Management," *American Sociological Review* 51, no. 2 (1986): 184–200.
40. Michael Useem, "Corporations and the Corporate Elite," *Annual Review of Sociology* 6 (1980): 41–77.

41. Thomas R. Dye, *Who's Running America?: The Clinton Years* (Englewood Cliffs, N.J.: Prentice Hall, 1995).
42. Michael Useem, "Corporations and the Corporate Elite," *Annual Review of Sociology* 6 (1980): 41–77.
43. Richard L. Zweigenhaft and G. William Domhoff, *Diversity in the Power Elite: Have Women and Minorities Reached the Top?* (New Haven: Yale University Press, 1998).
44. Rosabeth Moss Kanter, *Men and Women of the Corporation* (New York: Basic Books, 1993), p. 49.
45. Andrew Hacker, "The Elected and the Anointed: Two American Elites," *American Political Science Review* 55 (1961): 539–549.
46. Michael Useem, "Corporations and the Corporate Elite," *Annual Review of Sociology* 6 (1980): 41–77.
47. Lisa Keister, *Wealth in America* (New York: Cambridge University Press, 2000).
48. Edward Wolff, "Recent Trends in the Size Distribution of Household Wealth," *Journal of Economic Perspectives* 12 (1998): 131–150.
49. Edward Wolff, "Recent Trends in Wealth Ownership, 1983–1998," (Cambridge, Mass.: Jerome Levy Economics Institute, 2000).
50. Edward Wolff, "Recent Trends in Wealth Ownership, 1983–1998," (Cambridge, Mass.: Jerome Levy Economics Institute, 2000), p. 9.
51. Laurence Kotlikoff and Jagadeesh Gokhale, *The Baby Boomers' Mega-Inheritance: Myth or Reality?* (Cleveland: Federal Reserve Bank of Cleveland, 2000).
52. E. Digby Baltzell, *Philadelphia Gentlemen: The Making of a National Upper Class* (Glencoe, Ill.: Free Press, 1958).
53. G. William Domhoff, *Who Rules America?* 1st ed. (Englewood Cliffs, N.J.: Prentice-Hall, 1967); C. W. Mills, *The Power Elite* (New York: Oxford University Press, 1956).

Chapter 4: The Policy-Planning Network

1. G. William Domhoff, *Who Rules America?*, 1st ed. (Englewood Cliffs, N.J.: Prentice-Hall, 1967).
2. Harold Salzman and G. William Domhoff, "Nonprofit Organizations and the Corporate Community," *Social Science History* 7 (1983): 205–216.
3. Eban Goodstein, *The Trade-Off Myth: Fact and Fiction about Jobs and the Environment* (Washington, D.C.: Island Press, 1999); Irvine Alpert and Ann Markusen, "Think Tanks and Capitalist Policy," in *Power Structure Research*, ed. G. William Domhoff (Beverly Hills: Sage Publications, 1980), 173–197.
4. Marshall Robinson, "The Ford Foundation: Sowing the Seeds of a Revolution," *Environment* 10 (April 1993): 1–10.
5. Robert C. Mitchell, "From Conservation to Environmental Movement: The Development of the Modern Environmental Lobbies," in *Governmental and Environmental Politics*, ed. Michael Lacey (Baltimore: Johns Hopkins University Press, 1991), 81–113; NRDC *Twenty Years Defending the*

Environment (New York: Natural Resources Defense Council, 1990); David Vogel, *Fluctuating Fortunes: The Political Power of Business in America* (New York: Basic Books, 1989).

6. Mark Dowie, *Losing Ground: American Environmentalism at the Close of the Twentieth Century* (Cambridge: MIT Press, 1995).

7. Berkeley Miller and William Canak, "There Should Be No Blanket Guarantee: Employers' Reactions to Public Employee Unionism, 1965–1975," *Journal of Collective Negotiations in the Public Sector* 24 (1995): 17–35.

8. Richard Magat, *Unlikely Partners: Philanthropic Foundations and the Labor Movement* (Ithaca, N.Y.: ILR Press, 1999).

9. Berkeley Miller and William Canak, "Laws As a Cause and Consequence of Public Employee Unionism," *Industrial Relations Research Association Series* (1995): 346–357.

10. Joseph G. Peschek, *Policy-Planning Organizations: Elite Agendas and America's Rightward Turn* (Philadelphia: Temple University Press, 1987).

11. James A. Smith, *The Idea Brokers: Think Tanks and the Rise of the New Policy Elite* (New York: The Free Press, 1991), p. 264.

12. Joseph G. Peschek, *Policy-Planning Organizations: Elite Agendas and America's Rightward Turn* (Philadelphia: Temple University Press, 1987).

13. Peter Passell, "Economic Scene: A New Project Will Measure the Cost and Effect of Regulation," *New York Times*, 30 July 1998, C2.

14. Russ Bellant, *The Coors Connection: How Coors Family Philanthropy Undermines Democratic Pluralism* (Boston: South End Press, 1991).

15. Mary Anna Culleton Colwell, *Private Foundations and Public Policy: The Political Role of Philanthropy* (New York: Garland, 1993).

16. Michael P. Allen, "Elite Social Movement Organizations and the State: The Rise of the Conservative Policy-Planning Network," *Research in Politics and Society* 4 (1992): 87–109.

17. Robert Kaiser and Ira Chinoy, "The Right's Funding Father," *Washington Post Weekly*, 17 May 1999, 6.

18. "Buying a Movement: Right-Wing Foundations and American Politics," (Washington, D.C.: People for the American Way, 1996); David Callahan, "$1 Billion for Ideas: Conservative Think Tanks in the 1990s," (Washington, D.C.: National Committee for Responsive Philanthropy, 1999).

19. Val Burris, "Elite Policy-Planning Networks in the United States," *Research in Politics and Society* 4 (1992): 111–134.

20. G. William Domhoff, *Who Rules America?*, 1st ed. (Englewood Cliffs, NJ: Prentice-Hall, 1967); Laurence Shoup and William Minter, *Imperial Brain Trust* (New York: Monthly Review Press, 1977).

21. Harold Salzman and G. William Domhoff, "The Corporate Community and Government: Do They Interlock?," in *Power Structure Research*, ed. G. William Domhoff (Beverly Hills: Sage Publications, 1980), 227–254.

22. G. William Domhoff, *The Power Elite and the State: How Policy Is Made in America* (Hawthorne, N.Y.: Aldine de Gruyter, 1990), chapter 5.

23. David Eakins, "The Development of Corporate Liberal Policy Research in the United States, 1885–1965," Ph.D. Dissertation, University of Wisconsin, 1966, p. 346.

24. William Frederick, "Free Market vs. Social Responsibility: Decision Time at the CED," *California Management Review* 23 (1981): 20–28.
25. "Rehabilitation Project: Once-Mighty CED Panel of Executives Seeks a Revival, Offers Advice to Carter," *Wall Street Journal,* 17 December 1976, 38.
26. Kim McQuaid, *Big Business and Presidential Power: From FDR to Reagan* (New York: Morrow, 1982).
27. G. William Domhoff, *The Bohemian Grove and Other Retreats: A Study in Ruling-Class Cohesiveness* (New York: Harper & Row, 1974), pp. 107–109.
28. Mark J. Green and Andrew Buchsbaum, "The Corporate Lobbies: Political Profiles of the Business Roundtable and the Chamber of Commerce," (Washington, D.C.: Public Citizen, 1980); James A. Gross, *Broken Promise: The Subversion of U.S. Labor Relations Policy, 1947–1994* (Philadelphia: Temple University Press, 1995).
29. David Vogel, *Fluctuating Fortunes: The Political Power of Business in America* (New York: Basic Books, 1989).
30. George Gonzalez, "Capitalism and the Environment: An Analysis of U.S. Environmental Policy Via Competing Theories of the State," Ph.D. Dissertation, University of Southern California, 1998), chapter 4.
31. "Raging at the Roundtable," *Fortune,* 16 May 1983, 19–22; "Business Groups Urge Cut in Pentagon Funds," *New York Times,* 23 February 1985, 9.
32. Herman Belz, *Equality Transformed* (New Brunswick, N.J.: Transaction Books, 1991).
33. Herman Belz, *Equality Transformed* (New Brunswick, N.J.: Transaction Books, 1991).
34. Beth Mintz, "The Failure of Health Care Reform: The Role of Big Business in Policy Formation," in *Social Policy and the Conservative Agenda,* ed. Clarence Lo and Michael Schwartz (Malden, Mass.: Blackwell, 1998), 210–224; Cathie Jo Martin, "Stuck in Neutral: Big Business and the Politics of National Health Reform," *Journal of Health Politics, Policy and Law* 20, no. 2 (1995): 431–436.
35. Michael Dreiling, "Forging Solidarity in the Struggle over the North American Foreign Trade Agreement: Strategy and Action for Labor, Nature, and Capital," Ph.D. Dissertation, University of Michigan, 1997; John R. MacArthur, *The Selling of "Free Trade": NAFTA, Washington, and the Subversion of American Democracy* (New York: Hill & Wang, 2000).

Chapter 5: The Role of Public Opinion

1. Lawrence Jacobs and Robert Shapiro, *Politicians Don't Pander* (Chicago: University of Chicago Press, 2000).
2. S. Herbst, *Numbered Voices: How Opinion Polling Has Shaped American Politics* (Chicago: University of Chicago Press, 1993), p. 166.
3. Benjamin I. Page and Robert Y. Shapiro, *The Rational Public: Fifty Years of Trends in Americans' Policy Preferences* (Chicago: University of Chicago Press, 1992).
4. John Zaller, *The Nature and Origins of Mass Opinion* (Cambridge, England and New York: Cambridge University Press, 1992).

5. Michael Wala, *The Council on Foreign Relations and American Foreign Policy in the Early Cold War* (Providence: Berghahn Books, 1994).

6. Jerry Sanders, *Peddlers of Crisis: The Committee on the Present Danger and the Politics of Containment* (Boston: South End Press, 1983).

7. Linda Bergthold, *Purchasing Power in Health: Business, the State, and Health Care Politics* (New Brunswick, N.J.: Rutgers University Press, 1990); C. Estes, "Privatization, the Welfare State, and Aging: The Reagan-Bush Legacy," in *The Nation's Health*, 5th ed. (Boston: Jones & Bartlett, 1997), 199–209.

8. Seymour M. Lipset, *The First New Nation: The United States in Historical and Comparative Perspective* (New York: Basic Books, 1963); Louis Hartz, *The Liberal Tradition in America; An Interpretation of American Political Thought since the Revolution* (New York: Harcourt Brace, 1955).

9. William Ryan, *Blaming the Victim* (New York: Random House, 1971); Robert E. Lane, *Political Ideology: Why the American Common Man Believes What He Does* (New York: Free Press of Glencoe, 1962).

10. Richard Sennett and Jonathan Cobb, *The Hidden Injuries of Class* (New York: Norton, 1993), pp. 250–251.

11. Richard Sennett and Jonathan Cobb, *The Hidden Injuries of Class* (New York: Norton, 1993), p. 251.

12. John C. Stauber and Sheldon Rampton, *Toxic Sludge Is Good for You: Lies, Damn Lies, and the Public Relations Industry* (Monroe, Maine: Common Courage Press, 1995).

13. Shawn Zeller, "Thriving in a Crisis," *National Journal*, 14 October 2000, 3262.

14. John C. Stauber and Sheldon Rampton, *Toxic Sludge Is Good for You: Lies, Damn Lies, and the Public Relations Industry* (Monroe, Maine: Common Courage Press, 1995).

15. Beth Ghiloni, "The Velvet Ghetto: Women, Power, and the Corporation," in *Power Elites and Organizations*, ed. G. William Domhoff and Thomas Dye (Beverly Hills: Sage Publications, 1987), pp. 21–36.

16. Jerome L. Himmelstein, *Looking Good and Doing Good: Corporate Philanthropy and Corporate Power.* (Bloomington: Indiana University Press, 1997).

17. Jerome L. Himmelstein, *Looking Good and Doing Good: Corporate Philanthropy and Corporate Power.* (Bloomington: Indiana University Press, 1997), p. 151.

18. Joseph Galaskiewicz and Ronald S. Burt, "Interorganization Contagion in Corporate Philanthropy," *Administrative Science Quarterly* 36, no. 1 (1991): 88–105; M. David Ermann, "The Operative Goals of Corporate Philanthropy: Contributions to the Public Broadcasting Service, 1972–1976," *Social Problems* 25, no. 5 (1978): 504–514.

19. J. Allen Whitt and Gwen Moore, "Network Ties between National Charities and Large Corporations" (paper presented at the Sunbelt Social Network Conference, San Diego, 1997).

20. David Vogel, *Fluctuating Fortunes: The Political Power of Business in America* (New York: Basic Books, 1989).

21. Ruth Wooden, "WWII Spawned the Ad Council. Today, the Public Service Agency Continues to Fight the Nation's Social Ills," *Advertising Age,* 29 March 1999, C122.

22. Warren Berger, "Source of Classic Images Now Struggles to Be Seen," *New York Times,* 20 November 2000, D6.

23. Glenn K. Hirsch, "Only You Can Prevent Ideological Hegemony: The Advertising Council and Its Place in the American Power Structure," *Insurgent Sociologist* 5, no. 3 (1975): p. 69.

24. Glenn K. Hirsch, "Only You Can Prevent Ideological Hegemony: The Advertising Council and Its Place in the American Power Structure," *Insurgent Sociologist* 5, no. 3 (1975): p. 78.

25. Benjamin I. Page and Robert Y. Shapiro, *The Rational Public: Fifty Years of Trends in Americans' Policy Preferences* (Chicago: University of Chicago Press, 1992), p. 205.

26. John E. Mueller, *War, Presidents, and Public Opinion* (New York: Wiley, 1973); Robert Erikson and Kent Tedin, *American Public Opinion,* 5th ed. (Boston: Allyn & Bacon, 1995).

27. John E. Mueller, *War, Presidents, and Public Opinion* (New York: Wiley, 1973); Daniel Wirls, *Buildup: The Politics of Defense in the Reagan Era* (Ithaca: Cornell University Press, 1992).

28. Elizabeth Fones-Wolf, *Selling Free Enterprise: The Business Assault on Labor and Liberalism, 1945–1960* (Urbana: University of Illinois Press, 1994).

29. NCEE, *EconomicsAmerica: Directory* (New York: National Council for Economic Education, 1997), p. i.

30. Dave Kansas, "Economic Illiteracy Abounds in U.S., New Survey Shows; Respondents Say They Glean Most Information Via TV," *Wall Street Journal,* 11 September 1992, B14A(W), A11E(E).

31. Benjamin I. Page and Robert Y. Shapiro, *The Rational Public: Fifty Years of Trends in Americans' Policy Preferences* (Chicago: University of Chicago Press, 1992), p. 117.

32. Howard J. Gold, *Hollow Mandates: American Public Opinion and the Conservative Shift* (Boulder, Colo.: Westview Press, 1992).

33. Edward G. Carmines and James A. Stimson, *Issue Evolution: Race and the Transformation of American Politics* (Princeton: Princeton University Press, 1989).

34. Ben H. Bagdikian, *The Media Monopoly* (Boston: Beacon Press, 2000).

35. Herbert Gans, "Are U.S. Journalists Dangerously Liberal?," *Columbia Journalism Review* (November–December 1985), 29–33; Michael Schudson, *The Power of News* (Cambridge: Harvard University Press, 1995).

36. Peter Dreier, "The Position of the Press in the U.S. Power Structure," *Social Problems* 29, no. 3 (1982): 298–310.

37. Thomas R. Dye, *Who's Running America? The Clinton Years* (Englewood Cliffs, N.J.: Prentice Hall, 1995), pp. 108, 120.

38. Herbert J. Gans, *Deciding What's News: A Study of* CBS Evening News, NBC Nightly News, Newsweek, *and* Time, 1st ed. (New York: Pantheon Books, 1979).

39. John Zaller, *The Nature and Origins of Mass Opinion* (Cambridge, England and New York: Cambridge University Press, 1992), p. 319.
40. John Zaller, *The Nature and Origins of Mass Opinion* (Cambridge, England and New York: Cambridge University Press, 1992), p. 15.
41. Jerry Sanders, *Peddlers of Crisis: The Committee on the Present Danger and the Politics of Containment* (Boston: South End Press, 1983).
42. L. Heath and K. Gilbert, "Mass Media and Fear of Crime," *American Behavioral Scientist* 39 (1996): 379–386; M. MacKuen and S. Coombs, *More Than News* (Beverly Hills: Sage Publications, 1981).
43. Shanto Iyengar and Adam F. Simon, "New Perspectives and Evidence on Political Communication and Campaign Effects," *Annual Review of Psychology* 51 (2000): 149–162.
44. Robert Erikson and Kent Tedin, *American Public Opinion*, 5th ed. (Boston: Allyn & Bacon, 1995).
45. David Demers, *The Menace of the Corporate Newspaper: Fact or Fiction?* (Ames: University of Iowa Press, 1996).
46. William Schneider, "And Lo, the Momentum Shifted," *National Journal*, 3 October 1998, 2350.
47. C. Glynn et al., *Public Opinion* (Boulder, Col.: Westview Press, 1999).
48. Robert Erikson and Kent Tedin, *American Public Opinion*, 5th ed. (Boston: Allyn & Bacon, 1995), p. 247.
49. William A. Gamson, *Talking Politics* (Cambridge, England and New York: Cambridge University Press, 1992), p. 4.
50. Jeffrey Berry, *The New Liberalism* (Washington, D.C.: Brookings Institution Press, 1999).
51. Lawrence Jacobs and Robert Shapiro, *Politicians Don't Pander* (Chicago: University of Chicago Press, 2000).
52. Richard Morin, "What Informed Opinion? A Survey Trick Points Out the Hazards Facing Those Who Take the Nation's Pulse," *Washington Post Weekly*, 10 April 1995, 36.
53. David Rosenbaum, "Deficit: Public Enemy No. 1, It's Not," *New York Times*, 16 February 1997, D1.
54. Richard Rothstein, "Education Policymaking Requires More Than Polls," *New York Times*, 15 November 2000, A25.
55. John Zaller, *The Nature and Origins of Mass Opinion* (Cambridge, England and New York: Cambridge University Press, 1992), chapter 5.
56. John Zaller, *The Nature and Origins of Mass Opinion* (Cambridge, England and New York: Cambridge University Press, 1992).
57. Stanley Milgram, *Obedience to Authority: An Experimental View* (New York: Harper & Row, 1974); Elliot Aronson, *The Social Animal* (New York: W.H. Freeman & Co., 1992).
58. T. D. Miethe, *Whistleblowing at Work: Tough Choices in Exposing Fraud, Waste, and Abuse on the Job* (Boulder, Colo.: Westview Press, 1999).
59. "Ralph Nader," in *Current Biography* (New York: H.H. Wilson, 1968), 280.
60. Richard Flacks, *Making History: The Radical Tradition in American Life* (New York: Columbia University Press, 1988); M. Mann, "The Ideology of Intellectuals and Other People in the Development of Capitalism,"

in *Stress and Contradiction in Modern Capitalism,* ed. L. Lindberg and R. Alford (Lexington, Mass.: Lexington Books, 1975).

61. Harvey Molotch, "Oil in Santa Barbara and Power in America," *Sociological Inquiry* 40 (1970): 131–144.

Chapter 6: Parties and Elections

1. John Higley et al., "Elite Integration in Stable Democracies: A Reconsideration," *European Sociological Review* 7, no. 1 (1991): 35–53; Michael G. Burton and John Higley, "Elite Settlements," *American Sociological Review* 52, no. 3 (1987): 295–307.

2. Seymour M. Lipset and Gary W. Marks, *It Didn't Happen Here: Why Socialism Failed in the United States* (New York: W.W. Norton & Co., 2000); Steven J. Rosenstone, Roy L. Behr, and Edward H. Lazarus, *Third Parties in America: Citizen Response to Major Party Failure,* 2nd rev. and expanded ed. (Princeton: Princeton University Press, 1996).

3. Richard Hofstadter, *The Idea of a Party System: The Rise of Legitimate Opposition in the United States, 1780–1840* (Berkeley: University of California Press, 1969).

4. Seymour M. Lipset and Gary W. Marks, *It Didn't Happen Here: Why Socialism Failed in the United States* (New York: W.W. Norton & Co., 2000).

5. G. William Domhoff, *The Power Elite and the State: How Policy Is Made in America* (Hawthorne, N.Y.: Aldine de Gruyter, 1990), chapter 9.

6. Kenneth Baer, *Reinventing Democrats* (Lawrence: University of Kansas Press, 2000); Jeff Manza and Clem Brooks, Social Cleavages and *Political Change: Voter Alignments and U.S. Party Coalitions* (New York: Oxford University Press, 1999); William Mayer, *The Divided Democrats* (Boulder, Colo.: Westview Press, 1996).

7. C. Vann Woodward, *Reunion and Reaction: The Compromise of 1877 and the End of Reconstruction* (Boston: Little Brown, 1966).

8. Lee J. Alston and Joseph P. Ferrie, *Southern Paternalism and the American Welfare State* (New York: Cambridge University Press, 1999); Michael Webber, *New Deal Fat Cats: Business, Labor, and Campaign Finance in the 1936 Presidential Election* (New York: Fordham University Press, 2000).

9. David Brady and Charles Bullock, "Is There a Conservative Coalition in the House?," *Journal of Politics* 42 (1980): 549–559; James T. Patterson, *Congressional Conservatism and the New Deal: The Growth of the Conservative Coalition in Congress, 1933–1939* (Westport, Conn.: Greenwood Press, 1981); David M. Potter, *The South and the Concurrent Majority* (Baton Rouge: Louisiana State University Press, 1972).

10. Michael K. Brown, *Race, Money and the American Welfare State* (Ithaca: Cornell University Press, 1999); Alan Brinkley, *The End of Reform: New Deal Liberalism in Recession and War,* 1st ed. (New York: Alfred A. Knopf, 1995); Aage R. Clausen, *How Congressmen Decide: A Policy Focus* (New York: St. Martin's Press, 1973).

11. Mack C. Shelley, *The Permanent Majority: The Conservative Coalition in the United States Congress* (University, Ala.: University of Alabama Press, 1983).

12. Lawrence Jacobs and Robert Shapiro, *Politicians Don't Pander* (Chicago: University of Chicago Press, 2000), see chapter 1 for an excellent analysis.

13. Michael Janofsky, "Town Becomes a Laboratory for Rule by Greens," *New York Times*, 3 January 2001, A8.

14. Allen F. Lovejoy, *La Follette and the Establishment of the Direct Primary in Wisconsin, 1890–1904* (New Haven: Yale University Press, 1941), V. O. Key, *Southern Politics in State and Nation* (New York: Random House, 1949).

15. Robert L. Morlan, *Political Prairie Fire: The Nonpartisan League, 1915–1922* (St. Paul: Minnesota Historical Society Press, 1985), p. 1.

16. Charles L. Fontenay, *Estes Kefauver: A Biography* (Knoxville: University of Tennessee Press, 1980).

17. Jerome L. Himmelstein, *To the Right: The Transformation of American Conservatism* (Berkeley: University of California Press, 1990); George Rising, *Clean for Gene: Eugene McCarthy's 1968 Presidential Campaign* (Westport, Conn.: Praeger, 1997).

18. Lucius J. Barker and Ronald W. Walters, *Jesse Jackson's 1984 Presidential Campaign: Challenge and Change in American Politics* (Urbana: University of Illinois Press, 1989); Teresa Noel Celsi, *Jesse Jackson and Political Power* (Brookfield, Conn.: Millbrook Press, 1992).

19. Greg Mitchell, *The Campaign of the Century: Upton Sinclair's Race for Governor of California and the Birth of Media Politics* (New York: Random House, 1992).

20. James Weinstein, *The Decline of Socialism in America, 1912–1925* (New York: Monthly Review Press, 1967).

21. Samuel Hays, "The Politics of Reform in the Progressive Era," *Pacific Northwest Review* 55 (1964): 157–169; Martin J. Schiesl, *The Politics of Efficiency: Municipal Administration and Reform in America, 1800–1920* (Berkeley: University of California Press, 1977); James Weinstein, "Organized Business and the Commission and Manager Movements," *Journal of Southern History* 28 (1962): 166–182.

22. G. William Domhoff, *Who Really Rules? New Haven and Community Power Re-examined* (New Brunswick, N.J.: Transaction Books, 1978), chapter 5; Alasdair Roberts, "Demonstrating Neutrality: The Rockefeller Philanthropies and the Evolution of Public Administration, 1927–1936," *Public Administration Review* (May–June 1994): 221–228.

23. James Weinstein, *The Decline of Socialism in America, 1912–1925* (New York: Monthly Review Press, 1967); James Weinstein, "Organized Business and the Commission and Manager Movements," *Journal of Southern History* 28 (1962): 166–182.

24. Tari Renner and Victor DeSantis, "Contemporary Patterns and Trends in Municipal Government Structures," in *The Municipal Yearbook 1993* (Washington, D.C.: International City Managers Association, 1994); Raymond E. Wolfinger, *The Politics of Progress* (Englewood Cliffs, N.J.: Prentice-Hall, 1973).

25. G. William Domhoff, *Who Rules America Now?* (New York: Simon & Schuster, 1983), chapter 6; John R. Logan and Harvey Molotch, *Urban*

Fortunes: The Political Economy of Place, (Berkeley: University of California Press, 1987).

26. Richard Gendron, "The Fault Lines of Power: Post-Earthquake Development in a Progressive City," Ph.D. Dissertation, University of California, Santa Cruz, (1998); John Logan, Rachel Whaley, and Kyle Crowder, "The Character and Consequences of Growth Regimes," *Urban Affairs Review* 32 (1997): 603–630.

27. Warren Miller and J. Merrill Shanks, *The New American Voter* (Cambridge: Harvard University Press, 1996).

28. Jeffrey Birnbaum, *The Money Men* (New York: Crown, 2000).

29. Center for Responsive Politics (opensecrets.org, 2000).

30. Alan Neustadtl, Denise Scott, and Dan Clawson, "Class Struggle in Campaign Finance? Political Action Committee Contributions in the 1984 Elections," *Sociological Forum* 6 (1991): 219–238.

31. Dan Clawson, Alan Neustadtl, and Denise Scott, *Money Talks: Corporate PACS and Political Influence* (New York: Basic Books, 1992); Dan Clawson, Alan Neustadtl, and Mark Weller, *Dollars and Votes: How Business Campaign Contributions Subvert Democracy* (Philadelphia: Temple University Press, 1998).

32. Val Burris, "The Political Partisanship of American Business: A Study of Corporate Political Action Committees," *American Sociological Review* 52, no. 6 (1987): 732–744; Val Burris and James Salt, "The Politics of Capitalist Class Segments: A Test of Corporate Liberalism Theory," *Social Problems* 37, no. 3 (1990): 341–359.

33. Center for Responsive Politics (opensecrets.org, 2000).

34. Stephen Isaacs, *Jews and American Politics* (New York: Doubleday, 1974); Seymour Lipset and Earl Raab, "The American Jews, the 1984 Elections, and Beyond," *Tocqueville Review* 6 (1984): 401–419.

35. Dan Clawson, Alan Neustadtl, and Mark Weller, *Dollars and Votes: How Business Campaign Contributions Subvert Democracy* (Philadelphia: Temple University Press, 1998).

36. Nicholas Horrock, "Reagan Resists Financial Disclosure," *New York Times,* 13 August 1976, A10.

37. Paul Hoffman, *Lions in the Street* (New York: Saturday Review Press, 1973), p. 106.

38. Phil Kuntz, "Perfectly Legal," *Wall Street Journal,* 10 October 1996, A1(W), A1(E).

39. Douglas Frantz, "Influential Group Brought into Campaign by Kemp," *New York Times,* 1 September 1996, 15(N), 32(L).

40. Karen Foerstel, "Grass Greener after Congress," *National Journal,* 11 March 2000, 515–519.

41. Marc Lacey, "First Asian-American Picked for Cabinet," *New York Times,* 30 June 2000, A15; Alan Greenblatt, "Gingrich, Inc.: Making a Living," *CQ Weekly,* 9 January 1999, 39.

42. Richard L. Zweigenhaft, "Who Represents America?" *Insurgent Sociologist* 5, no. 3 (1975): 119–130; Donald R. Matthews, *The Social Background of Political Decision-Makers* (New York: Random House, 1967); Suzanne

Keller, *Beyond the Ruling Class: Strategic Elites in Modern Society* (New York: Random House, 1963).

43. Edward Pessen, *The Log Cabin Myth: The Social Backgrounds of the Presidents* (New Haven: Yale University Press, 1984), p. 81.

44. Heinz Eulau and John D. Sprague, *Lawyers in Politics: A Study in Professional Convergence* (Westport, Conn.: Greenwood Press, 1984); Mark C. Miller, *The High Priests of American Politics: The Role of Lawyers in American Political Institutions* (Knoxville: University of Tennessee Press, 1995).

45. Morgens Pederson, "Lawyers in Politics: The Danish Folketing and United States Legislatures," *Comparative Legislative Behavior,* ed. Samuel Patterson and John Wahlke (New York: Wiley & Sons, 1972), 25–63.

46. "Congress of Relative Newcomers Poses Challenges to Bush Leadership," *CQ Weekly,* 20 January 2001, 178–182.

47. Joseph A. Schlesinger, *Ambition and Politics: Political Careers in the United States* (Chicago: Rand McNally, 1966), p. 5.

48. Warren Miller and J. Merrill Shanks, *The New American Voter* (Cambridge: Harvard University Press, 1996).

49. "Will the Rise of 'Blue Dogs' Revive Partisan Right?" *Congressional Quarterly,* 21 December 1996, 3436–3438.

50. Kirk Victor and David Baumann, "Looking to the Middle," *National Journal,* 16 December 2000, 3878–3882.

51. Michael Pertschuk, *Giant Killers* (New York: Norton, 1986).

52. Michael Pertschuk and Wendy Lesko, *The People Rising: The Campaign against the Bork Nomination* (St. Paul, Minn.: Thunder's Mouth Press, 1989).

Chapter 7: How the Power Elite Dominate Government

1. Michael Mann, "The Autonomous Power of the State: Its Origins, Mechanisms, and Results," *Archives of European Sociology* 25 (1984): 185–213; Michael Mann, *The Sources of Social Power: A History of Power From the Beginning to A.D. 1760,* vol. 1 (New York: Cambridge University Press, 1986).

2. Roger Friedland and A. F. Robertson, *Beyond the Marketplace: Rethinking Economy and Society.* (New York: Aldine de Gruyter, 1990).

3. Steve Lohr, "U.S. Pursuit of Microsoft: Rare Synergy With Company's Rivals," *New York Times,* 12 June 2000, C1.

4. James Livingston, *Origins of the Federal Reserve System: Money, Class, and Corporate Capitalism, 1890–1913* (Ithaca: Cornell University Press, 1986).

5. Bob Woodward, *Maestro: Greenspan's Fed and the American Boom* (New York: Simon & Schuster, 2000).

6. Timothy Egan, "Failing Farmers Learn to Profit From Wealth of U.S. Subsidies," *New York Times,* 25 December 2000, 1.

7. John Myles and Jill Quadagno, "Envisioning a Third Way: The Welfare State in the Twenty-First Century," *Contemporary Sociology* 29 (2000): 156–167.

8. G. William Domhoff, *Who Rules America?,* 1st ed. (Englewood Cliffs, N.J.: Prentice-Hall, 1967); G. William Domhoff, *Who Rules America Now?* (New

York: Simon & Schuster, 1983); Harold Salzman and G. William Domhoff, "The Corporate Community and Government: Do They Interlock?," in *Power Structure Research,* ed. G. William Domhoff (Beverly Hills: Sage Publications, 1980), 227–254.

9. Philip H. Burch, *Elites in American History: The New Deal to the Carter Administration,* vol. 3 (New York: Holmes & Meier, 1980); Philip H. Burch, *Elites in American History: The Civil War to the New Deal,* vol. 2 (New York: Holmes & Meier, 1981); Philip H. Burch, *Elites in American History: The Federalist Years to the Civil War,* vol. 1 (New York: Holmes & Meier, 1981).

10. Beth Mintz, "The President's Cabinet, 1897–1972: A Contribution to the Power Structure Debate," *Insurgent Sociologist* 5 (1975): 131–148.

11. Michael Useem, "Which Business Leaders Help Govern?," in *Power Structure Research,* ed. G. William Domhoff (Beverly Hills: Sage Publications, 1980), 199–225; Michael Useem, *The Inner Circle: Large Corporations and the Rise of Business Political Activity in the U.S. and U.K.* (New York: Oxford University Press, 1984).

12. James Grimaldi, "The Antitrust Administration," *Washington Post Weekly,* 10 July 2000, 18.

13. David Kessler, *A Question of Intent: How a Small Government Agency Took on America's Most Powerful and Deadly Industry* (New York: Public Affairs Press, 2000).

14. Joe Conason, "Notes on a Native Son: The George W. Bush Success Story," *Harper's Magazine,* February 2000, 39–53.

15. Thomas Toch, "A Savior for Washington's Has-Beens," *New Republic,* 21 December 1998, 10.

16. Richard L. Zweigenhaft and G. William Domhoff, *Diversity in the Power Elite: Have Women and Minorities Reached the Top?* (New Haven: Yale University Press, 1998).

17. Michael Mann, *The Sources of Social Power: The Rise of Classes and Nation-States, 1760–1914,* vol. 2 (New York: Cambridge University Press, 1993).

18. Morris Leopold Ernst, *The Great Reversals: Tales of the Supreme Court* (New York: Weybright & Talley, 1973).

19. Richard Cortner, *The Wagner Act Cases* (Knoxville: University of Tennessee Press, 1964).

20. Robert Carp and Ronald Stidham, *Judicial Process in America,* 4th ed. (Washington: CQ Press, 1998); Lawrence Baum, *The Supreme Court,* 6th ed. (Washington, D.C.: CQ Press, 1998).

21. Robert Carp and Ronald Stidham, *Judicial Process in America,* 4th ed. (Washington, D.C.: CQ Press, 1998), p. 217.

22. Lawrence Baum, *The Supreme Court,* 6th ed. (Washington, D.C.: CQ Press, 1998).

23. Kenneth M. Goldstein, *Interest Groups, Lobbying, and Participation in America* (Cambridge, England and New York: Cambridge University Press, 1999).

24. Shawn Zeller, "Cassidy Captures the Gold," *National Journal,* 21 October 2000, 3332–3334.

25. David Johnston, "Study Finds That Many Large Corporations Pay No Taxes," *New York Times,* 29 October 2000, C2.

26. James Dao, "After a Crash in North Carolina, Marines Ground Osprey Program," *New York Times*, 13 December 2000, 1; Stephen Labaton, "Congress Severely Curtails Plan for Low-Power FM Stations," *New York Times*, 19 December 2000, 1.

27. Peter Stone, "A Bermuda Brouhaha for Insurers," *National Journal*, 14 October 2000, 3262.

28. Dan Clawson, Alan Neustadtl, and Mark Weller, *Dollars and Votes: How Business Campaign Contributions Subvert Democracy* (Philadelphia: Temple University Press, 1998), p. 6.

29. Dan Clawson, Alan Neustadtl, and Mark Weller, *Dollars and Votes: How Business Campaign Contributions Subvert Democracy* (Philadelphia: Temple University Press, 1998), p. 7.

30. Mark Green, ed., *The Monopoly Makers* (New York: Grossman, 1973); David Vogel, *Fluctuating Fortunes: The Political Power of Business in America* (New York: Basic Books, 1989).

31. Ilana DeBare, "A Time for Caring," *San Francisco Chronicle*, 3 August 1998, B1–B3.

32. David Vogel, *Fluctuating Fortunes: The Political Power of Business in America* (New York: Basic Books, 1989); G. William Domhoff, *The Power Elite and the State: How Policy Is Made in America* (Hawthorne, N.Y.: Aldine de Gruyter, 1990), chapter 10.

33. G. William Domhoff, *The Power Elite and the State: How Policy Is Made in America* (Hawthorne, N.Y.: Aldine de Gruyter, 1990), chapter 8.

34. David C. Jacobs, *Business Lobbies and the Power Structure in America: Evidence and Arguments* (Westport, Conn.: Quorum Books, 1999).

35. G. William Domhoff, *The Power Elite and the State: How Policy Is Made in America* (Hawthorne, N.Y.: Aldine de Gruyter, 1990), chapter 7; G. William Domhoff, *State Autonomy or Class Dominance? Case Studies on Policy Making in America* (Hawthorne, N.Y.: Aldine de Gruyter, 1996), chapter 3; James Weinstein, *The Corporate Ideal in the Liberal State, 1900–1918* (Boston: Beacon Press, 1968); Michael E. Parrish, *Securities Regulation and the New Deal* (New Haven: Yale University Press, 1970).

36. G. William Domhoff, *State Autonomy or Class Dominance? Case Studies on Policy Making in America* (Hawthorne, N.Y.: Aldine de Gruyter, 1996), chapter 5.

37. James Douglas Brown, *An American Philosophy of Social Security: Evolution and Issues* (Princeton: Princeton University Press, 1972), pp. 90–91.

38. David Loth, *Swope of GE* (New York: Simon & Schuster, 1958), pp. 234ff.

39. Lee J. Alston and Joseph P. Ferrie, *Southern Paternalism and the American Welfare State* (New York: Cambridge University Press, 1999).

40. James D. Brown, *An American Philosophy of Social Security: Evolution and Issues* (Princeton: Princeton University Press, 1972).

41. G. William Domhoff, *State Autonomy or Class Dominance? Case Studies on Policy Making in America* (Hawthorne, N.Y.: Aldine de Gruyter, 1996), p. 160.

42. William Graebner, *A History of Retirement* (New Haven: Yale University Press, 1980).

43. Jill S. Quadagno, *The Transformation of Old Age Security: Class and Politics in the American Welfare State* (Chicago: University of Chicago Press, 1988).

44. Donald Fisher, *Fundamental Development of the Social Sciences* (Ann Arbor: University of Michigan Press, 1993).

45. Jeff Manza, "Policy Experts and Political Change during the New Deal" (Ph.D. Dissertation, University of California, 1995).

46. G. William Domhoff, *The Power Elite and the State: How Policy Is Made in America* (Hawthorne, N.Y.: Aldine de Gruyter, 1990), chapter 4; James Weinstein, *The Corporate Ideal in the Liberal State, 1900–1918* (Boston: Beacon Press, 1968); Bruno Ramirez, *When Workers Fight* (Westport, Conn.: Greenwood, 1978).

47. G. William Domhoff, *State Autonomy or Class Dominance? Case Studies on Policy Making in America* (Hawthorne, N.Y.: Aldine de Gruyter, 1996), chapter 4.

48. G. William Domhoff, *The Power Elite and the State: How Policy Is Made in America* (Hawthorne, N.Y.: Aldine de Gruyter, 1990); chapter 4; Rhonda F. Levine, *Class Struggle and the New Deal* (Lawrence: University of Kansas Press, 1988).

49. J. Joseph Huthmacher, *Senator Robert F. Wagner and the Rise of Urban Liberalism* (New York: Atheneum, 1968).

50. Kim McQuaid, *Big Business and Presidential Power: From FDR to Reagan* (New York: Morrow, 1982).

51. Leo Huberman, *The Labor Spy Racket* (New York: Modern Age Books, 1937).

52. Jerrold Auerbach, *Labor and Liberty: The LaFollette Committee and the New Deal* (Indianapolis: Bobbs Merrill, 1966).

53. Carey McWilliams, *Ill Fares the Land: Migrants and Migratory Labor in the United States* (Boston: Little, Brown, 1942), p. 356.

54. G. William Domhoff, *The Power Elite and the State: How Policy Is Made in America* (Hawthorne, N.Y.: Aldine de Gruyter, 1990), p. 98.

55. James A. Gross, *The Reshaping of the National Labor Relations Board: National Labor Policy in Transition, 1937–1947* (Albany: State University of New York Press, 1981).

56. James A. Gross, *Broken Promise: The Subversion of U.S. Labor Relations Policy, 1947–1994* (Philadelphia: Temple University Press, 1995); Holly J. McCammon and Melinda D. Kane, "Shaping Judicial Law in the Post-World War II Period: When Is Labor's Legal Mobilization Successful?," *Sociological Inquiry* 67, no. 3 (1997): 275–298; Holly J. McCammon, "From Repressive Intervention to Integrative Prevention: The U.S. State's Legal Management of Labor Militancy, 1881–1978," *Social Forces* 71, no. 3 (1993): 569–601; Holly J. McCammon, "Disorganizing and Reorganizing Conflict: Outcomes of the State's Legal Regulation of the Strike Since the Wagner Act," *Social Forces* 72, no. 4 (1994): 1011–1049.

57. Charles Noble, *Liberalism at Work: The Rise and Fall of OSHA* (Philadelphia: Temple University Press, 1986).

58. Charles Noble, *Liberalism at Work: The Rise and Fall of OSHA* (Philadelphia: Temple University Press, 1986); Andrew Szasz, "Industrial Resistance to Occupational Safety and Health Regulation: 1971–1981," *Social Problems* 32 (1984): 103–116.

59. Helen Dewar and Cindy Skrzycki, "Business Flexes Its Muscles," *Washington Post Weekly*, 18 March, 2001, p. 13.

60. Leonard S. Silk and David Vogel, *Ethics and Profits: The Crisis of Confidence in American Business* (New York: Simon & Schuster, 1976), pp. 50, 75.

61. Leonard S. Silk and David Vogel, *Ethics and Profits: The Crisis of Confidence in American Business* (New York: Simon & Schuster, 1976), p. 64.

62. Leonard S. Silk and David Vogel, *Ethics and Profits: The Crisis of Confidence in American Business* (New York: Simon & Schuster, 1976), p. 193.

63. James W. Prothro, *The Dollar Decade: Business Ideas in the 1920's* (Baton Rouge: Louisiana State University Press, 1954).

64. Grant McConnell, *Private Power & American Democracy* (New York: Alfred A. Knopf, 1966), p. 294.

65. David Vogel, "Why Businessmen Mistrust Their State: The Political Consciousness of American Corporate Executives," *British Journal of Political Science* 8 (1978): 45–78.

66. Frances Fox Piven and Richard A. Cloward, *Regulating the Poor: The Functions of Public Welfare,* updated ed. (New York: Vintage Books, 1993); Nancy Ellen Rose, *Put to Work: Relief Programs in the Great Depression* (New York: Monthly Review Press, 1994).

67. Frances Fox Piven and Richard A. Cloward, *The New Class War: Reagan's Attack on the Welfare State and Its Consequences* (New York: Pantheon Books, 1982).

Chapter 8: The Big Picture

1. Jeffrey Berry, *The New Liberalism* (Washington, D.C.: Brookings Institution Press, 1999).

2. Mark Dowie, *Losing Ground: American Environmentalism at the Close of the Twentieth Century* (Cambridge: MIT Press, 1995).

3. David Vogel, *Fluctuating Fortunes: The Political Power of Business in America* (New York: Basic Books, 1989).

4. Michael Pertschuk, *Revolt against Regulation: The Rise and Pause of the Consumer Movement* (Berkeley: University of California Press, 1982).

5. Ardith Maney and Loree Gerdes Bykerk, *Consumer Politics: Protecting Public Interests on Capitol Hill,* Contributions in Political Science no. 343. (Westport, Conn.: Greenwood Press, 1994).

6. Andrew Szasz, "Industrial Resistance to Occupational Safety and Health Regulation: 1971–1981," *Social Problems* 32 (1984): 103–116; Charles Noble, *Liberalism at Work: The Rise and Fall of OSHA* (Philadelphia: Temple University Press, 1986).

7. John Higley and Michael G. Burton, "The Elite Variable in Democratic Transitions and Breakdowns," *American Sociological Review* 54, no. 1 (1989): 17–32; Michael Burton and John Higley, "Invitation to Elite Theory: The Basic Contentions Reconsidered," in *Power Elites and Organizations,* ed. G. William Domhoff and Thomas Dye (Beverly Hills: Sage Publications, 1987), 219–238.

8. Mattei Dogan and John Higley, eds., *Elites, Crises, and the Origins of Regimes* (New York: Rowman & Littlefield, 1998); John Higley et al., "Elite Integration in Stable Democracies: A Reconsideration," *European Sociological Review* 7, no. 1 (1991): 35–53.

9. Nancy DiTomaso, "Organizational Analysis and Power Structure Research," in *Power Structure Research*, ed. G. William Domhoff (Beverly Hills: Sage Publications, 1980), 255–268.

10. G. William Domhoff and Thomas R. Dye, eds., *Power Elites and Organizations* (Beverly Hills: Sage Publications, 1987); G. William Domhoff, ed., *Power Structure Research* (Beverly Hills: Sage Publications, 1980); Floyd Hunter, *Community Power Structure: A Study of Decision Makers* (Chapel Hill: University of North Carolina Press, 1953); C. Wright Mills, *The Power Elite* (New York: Oxford University Press, 1956).

11. Gregory Hooks, *Forging the Military-Industrial Complex* (Urbana: University of Illinois Press, 1991); Theda Skocpol, *Protecting Soldiers and Mothers: The Political Origins of Social Policy in the United States* (Cambridge, Mass.: Belknap Press of Harvard University Press, 1992); Theda Skocpol, *States and Social Revolutions: A Comparative Analysis of France, Russia, and China* (Cambridge, England and New York: Cambridge University Press, 1979).

12. Kenneth Finegold and Theda Skocpol, *State and Party in America's New Deal* (Madison: University of Wisconsin Press, 1995).

13. William D. Berry and David Lowery, *Understanding United States Government Growth: An Empirical Analysis of the Post-War Era* (New York: Praeger, 1987).

14. G. William Domhoff, *State Autonomy or Class Dominance? Case Studies on Policy Making in America* (Hawthorne, N.Y.: Aldine de Gruyter, 1996), chapter 6.

15. Gwendolyn Mink, *Old Labor and New Immigrants in American Political Development, 1870–1925* (Ithaca: Cornell University Press, 1986).

16. Arno Mayer, *The Persistence of the Old Regime* (New York: Pantheon, 1981); Richard F. Hamilton, *The Bourgeois Epoch: Marx and Engels on Britain, France, and Germany* (Chapel Hill: University of North Carolina Press, 1991); Kim Voss, *The Making of American Exceptionalism: The Knights of Labor and Class Formation in the Nineteenth Century* (Ithaca: Cornell University Press, 1993).

17. Sidney Fine, *Sit-Down: The General Motors Strike of 1936–1937* (Ann Arbor: University of Michigan Press, 1969).

18. Frances Fox Piven and Richard A. Cloward, *Poor People's Movements: Why They Succeed, How They Fail.* (New York: Pantheon Books, 1977).

19. James Weinstein, *Ambiguous Legacy: The Left in American Politics* (New York: New Viewpoints, 1975), pp. 80–81.

20. Seymour M. Lipset and Gary W. Marks, *It Didn't Happen Here: Why Socialism Failed in the United States* (New York: W.W. Norton, 2000).

21. Theda Skocpol, *Protecting Soldiers and Mothers: The Political Origins of Social Policy in the United States* (Cambridge, Mass.: Belknap Press of Harvard University Press, 1992).

22. Alan Brinkley, *The End of Reform: New Deal Liberalism in Recession and War.* (New York: Alfred A. Knopf, 1995).

23. Martin Oppenheimer, *The State in Modern Society* (New York: Humanity Books, 2000); Ralph Miliband, *Marxism and Politics* (Oxford: Oxford University Press, 1977); Gary Teeple, *Marx's Critique of Politics, 1842–1847* (Toronto: University of Toronto Press, 1984).

24. Arno Mayer, *The Persistence of the Old Regime* (New York: Pantheon, 1981); Richard F. Hamilton, *The Bourgeois Epoch: Marx and Engels on Britain, France, and Germany* (Chapel Hill: University of North Carolina Press, 1991); Michael Mann, *The Sources of Social Power*, vol. 1 (New York: Cambridge University Press, 1986).

25. William A. Gamson, *The Strategy of Social Protest*, 2nd ed. (Belmont, Calif.: Wadsworth, 1990); Thomas Wellock, *Critical Masses: Opposition to Nuclear Power in California, 1958–1978* (Madison: University of Wisconsin Press, 1998); Christian Joppke, *Mobilizing against Nuclear Energy: A Comparison of Germany and the United States,* (Berkeley: University of California Press, 1993).

26. Jack M. Bloom, *Class, Race, and the Civil Rights Movement.* (Bloomington: Indiana University Press, 1987); L. Alston and J. Ferrie, *Southern Paternalism and the American Welfare State* (New York: Cambridge University Press, 1999).

27. Charles W. Whalen and Barbara Whalen, *The Longest Debate: A Legislative History of the 1964 Civil Rights Act* (Washington, D.C.: Seven Locks Press, 1985).

28. Richard E. Cohen, "A Congress Divided," *National Journal,* 5 February 2000, 382–404; Keith T. Poole and Howard Rosenthal, *Congress: A Political-Economic History of Roll Call Voting* (New York: Oxford University Press, 1997).

29. James Glaser, *Race, Campaign Politics, and Realignment in the South* (New Haven: Yale University Press, 1996).

30. Charles Lindblom, *Politics and Markets: The World's Political Economic Systems* (New York: Basic Books, 1977); Robert Kuttner, *Everything for Sale: The Virtues and Limits of Markets.* (New York: Alfred A. Knopf, 1997).

Appendix A

1. The best starting point for content analysis using search software and the Internet is Carl Roberts, ed., *Text Analysis for the Social Sciences* (Mahwah, N.J.: Erlbaum, 1997). See also the excellent papers by Roberto Franzosi, "Computer-Assisted Coding of Textual Data: An Application of Semantic Grammars," *Sociological Methods and Research* 19 (1990): 225–257, and "Narrative as Data: Linguistic and Statistical Tools for the Quantitative Study of Historical Events," *International Review of Social History* 43, supplement 6 (1998): 81–104.

2. The two American studies are by Floyd Hunter, *Top Leadership USA* (Chapel Hill: University of North Carolina Press, 1957) and Gwen Moore, "The Structure of a National Elite Network," *American Sociological Review,* 44 (1979): 673–92. The Australian study is by John Higley, Desley Deacon, and Don Smart, *Elites in Australia* (London: Routledge and Kegan Paul, 1979). The Norwegian study is by John Higley, G. Lowell Field, and Knut Groholt, *Elite Structure and Ideology* (New York: Columbia University Press, 1976). For a summary of reputational studies at the local level in the United States, see G. William Domhoff, *Who Really Rules? New Haven and Community Power Re-Examined* (New Brunswick, N.J.: Transaction Books, 1978).

Index

The letter "n" after a page reference indicates a note.